THE TENNESSEE THEATRE

A GRAND ENTERTAINMENT PALACE

BY JACK NEELY

AUTHOR ◆ *Jack Neely*
BOOK DESIGN ◆ *Robin Easter Design / Whitney Hayden*
COPY EDITOR ◆ *Evelyn Bennett*
RESEARCH ◆ *Tim Burns, Hollie Cook, Jen Mowrer, Tom Whisman*
PRINT MANAGER ◆ *Chris Hoosier*
PRINTING ◆ *Lithographics, Nashville, Tennessee*
DISTRIBUTION ◆ *University of Tennessee Press*
PROJECT MANAGER ◆ *Becky Hancock, Executive Director, Historic Tennessee Theatre Foundation*

604 S. Gay Street, Knoxville, TN 37902

Photo permissions / credits listed on page 199.

ISBN 978-0-692-32001-3

CONTENTS

Foreword ✢ I   *Preface* ✢ II   *Introduction* ✢ XI

CHAPTER 1 BEFORE THE TENNESSEE → 1

CHAPTER 2 PLANNING A MOVIE PALACE → 13

CHAPTER 3 CURTAIN → 31

CHAPTER 4 ON STAGE AND SCREEN → 61

CHAPTER 5 PREMIERES AND THE POSTWAR ERA → 85

CHAPTER 6 TRANSITION AT THE TENNESSEE → 103

CHAPTER 7 A NOSTALGIC ERA → 123

CHAPTER 8 NEW DIRECTIONS → 137

CHAPTER 9 REBIRTH IN A NEW CENTURY → 163

Appendix & Acknowledgments ✢ 197   *Index* ✢ 207

As mayor of Knoxville in 2005, I was proud to be able to lend my support to the restoration of the historic Tennessee Theatre—a cause near and dear to my heart. The city donated $4 million toward the more than $25 million raised for the restoration of the Official State Theatre of Tennessee to its original 1928 splendor. As someone who grew up loving this theater, I will always think of it as one of Tennessee's treasures.

During my term as mayor, I placed a high priority on downtown redevelopment and preservation of key historic landmarks. Knoxville's historic places, like the Tennessee Theatre, make our city a unique place to live, work and visit. The restoration of the Tennessee Theatre was a catalyst for the revitalization of the entire downtown.

It's been a decade since James A. Dick, the board of the Historic Tennessee Theatre Foundation and the support of an entire community saved the theater for future generations. Through their dedication, more than one million people have rediscovered the magic of the Tennessee Theatre.

Congratulations to the Tennessee Theatre on over eight decades of unforgettable entertainment. On behalf of the State of Tennessee, I extend sincere wishes for another 85 years and more of serving the people of East Tennessee.

Bill Haslam

BILL HASLAM
GOVERNOR OF TENNESSEE

PREFACE

If I hadn't actually seen the Tennessee this week with my own two eyes, I would have assumed my childhood memories of it were some exaggerated dream.

The Tennessee has always seemed very old to me, hailing from several eras ago, when everything was altogether different. When it was built, most movies were silent, television was a science-fiction fantasy, air conditioning was rare, jazz was for dancing, and there was no such thing as rock 'n' roll. Even the form of music known as bluegrass didn't exist. Although the Tennessee evokes a brief era of grand movie palaces, so many have been lost or ruined in one way or another that most cities today have nothing comparable.

Considering its age, I'm having a hard time processing the fact that I've personally witnessed more than half of the Tennessee Theatre's history. I grew up with the Tennessee Theatre. I can't swear to remember the first movie I ever saw there, but somehow I do remember being there just after Christmas 1966, to watch the first movie shown after its first big remodel: *Follow Me, Boys*, the Disney comedy about scouting starring Fred MacMurray and Kurt Russell. For 8-year-old boys, the television star Kurt Russell (the Jungle Boy on Gilligan's Island) was our avatar. And this same movie featured, of all people, Lillian Gish. At 8, I did not know Hetty, the old lady in the movie, had been a screen goddess of the silent days. Or that Charlie Ruggles, who played old man Hughes, was the same puffed-up fellow who, 30 or 40 years later, my future kids and I would laugh at in a much, much older classic screwball comedy called *Bringing Up Baby*. Or that Fred MacMurray, everybody's favorite dad and absent-minded professor, had ever played a convincing murderer in an iconic film-noir thriller called *Double Indemnity*.

That silly Disney movie that greeted a facelifted Tennessee Theatre was a study in the history of motion pictures — and more so in the Tennessee itself, which introduced tens of thousands to the film legends of Hollywood's Golden Age: John Wayne, Humphrey Bogart, Katharine Hepburn, Gene Kelly, Bette Davis, the Marx Brothers.

My family went to the Tennessee a lot. It's funny how some movies you remember so well you remember where you saw them. *The Computer Wore Tennis Shoes*, *Chitty Chitty Bang Bang*, *Blackbeard's Ghost*, *On Her Majesty's Secret Service*. It was always brightly lit and friendly and busy.

But somehow we stopped going. I hadn't been there for years, in the summer of 1975, when a high school chum talked me into going to see a James Caan movie called *Rollerball*. Maybe the movie's dystopian scenario was part of my perception, but that summer the old Tennessee didn't seem like itself: darker, quieter, almost funereal. The movie was moderately popular, but there were few people in the cavernous theater. When we got out, downtown was empty and spooky. We shouted in the streets to hear the echo. No one was there to be bothered. I never saw another new movie at the Tennessee.

It seems like much more than three years later that I began a habit of returning, often by myself. The Tennessee was showing old black-and-white movies, to capitalize on the 1970s nostalgia craze. I'd go no matter what they were playing. To me those movies weren't "nostalgic." The movies that interested me were those made long before I was born. *Captain Blood*, *Grand Hotel*, *In a Lonely Place*. I had never heard of most of them, and had no memories associated with them. (The Knoxville of my youth was not one of the many TV markets that offered old movies on late-late shows.) But they had a hold on me. Each offered a conducted tour of an exotic place, even if it was just an American city in the 1930s. An old movie was to me like a fantasy world where everything was sort of familiar, but intricately different. I was fascinated. In those days, before cable and any variety of movies you could watch at home, the Tennessee was my only access to cinema heritage, but also a portal to a parallel universe.

The first time I ever saw *Casablanca* was at the Tennessee. In fact, all the times I've ever seen *Casablanca* were at the Tennessee, and I've seen it so many times I can quote dozens of words of dialogue. The Tennessee's design could be a set for *Casablanca*, perhaps a deleted scene in which Rick and Ilsa try to forget about the Nazis and Ilsa's inconvenient marital status with a night at the movies. I've avoided ever watching more than a few minutes of the movie on a TV screen; the experience is diminished.

Old movies made the Tennessee a handy introduction to my hometown. There was a time that the interior of the Tennessee was the only thing in Knoxville that dependably impressed strangers. Meeting a young tourist from England, I immediately invited her to a Three Stooges festival at the Tennessee. She was more impressed with the theater than the Stooges.

I returned again, to see John Cullum in *Drumwright* during the 1982 World's Fair. It was a novelty to see live performers within that old proscenium where, despite my 20 years' experience with the old theater, I'd seen only movies.

Everybody remembers the first date with a future spouse there. I do too, going with my wife, Janet, to see a screening of *It Happened One Night* in 1983. Even if, to this day, she adamantly insists she did not consider it a date.

I've seen about 30 operas at the Tennessee, which constitutes most of the operas I've ever seen. Probably 100 symphony performances. And dozens and dozens of other shows. On that stage I've seen Chet Atkins, Bob Dylan, the Everly Brothers, Elvis Costello, Esperanza Spalding, Morrissey, David Byrne.

I was there as a reporter, just over a decade ago now, covering the massive renovation in detail for Metro Pulse. Among cover story subjects, it was one of our closest-at-hand. When the Tennessee was closed for all that work, Metro Pulse moved into the adjacent Burwell Building. So for years my office overlooked the Tennessee's marquee. Whether I was going to a show or not, I was always aware of it. Just leaving the office after work often called for wading through a crowd, sometimes having to convince strangers I wasn't trying to cut line.

I've spoken on the Tennessee's stage a couple of times, about some old movie or historical subject or other, but never drew a crowd like I faced when I appeared with the V-Roys for their last sellout New Year's Eve show, about three seconds after midnight, January 1, 2012. I was the one wearing a diaper, representing the new year. I can assure our readers that there are no pictures of that episode in this book.

That's all just to say I had every reason to think I knew the place. Researching this book convinced me I did not.

The subject may be more complex than you'd expect, considering it's about one address. Both at the library and through the personal memories of several leaders and witnesses, I found an abundance of information from the 1970s forward, when the theater has been the center of public attention, recognized as a local treasure. There are thick files about the theater during that era, and memories are mostly clear.

But to make it a full history requires wading into the theater's murky earlier years, especially concerning certain legendary performances remembered clearly by no one who's still able to talk about them. For those there were only a handful of yellowing clippings and secondhand lore, mostly passed down from witnesses who are no longer among us. Contrary to assumptions, local 20th-century newspapers are not indexed, either in paper or electronically, so even performances that made a big splash at the time aren't often easy to look up. Some legends we began to consider apocryphal, like the one that exotic singer and dancer Fifi D'Orsay once performed at the Tennessee. Much of what I found was in old newspapers available on microfilm, the dates found by connecting clues turned up by researchers working on this book just this year, or by dead reckoning. We eventually tracked down almost everything I was looking for; every one of the legends I had begun to question turned out to be true, and each one is documented in this book.

The Tennessee's history can surprise even its historians. Plans to build a grand landmark theater on this site seem to have commenced soon after World War I, and there were unexpected turns in the Tennessee's multi-year planning period, which included a well-known architect's abandoned proposal I'd never heard about. There were interesting personal dynamics in its perhaps unique final design, a rare survivor of a fleeting high-profile partnership. The amount and quality of live entertainment staged at the theater during its first dozen years, when it was open daily as a movie theater, was a surprise. To a degree I didn't realize, the Tennessee witnessed the final days of vaudeville in Knoxville and somehow, in the midst of history's worst Depression, a brief flowering of Broadway-quality extravaganzas. And I didn't appreciate the esteem with which the theater is held in the entertainment industry today. After the seismic improvements unveiled in 2005, it's counted as one of the finest and most popular theater venues in the world.

A few answers still elude us, maybe something for a future historian to work on. There's much still unknown about the decision-making process concerning the theater's design and construction. Few locals were associated with the project for very long. Paramount Studios in Hollywood was ultimately in charge of creating the Tennessee Theatre, and their archives are not available to researchers. Newspaper reporters, who are distracted by other deadlines and constrained by space issues, are our only sources for most of the Tennessee's performances, our only proof they even happened. In some cases these articles were vivid and thorough, especially when the byline belonged to Journal critic Malcolm Miller, a thespian himself who would later, unexpectedly, find himself manager of the Tennessee. In some cases we can only wish the reporters had described more of what they saw. Tom Mix's small rodeo, which apparently involved multiple full-grown horses on stage in 1933, did not yield descriptions that might help skeptical stagehands understand just what they did and how they did it. In 1935 a rare midnight appearance by the actual first-generation Grand Old Opry, heretofore unknown to local historians, apparently was not attended by reporters at all. All we have is the impressive lineup.

And I've always wondered what was in those big jars in the alcoves. Even after all this research, I still don't know the answer to that.

My half-century acquaintance with the Tennessee hasn't made me an expert on the theater, but I've been grateful to have known several experts personally.

I was fortunate to have grown up knowing a couple of the theater's historians. Librarian David J. Harkness (1913 – 2004) was a close family friend, often a guest at our dinner table when I was growing up. He began frequenting the theater when he moved to Knoxville from Jellico to go to school in 1931 and had personal memories of many of its legendary years. He was personally involved in organizing some of the Tennessee's hallmark events, especially the 1953 premiere of *So This Is Love*. And he was also a historian, with a particular interest in show business. He would have been an invaluable consultant, but I trust his memories, conveyed in old newspaper articles, about performers who appeared at the Tennessee. I'm sorry he didn't get to see the renovated Tennessee Theatre, much of its interior looking perhaps about like it did when he first saw it during the Hoover administration.

And for most of my life I knew the late Wallace Baumann (1925 – 2009). Perhaps the most prominent supporter of the Tennessee in the theater's history, Wallace had worked toward the revival of the theater beginning in the 1960s, when it was still a movie house, and lived to witness its revival, which might not have happened without his decades of personal and financial support. As a columnist I kept his number handy, and more than a few times he was helpful with a story, especially when it involved 20th-century show business, and of course when it involved the Tennessee Theatre. He died before I began working on this project, but his large collection of Tennessee memorabilia and records, on file at the Calvin M. McClung Historical Collection, was invaluable. Going over his notes reminded me of our dozens of conversations over the years. A part of his persona is still there, in all those boxes.

Tim Burns, the Tennessee's longtime technical director, has kept the theater running all these years, knows its nooks and crannies better than anybody, and along the way has become a student of the history of the American movie palace. He was a great deal of help in putting together the complicated chronology of the last 40 years and also directing me to trade-publication stories relevant to the Tennessee. Toward the end of my research, he also helped direct me to confirm some particularly elusive legends, like the ones concerning the young Cuban rumba sensation Desi Arnaz. And by poring over Baumann's collection as well as through his own resources, Tim found a great many images no one else could have.

Bill Snyder is the guy singly most responsible for motivating this book. The former engineering professor and chancellor of the University of Tennessee is more recognizable to thousands as the longest-tenured organist in the Tennessee's history. He's one of the theater's greatest champions. Bill was the first one who brought up the prospect of a book about the theater's history, over drinks at Sapphire several years ago, probably soon after the big renovation. At that time both of us were a little skeptical about whether we could marshal the resources to make a book-length history of the theater happen, but I'm glad we did.

Former executive director Tom Cervone helped get this ball rolling. However, current executive director Becky Hancock — whom I first knew as the pretty blonde in jeans who announced old movies years ago — is the one who saw it through and coordinated these several efforts, keeping us all on deadline to make this an expeditious reality. She even pitched in with some photo research.

Bradley Reeves, of the Tennessee Archive of Moving Image and Sound, has become an authority on his subject and is generous with his resources; he helped me with perspective and also supplied several of the images we've used. Others who helped with images were photo researcher Jen Mowrer, who was enlisted for this purpose, and Paul Efird of the Knoxville News Sentinel, who assisted in gathering images from that daily newspaper's substantial archive. Artist Joe Parrott Jr. provided access to the archives of his father, the Tennessee's first and only staff artist; Joe still runs the commercial art business his father started in 1932.

I spoke at length with music promoter Ashley Capps, architect Doug McCarty, publisher Bruce Hartmann, and several others who offered insight into the complexity of the theater's later years. Don Townsend helped with the history of the Knoxville Opera in this place. Historian Betsey Creekmore, a member of the theater's board, straightened me out on a few issues. For some background, I reviewed Dean Novelli's comprehensive research on the Bijou Theatre, published in his 1986 essay, "On a Corner of Gay Street," supplemented with some recent conversations concerning his research into the theater's practical origins.

I'm lucky that Robin Easter, whose talent and grace first impressed me when we worked at Whittle Communications a couple of decades ago, is in charge of designing the book. I got to work with another Whittle colleague, Evelyn Bennett, whose skills with detail were redoubtable then as they are now.

Hollie Cook (who also worked with me a few years ago on my Market Square book) compiled the index.

And two weeks before the deadline, when we were despairing of finding dates and descriptions of some oft-cited legendary performances, retired librarian Tom Whisman took to the microfilm viewers to do some painstaking (but fascinating) week-by-week newspaper research. I'm grateful that his discoveries forced me to delete some paragraphs I'd already written expressing regret that we never nailed down certain legendary live performances of the 1930s, like the Ziegfeld Follies and the Tennessee's first real Broadway show, the Helen Hayes hit Mary of Scotland.

This would of course be impossible without handy libraries. I did more than half the research in the Knox County Library System's Calvin M. McClung Collection, Steve Cotham, director — which is, conveniently, directly across Gay Street from the Tennessee. McClung is custodian of Wallace Baumann's copious papers, including hundreds of photographs, but they've been keeping a file on the Tennessee Theatre since the 1960s and also have files on several of the people involved in the theater over the years.

I did some general show biz research through histories and especially biographies at Lawson McGhee Library. And I found a couple of occasions to visit the University of Tennessee Hodges Library Special Collections, where research specialist Bill Eigelsbach was especially helpful.

And I almost hate to say it, but I'm grateful to YouTube, which offers insights that wouldn't have been available to previous generations. The Internet in general can sometimes come across as a minefield of misinformation, but thanks to YouTube, we can actually see some of the Tennessee's live performers of the late '20s and '30s. We can actually watch Fifi D'Orsay dance, hear Gene Austin sing, and witness Hadji Ali regurgitate.

That Sanctuary of Desire — or Bordello for Pterodactyls, as I once described it in print, in my impudent youth — still seems huge, and exotic, and a little mysterious, and even after working on a book about it for the better part of a year, the Tennessee still keeps many of its secrets. Still, I hope we've revealed enough of them to tell a satisfying story about a place like no other.

JACK NEELY

One of the most exuberant movie palaces of the South,

THE TENNESSEE THEATRE IS A JAZZ AGE SPECTACLE, A GLIMMER OF A BRIEFLY EXTRAVAGANT ERA,

a bold architectural celebration of an astonishing and suddenly popular new form of art.

INTRODUCTION

The motion picture changed the way Americans experienced their world; within its broad region, the Tennessee became the superlative venue for that experience.

After almost a century, the Tennessee is still obligatory on any trip to Knoxville, one of those sights you have to witness at least once. Designed with dozens of shapes and countless colors to awe, it is distinct in appearance from every other theater in the world. It's a complex and fascinating artifact. But the Tennessee is also a practical edifice, a modern venue for classical music, opera, rock, jazz, bluegrass, and dozens of other genres that benefit from the old theater's excellent acoustics, praised in the national media for the quality of its sound.

Its history is just as distinctive. In its 49 years as a first-run cinema, the Tennessee introduced several thousand feature films to the Knoxville market, coinciding almost perfectly with Hollywood's Golden Age. In this room many East Tennesseans witnessed their first talking pictures and encountered the first stars of the sound era. Despite its reputation as the finest, the most expensive, the theater with chandeliers and original art and antiques in its lobby, the Tennessee was also the largest, the busiest, the most popular. In successive showings in a weeklong run of one popular movie, the theater might accommodate a crowd bigger than most modern football stadiums. In East Tennessee, even to this day, no single theater has shown more movies to more people. Exclusiveness is one of the Tennessee's most effective illusions.

But from its earliest days, the Tennessee was never just a movie theater. Its stage hosted thousands of live actors, singers, psychics, dancers, acrobats, magicians, comedians, and in the process witnessed the very end of vaudeville. Its rare Wurlitzer organ, original to 1928, has been played by local regulars as well as in special concerts by some of America's most celebrated organists. The Tennessee hosted at least one network radio broadcast of a live big-band-era performance, a show by Glenn Miller and his orchestra in 1940. It was once part of a world's fair, with the debut of a new musical drama seen by tens of thousands. In recent decades that same stage has presented some of the legends of American popular music: Bob Dylan, Chet Atkins, Johnny Cash, Ray Charles, Bert Bacharach, Diana Ross, Lionel Hampton, the Everly Brothers, Cab Calloway, Lou Reed. Speakers who have drawn crowds here have included legendary director Frank Capra, comedian Bill Cosby, actress Patricia Neal, novelist John Updike, poet Maya Angelou, author Elizabeth Gilbert, maverick chef Anthony Bourdain, radio personality Garrison Keillor. Major figures of modern classical, operatic, and minimalist music have performed here, including international violinists Midori and Joshua Bell, avant-garde composers Steve Reich and Terry Riley, and Metropolitan Opera stars Roberta Peters and Jerome Hines.

And many of them, even seasoned performers, look for words to describe the place, comparing it to a palace, a cathedral, the Taj Mahal, the interior of a genie's bottle, or a giant Fabergé egg.

It has hosted a handful of gala world premieres of Hollywood movies. It's been the distinctive setting of a few major artists' live recordings and videos. The national media have found reason to describe it when it has served as a venue for significant new-music festivals. The Tennessee has even appeared as a scene in one major motion picture, albeit briefly and with an altered name.

Its story is different from that of every other theater in the world.

AISLE 2
EXIT

BEFORE THE TENNESSEE

CHAPTER 1

If we can judge walls by the interesting scenes they've witnessed, there are hardly any walls more historic than those of the Tennessee Theatre. Still, the ground beneath the Tennessee was notably historic long before any movie house was built here. Although it may be difficult to picture today, this plot of land was once regarded as the northern outskirts of a frontier town that clustered itself near the river. The southeast corner of Gay Street and Clinch Avenue was precisely the spot where Pennsylvania-born Presbyterian minister Samuel Carrick (1760 – 1809) established one of the first public colleges west of the Appalachian Mountains.

Named to honor William Blount, President George Washington's appointed governor of the Southwestern Territory, Blount College had settled, by 1799, in a three-story frame house on this site. It moved half a mile west to "the Hill" in 1828 and later evolved into a much larger institution. But the University of Tennessee's first real campus was on this downtown plot of land. Much of the university's lore — about the mysterious five female students who have suggested to some researchers that UT has a claim to be America's first co-educational institution, and about its first alumni, like Clement Clay, who would become an early governor of Alabama — concerns the teaching that went on right here.

Rev. Carrick's old college building was probably torn down before the Civil War. By the 1860s it was an urban block of commercial buildings close together facing Gay Street, and a few small houses facing State.

Just across State Street is one relic of the collegiate era. In the First Presbyterian churchyard, one of the graves closest to the theater's backstage is that of Samuel Carrick, honored as the founder of the University of Tennessee.

During Knoxville's first 75 years, the town was a practical place. First the state capital, then not, it was an isolated settlement surviving on the edge of a rugged landscape. Entertainment was secondary, a song in a tavern or a choir in a church or an occasional cockfight or horse race. Dramatic performances were not unknown, but the city's first few generations never established a regular venue for them.

In the 1850s the city's railroad and new industries attracted newcomers from around the country and around the world. As soon as the Civil War was over, downtown Knoxville almost suddenly attracted entertainment. Swiss immigrant

GAY STREET · 1923

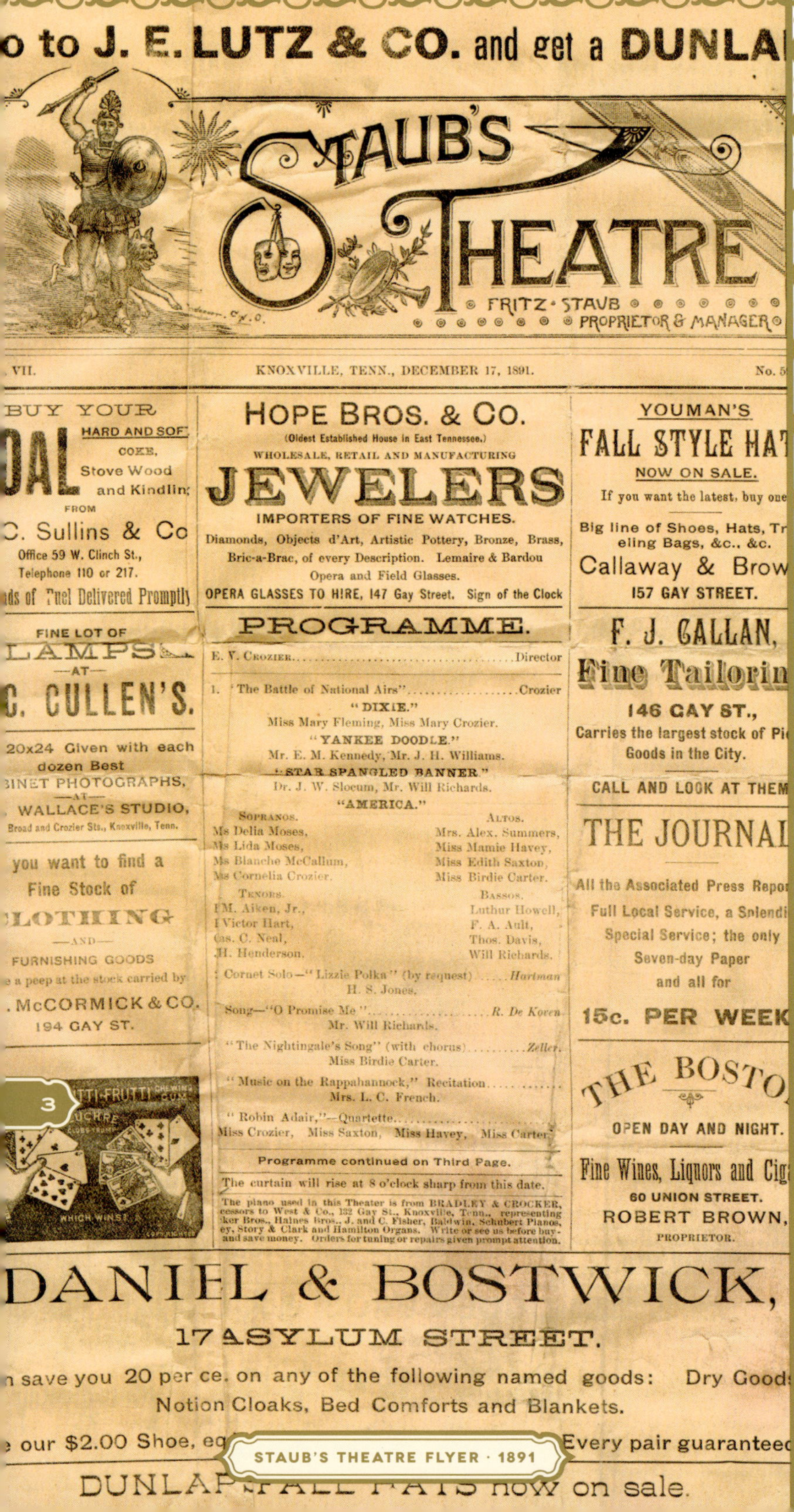

o to J. E. LUTZ & CO. and get a DUNLA

STAUB'S THEATRE

FRITZ · STAUB PROPRIETOR & MANAGER

VII. KNOXVILLE, TENN., DECEMBER 17, 1891. No. 5

BUY YOUR HARD AND SOF COKE, Stove Wood and Kindlin; FROM C. Sullins & Co Office 59 W. Clinch St., Telephone 110 or 217. ...ds of Fuel Delivered Promptly

HOPE BROS. & CO. (Oldest Established House in East Tennessee.) WHOLESALE, RETAIL AND MANUFACTURING JEWELERS IMPORTERS OF FINE WATCHES. Diamonds, Objects d'Art, Artistic Pottery, Bronze, Brass, Bric-a-Brac, of every Description. Lemaire & Bardou Opera and Field Glasses. OPERA GLASSES TO HIRE, 147 Gay Street. Sign of the Clock

YOUMAN'S FALL STYLE HAT NOW ON SALE. If you want the latest, buy one Big line of Shoes, Hats, Tr... eling Bags, &c., &c. Callaway & Brow... 157 GAY STREET.

FINE LOT OF LAMPS AT C. CULLEN'S.

PROGRAMME.

E. V. CROZIER.....Director

1. "The Battle of National Airs".....Crozier
"DIXIE." Miss Mary Fleming, Miss Mary Crozier.
"YANKEE DOODLE." Mr. E. M. Kennedy, Mr. J. H. Williams.
"STAR SPANGLED BANNER." Dr. J. W. Slocum, Mr. Will Richards.
"AMERICA."

SOPRANOS.	ALTOS.
Ms Delia Moses,	Mrs. Alex. Summers,
Ms Lida Moses,	Miss Mamie Havey,
Ms Blanche McCallum,	Miss Edith Saxton,
Ms Cornelia Crozier.	Miss Birdie Carter.
TENORS.	BASSOS.
M. Aiken, Jr.,	Luthur Howell,
Victor Hart,	F. A. Ault,
...as. C. Neal,	Thos. Davis,
H. Henderson.	Will Richards.

Cornet Solo—"Lizzie Polka" (by request).....Hartman
H. S. Jones.

Song—"O Promise Me".....R. De Koven
Mr. Will Richards.

"The Nightingale's Song" (with chorus).....Zeller.
Miss Birdie Carter.

"Music on the Rappahannock," Recitation.....
Mrs. L. C. French.

"Robin Adair,"—Quartette.
Miss Crozier, Miss Saxton, Miss Havey, Miss Carter.

Programme continued on Third Page.

The curtain will rise at 8 o'clock sharp from this date.

F. J. GALLAN, Fine Tailorin... 146 GAY ST., Carries the largest stock of Pi... Goods in the City.

CALL AND LOOK AT THEM

20x24 Given with each dozen Best ...BINET PHOTOGRAPHS, AT WALLACE'S STUDIO, Broad and Crozier Sts., Knoxville, Tenn.

you want to find a Fine Stock of CLOTHING AND FURNISHING GOODS ...a peep at the stock carried by ...McCORMICK & CO. 194 GAY ST.

THE JOURNAL All the Associated Press Repor... Full Local Service, a Splendi... Special Service; the only Seven-day Paper and all for 15c. PER WEEK

TUTTI-FRUTTI CHEWING GUM ... WHICH WINS?

THE BOSTO... OPEN DAY AND NIGHT. Fine Wines, Liquors and Cig... 60 UNION STREET. ROBERT BROWN, PROPRIETOR.

DANIEL & BOSTWICK, 17 ASYLUM STREET.

...n save you 20 per ce. on any of the following named goods: Dry Goods Notion Cloaks, Bed Comforts and Blankets.

...our $2.00 Shoe, eq... Every pair guaranteed

DUNLAP FALL HATS now on sale.

STAUB'S THEATRE FLYER · 1891

FIRST PRESBYTERIAN CHURCH, AT BOTTOM CENTER

Peter Staub built Knoxville's first big theater in 1872, on Gay Street at Cumberland. Staub's Opera House presented much more vaudeville than opera but established a tradition of regular, almost nightly, live entertainment on Gay Street. Named randomly, after an admired street of the same name in Baltimore, Gay Street was starting to seem gay, in the original sense of lighthearted, cheerful, and fun. Several other downtown streets changed their names, over the years, but Gay Street remained Gay Street. Its theaters, brightly lit well into the night, may have had something to do with that consistency.

Throughout the Victorian era, Staub's and multiple smaller theaters featured traveling vaudeville shows, so frequently that at the height of the season a local fan could watch a different performance every night for weeks without ever leaving Gay Street. On this one street, Knoxvillians got to see many of the great stars of the day, in person: Lily Langtree, Sarah Bernhardt, Will Rogers, Anna Pavlova, all three of the Barrymores. Late-19th-century Knoxville had railroads and a concentration of population, and that was enough to make it a respectable entertainment market.

SARAH BERNHARDT

ANNA PAVLOVA

AN UNLIKELY FILM PIONEER

William Gibbs McAdoo (1863 – 1941), who lived near Staub's Theatre in downtown Knoxville in his youth, graduated from UT, and as a young attorney founded the city's first electric streetcar system in 1890. McAdoo had a remarkable career that included a stint as Secretary of the Treasury under President Wilson and a long period as U.S. Senator from California. In 1919, as an attorney working with director D.W. Griffith and actors Charlie Chaplin, Douglas Fairbanks, and Mary Pickford, he helped found the major Hollywood studio United Artists.

THE STAUB WAS RENAMED LOEW'S IN 1920

Public showings of motion pictures first emerged in Europe in the mid-1890s. The first known exhibit of cinema in America was in New York in 1896.

By the account of one turn-of-the-century cinema operator, Knoxville was "known to be one of the first cities in the United States to have any moving pictures." Whether that statement is accurate or not, it does not mean movies were immediately popular here. Movies took years to catch on as a mainstream pastime.

At first, movies, or "magic lantern shows," were just another vaudeville novelty. A short film might be one of four or five attractions on a vaudeville bill. Researchers have argued about the first movie ever seen in Knoxville, whether it was a half-remembered outdoor showing in Turner Park along North Broadway in the late 1890s, as one old but hard-to-confirm story has it; or at Chilhowee Park, which was showing movies by 1905; or as part of a vaudeville show at Staub's; or in one of the shadowy nocturnal joints down on Central. By the early 1900s, movies were sometimes shown even at the roller-skating rink at Gay and Main, "just to give the skaters a rest."

LOEW'S INTERIOR

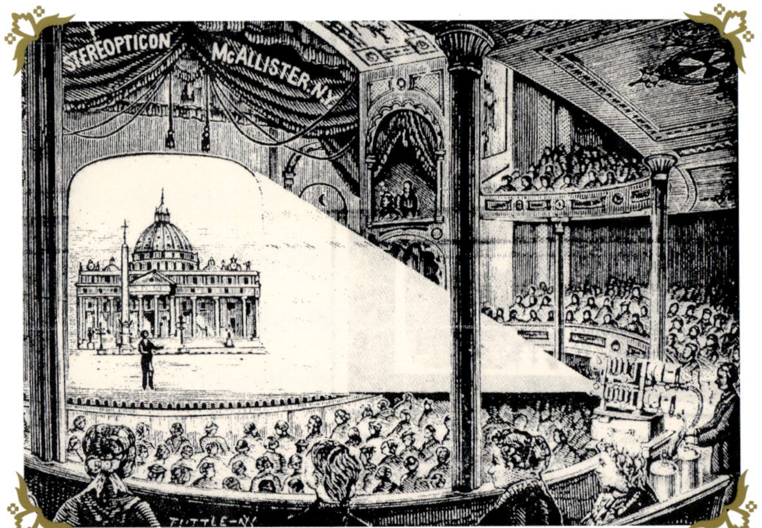

1897 ILLUSTRATION OF A MAGIC LANTERN SHOW

Some accounts outline a series of short-lived "magic-lantern shows" that coalesced along South Central, the old "Bowery" area, around 1905, when that urban thicket was still known mainly for saloons and whorehouses. Central, which connected the rail yards with the riverboat wharves, was Knoxville's cheap-entertainment district and might have seemed a natural for the latest gimmick. One particular "resort" known as the Arcade, located on Central near Church, showed some of Knoxville's first movies. Early cinema operators showed short, minutes-long films, often in combination with a live vaudeville comic. One of the earliest films mentioned in newspapers is Edison's grim four-minute documentary / re-enactment, *The Execution of Czolgosz*, which a Gay Street theater showed in 1902. Still, early movies proved to be less exciting than a regular night on the streets.

"A theater in the Bowery combined a show with a glass of beer," according to a paraphrased interview, about 30 years later, with early cinema operator Charlie Champe. "But the movies were practically booed out as just a little too tame.... Fights often started in the theaters, and the show was stopped as police were called. It was not a really popular business, although one that drew many out of mere curiosity."

Prohibition arrived in Knoxville early, first with a citywide saloon ban in 1907. Along with a new state law suppressing gambling, the new abstemiousness helped focus interest on legal entertainment, like movies. It also forced landlords to consider new uses for 106 saloon spaces suddenly emptied by the saloon ban. Some former saloons became small cinemas.

Cinemas suddenly proliferated that year, about nine of them popping up downtown, most of them on Gay Street. The Dixie Amusement Parlor at 315 South Gay promised "the best pictures in the city." The Wonderland was at 621 South Gay Street, on the same block as the future Tennessee, but across the street. It showed travel scenes shot from trains and in 1907 advertised a comedy short called *In the Haunts of Rip Van Winkle*.

Remarkably, one of Knoxville's earliest cinema operators was Cal Johnson, a former slave who'd prospered in the saloon business. Around 1907 he opened the Lincoln Theatre, a cinema set up in a former Central Street saloon. Aimed at the black audience, the Lincoln lasted only three or four years, but compared to most cinemas of the era, that was a good run. Few lasted more than a couple of years. That early rush to adapt may have overwhelmed the marketplace. Some pioneer cinemas shifted back to vaudeville, which, as it turned out, still had a few more decades of life.

KNOXVILLE'S LOST FIRST MOVIE

Local photographer Jim Thompson (1881 – 1976) experimented with making motion pictures. He completed one in 1915, a comedy called Aunt Sally Visits Knoxville. One of its "stars" was local artist Hugh Tyler, who was James Agee's uncle. Although released with some fanfare, it's considered "lost."

CAL JOHNSON

1844 - 1925

TOPPING-OUT CEREMONY WITH MAUD THE MULE · 1908

THE BURWELL

The Tennessee Theatre and the Burwell, the 10-story building on the corner of Clinch and Gay, are hard to speak of separately. Today, patrons enter beneath the face of the Burwell, to which the theater's famous vertical sign is attached. Many of the Burwell's offices and residences are directly above the Tennessee's lobby. However, the Burwell, originally known as the Knoxville Banking & Trust Building, was built 20 years before the theater, and without any dream there would ever be a theater attached to it.

Among the building's first tenants was J.E. Lutz, founder of an insurance company that lasted on the building's second floor for almost a century, and husband of Adelia Lutz, sometimes hailed as Tennessee's first female professional artist. Another was John Webb Green, attorney and author who was behind, among many other things, Fountain City Park, and his cousin, Clary Webb, who moved to Knoxville to join his firm. Webb's son Robert would found Knoxville's most durable private school.

The Burwell was, for four years, the tallest building in Knoxville. The new bank building's completion included a bizarre touch that earned it some national attention for its sheer oddity. Instead of the traditional Christmas tree, the construction company hoisted to the very top of the completed frame a favorite work mule named Maud. The picture made a collectible postcard, shown at left, with the caption, "Maud up in the air, 10 stories — 10,000 people view the sight."

continues on next page...

Former Knoxville mayor William Gass, president of the bank, was in charge of the project and noticed that one of Fuller's employees seemed especially at home in the building. Originally from Baltimore, Martin Quinn was a carpenter's foreman on the project. Gass surprised Quinn on the site with a proposal. "I guess you are 40-odd years old," Gass said. "You're old enough to settle down and rear your family. I want you to stay in Knoxville and manage this building."

Quinn wasn't crazy about the fact Knoxville had just voted itself dry. But he'd already learned how to deal with bootleggers. He accepted Gass's offer and spent the last 47 years of his life attending to the building he helped build. Quinn, who wore a thick mustache and carried a cane, became one of Gay Street's beloved characters. He raised two children in Knoxville and claimed he never regretted it.

One of the city's first mainstream movie theaters was the Edison Theatorium, named for cinema's presumed inventor, at 703 South Gay Street, in 1907. But that theater changed hands, and names, several times, and its emphasis on cinema may have been premature. By 1909 or 1910, the hall was hosting mostly vaudeville shows.

The first movie to draw a crowd patient enough to stand in line was reportedly a 1908 re-enactment of what the press had dubbed "the crime of the century," the recent murder of architect Stanford White by Harry Thaw, at New York's Madison Square Garden, concerning a beautiful woman. A 1912 showing of a Western about the Dalton gang was introduced by bank robber and ex-convict Emmett Dalton. Many early films seemed a safe way to witness violence.

Showing movies was an unstable business, and one barely a step removed from the wilder fringes of town. Movies were short, and movie theaters were generally short-lived, almost fly-by-night operations. Cinema wasn't taken very seriously, especially by the middle-class family seeking diversion.

A few hit on the right formula and lasted a decade or more. The Majestic, on Gay Street near Wall Avenue, was majestic in name only, one of a half-dozen cramped, often crowded storefront cinemas competing for the nickels of passersby who'd walk in to watch whatever was on for a few minutes regardless of showtimes, which were generally unannounced.

The Majestic is remembered better than others because it appears in James Agee's autobiographical novel, *A Death in the Family*. Its opening passage about a father and son walking to Gay Street to catch a movie, around 1916, may be literature's most famous

Gay Street was sprouting movie theaters soon after 1900, when Hollywood was still unknown — though most cinemas weren't nearly as grand as the Tennessee. Despite its name, the Majestic was a small theater, hardly bigger than a shoe store, but it became prominent in literature. In his Pulitzer-winning novel, "A Death in the Family," author James Agee remembered an evening watching a Charlie Chaplin film with his father, ca. 1916, a scene portrayed in motion pictures and television portrayals. In this rare photo of the northwestern corner of Gay and Wall, the Majestic is in the smaller building on the right — with a tailor shop upstairs. A sign in the foyer advertises the 1920 silent feature "Son of Tarzan."

THE MAJESTIC, AT RIGHT

depiction of downtown Knoxville. In the scene, the 6-year-old protagonist and his father watch a Charlie Chaplin short to the accompaniment of manic piano music. (The Pulitzer-winning novel, with its opening moviegoing scene, was later depicted in films, including one that had its world premiere at the Tennessee.)

AD FOR CRYSTAL THEATRE · CA. 1916

For Agee, movies became a lifelong fascination. The journalist and author went on to be a seminal movie critic, for both *Time* magazine and *The Nation*, and later wrote a couple of screenplays himself. His script for *The African Queen* earned an Oscar nomination. Agee became a personal friend of Chaplin and a prominent champion of his legacy.

Chaplin and others were making it obvious that moving pictures were sticking around, becoming part of America's mainstream popular culture, and perhaps even a wise business investment.

With the development of the feature film after 1915, cinema developers began reconsidering the concept. They emphasized comfort, concentrating more on large houses with plush seating, where people wouldn't mind sitting for a couple of hours at a time.

A few newer Gay Street cinemas — the Strand, the Queen, the Rex — suggested some pretentions of luxury and significance, or at least comfort and respectability.

THE STRAND THEATRE, GAY STREET · 1918

As early as 1915, multiple movie theaters competed for audiences along one remarkable street. The Rex and the Crystal were next-door cinemas on the 400 block of South Gay (just north of the Miller's building, near the far-right globes in this photo). The Crystal, on the left, appears to be advertising a Keystone Cops comedy; the Rex, a film featuring now-forgotten comic star Eddie Lyons. There was in fact a third cinema on the same block. Visible on the next block is an overhead banner advertising religious services at still another silent-era cinema, the Queen. Probably Knoxville's most sumptuous cinema before the Riviera, the Queen would close in 1928, the night before the Tennessee opened. The Burwell is visible in the background, to the left, and so is the Imperial Hotel, which burned down in 1916.

GAY STREET · CA. 1915

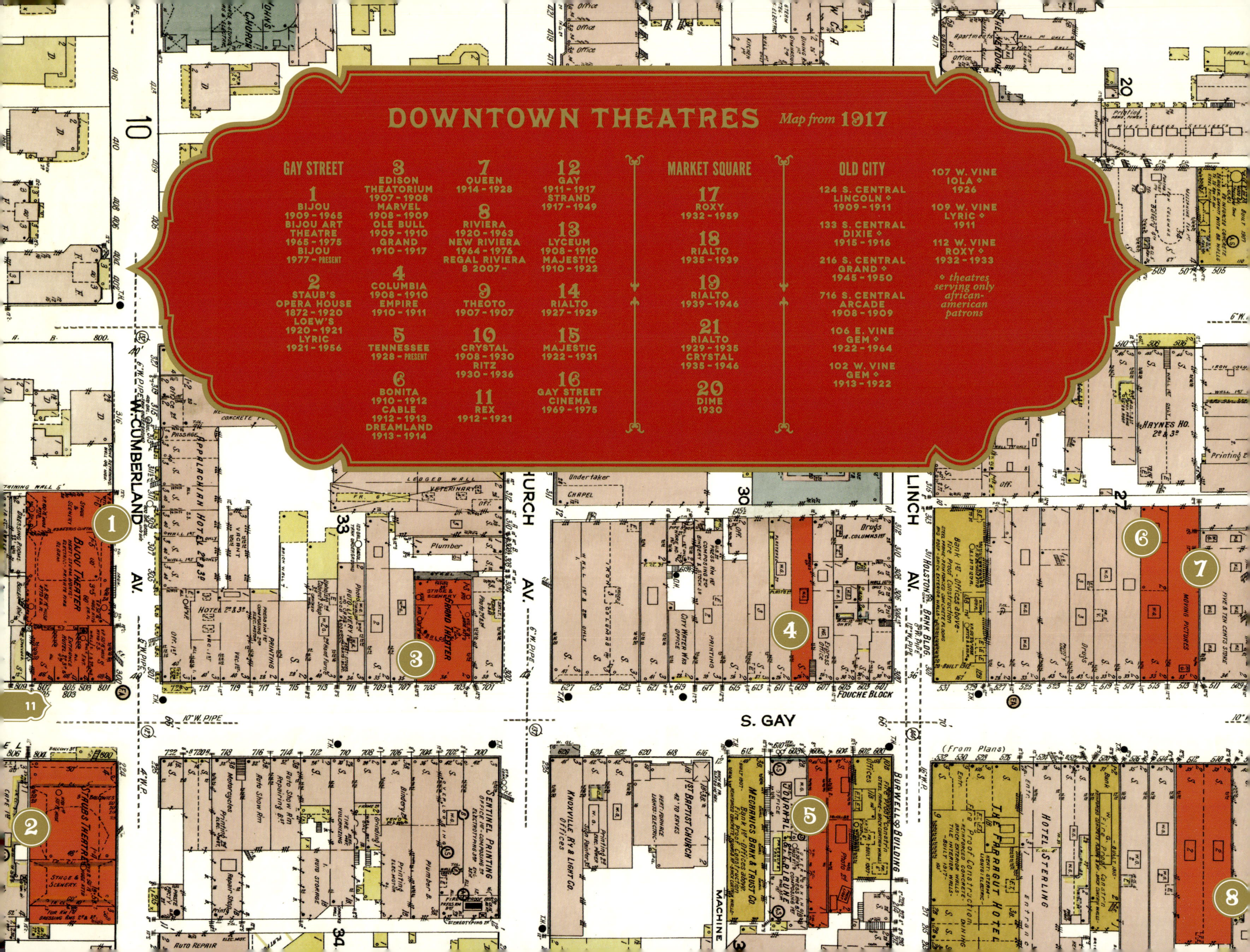
DOWNTOWN THEATRES
Map from 1917
GAY STREET
1
BIJOU
1909 - 1965
BIJOU ART THEATRE
1965 - 1975
BIJOU
1977 - PRESENT
2
STAUB'S OPERA HOUSE
1872 - 1920
LOEW'S
1920 - 1921
LYRIC
1921 - 1956
3
EDISON THEATORIUM
1907 - 1908
MARVEL
1908 - 1909
OLE BULL
1909 - 1910
GRAND
1910 - 1917
4
COLUMBIA
1908 - 1910
EMPIRE
1910 - 1911
5
TENNESSEE
1928 - PRESENT
6
BONITA
1910 - 1912
CABLE
1912 - 1913
DREAMLAND
1913 - 1914
7
QUEEN
1914 - 1928
8
RIVIERA
1920 - 1963
NEW RIVIERA
1964 - 1976
REGAL RIVIERA 8
2007 -
9
THEOTO
1907 - 1907
10
CRYSTAL
1908 - 1930
RITZ
1930 - 1936
11
REX
1912 - 1921
12
GAY
1911 - 1917
STRAND
1917 - 1949
13
LYCEUM
1908 - 1910
MAJESTIC
1910 - 1922
14
RIALTO
1927 - 1929
15
MAJESTIC
1922 - 1931
16
GAY STREET CINEMA
1969 - 1975
MARKET SQUARE
17
ROXY
1932 - 1959
18
RIALTO
1935 - 1939
19
RIALTO
1939 - 1946
21
RIALTO
1929 - 1935
CRYSTAL
1935 - 1946
20
DIME
1930
OLD CITY
124 S. CENTRAL
LINCOLN ◆
1909 - 1911
133 S. CENTRAL
DIXIE ◆
1915 - 1916
216 S. CENTRAL
GRAND ◆
1945 - 1950
716 S. CENTRAL
ARCADE
1908 - 1909
106 E. VINE
GEM ◆
1922 - 1964
102 W. VINE
GEM ◆
1913 - 1922
107 W. VINE
IOLA ◆
1926
109 W. VINE
LYRIC ◆
1911
112 W. VINE
ROXY ◆
1932 - 1933
◆ theatres serving only african-american patrons
W. CUMBERLAND AV.
S. GAY
BIJOU THEATER
STAUB'S THEATRE
GRAND THEATER

17
BAKERY
18
19
20
21
WALL AV.
WEST SIDE MARKET SQ.
M A R K E T H O
PUBLIC HALL 2D
POLICE HEADQUARTERS 2D
1ST CITY OFFICES 2D 3D
EAST SIDE MARKET SQ.
UNION AV.
Drugs
Moving Pictures
Bank
9
10
11
12
13
14
15
16
STRATFORD HOTEL
McCOY BUILDING
Flats Above
CURRY AV.
MARKET
COMMERCE AV.
LAWSON McGHEE PUBLIC LIBRARY
AUGUSTINE
VICTORIA
ST. MARY'S PAROCHIAL SCHOOL
LODGE HALL 4TH
MINNIS BLK.
Wall Paper & Paints
Fire Proof Constr'n (Built 1906)
THE ST. JAMES HOTEL
KNOXVILLE RY. & LIGHT CO.
MOORE HOME
PEOPLES TELEPHONE & TELEGRAPH CO
LODGE HALL 1ST
HAYNES BLK.
SANFORD BLK.
S. GAY
BRISCOE BLD'G
Dep't Store
Whol. Drugs
Whol. Milly
Furniture
Drugs
Printing
Tin Shop
FARM MACHINERY
AUTO SALES

PLANNING A MOVIE PALACE

CHAPTER 2

Born during the Civil War, Clay Brown Atkin (1864 – 1931) came from one of Knoxville's first prosperous industrial families. His father, Frank Atkin, a dealer in lumber and architectural wood, had built Knoxville's first railroad hotel, known as the Atkin House, which by the late 1860s sometimes hosted live music. Son Clay grew up in a suddenly booming industrial city and founded his own company principally involved in making high-class mantels for Edwardian homes. By 1900, C.B. Atkin's company had overseas contracts and claimed to be the biggest mantel manufacturer in the world. Atkin got involved in multiple real estate ventures, prominently a large hotel near the railroad station, the 1910 Hotel Atkin, which developed a reputation for hosting live classical music in the lobby.

The year before he'd been a partner in the construction of a new live-performance theater called the Bijou. Though right across the street from Staub's and not quite as big, it was a success, with a reputation as Knoxville's most modern theater; it was the city's first theater to accept reservations by telephone. It originally seated about 1,500, with two balconies. That figure was roughly cut in half with the passing decades, as seats got wider, and as the theater retired the second balcony. Though built for live performances, the Bijou was soon showing occasional movies.

Atkin later turned his attention to the tall building a couple of blocks away.

Originally known as the Knoxville Banking & Trust Building, the 10-story steel-frame building at Gay and Clinch was completed in 1908, a year before the Bijou, and was for four years Knoxville's tallest — by some accounts, Knoxville's first "skyscraper." The name of the contractor in charge of the job lent extra credit in the "skyscraper" claim. The George A. Fuller Company had practically invented the phenomenon. Five years earlier, it'd built New York's tallest building, the 22-story Flatiron Building.

The Knoxville Banking & Trust's future might have seemed assured. When the Holston Bank building, a little taller than the first skyscraper, was built diagonally across the street in 1913, the intersection of Gay and Clinch was becoming known as "the 100 Percent Corner," as if that were the one spot where the city was trying its hardest. The city's finest hotel, the Imperial, was on the intersection's northeast corner. When it burned down in a lightning fire in 1916, it was replaced with a larger hotel called the Farragut.

TENNESSEE THEATRE CONSTRUCTION · JANUARY 1928

BIJOU THEATRE INTERIOR

The Knoxville Banking & Trust Building became a prestigious address for Knoxville professionals, especially attorneys and insurance men. Several of its upper-floor tenants were firms that thrived there for decades. The bank on the ground floor didn't last long after the completion of its headquarters, however. Its president, William Gass, the former mayor who had directed the skyscraper's construction, disappeared from Knoxville's records soon after his bank did. Whether he moved away is a matter of speculation. He's the only 20th-century Knoxville mayor whose personal fate is unknown to historians.

In 1917, C.B. Atkin bought the skyscraper and gave it a more personal name, the Burwell. The name was in honor of his wife, Mary Burwell (1871 – 1949), originally of Schuylkill County, Pennsylvania. Atkin also bought a roughly mallet-shaped piece of acreage behind the Burwell stretching back to State Street. What he intended to do with the property was not immediately obvious.

When America joined the war in Europe, films rallied the home front, and idealistic young doughboys marched down Gay Street to board the troop trains at the station. One young country-club golf champ named McGhee Tyson saw a film on Gay Street about wartime heroism and enlisted as a Navy aviator. After his death in a plane crash over the North Sea, just months later, his mother offered the city Tyson Park, in trade for her son's name on the city's new airport.

By war's end, Knoxville was movie mad. Peace was at hand, the economy was booming, and veterans of one of the most horrible scenes in history were a ready market for diversion. Cities across America began building large, elegant movie theaters.

CLAY BROWN ATKIN

1864 – 1931

C. B. ATKIN IN "MEN OF AFFAIRS" 1921

Leading the charge was Paramount, the Hollywood studio associated with producer Adolph Zukor and the stars in his "Famous Players" strategy, casting familiar and beloved figures like Mary Pickford, Douglas Fairbanks, Gloria Swanson, and Rudolph Valentino. Paramount also pioneered national distribution, sending multiple new films each week to each of hundreds of Paramount cinemas around the nation. Paramount dominated many cities. Eventually through its distribution engine then known as Publix, Paramount would be in charge of 2,000 cinemas nationwide.

By 1920 Knoxville was a Paramount town, and nobody was complaining. (Loew's, a new name for Staub's, was an exception, but only for 20 months. Renamed the Lyric in late 1921, it became a Paramount theater.)

Knoxville's cinema supply, mostly consisting of small storefront theaters, suggested plenty of room in the market for a large first-run theater to accommodate the crowds who wanted to see the blockbuster movies when they were brand-new.

Regional business Tennessee Enterprises, a successor to an earlier organization called Signal Amusement Company, was the local management company associated with Paramount. Tennessee Enterprises announced a grand new theater on Gay Street and named it after a faraway place famous for its shows: the Riviera.

The construction of the Riviera, planned by local architects Manley & Young and built by local contractor Worsham Brothers, was almost stealthy. Work on the theater was hardly visible on Gay Street. Men worked behind the spruced-up brick façade of the circa 1880s Logan-Ernest Building.

BIJOU THEATRE IN 1912

Open on December 6, 1920, the Riviera was large, with 1,006 seats, and for several years it ruled as Knoxville's landmark movie house. It offered luxurious detailing, including a lobby of pink Tennessee marble and mahogany, modern ventilation (not yet air conditioning), modern bathrooms, and sconce-style lighting.

The Riviera was an elegant place, declared by the *Knoxville Journal* to be "one of the most modern and beautiful theaters in the country." Its beauty adhered to classical ideals of design. Still, there was nothing astonishingly unusual about it. The Riviera wasn't a spectacle in itself. Knoxville's booming population and the growing popularity of movies suggested the Riviera wouldn't be the last word. In fact, even before the Riviera was completed, plans were afoot for a much larger, much grander cinema half a block away.

A *Journal* article was headlined, "Riviera Theatre Opens Tomorrow: Beautiful Show House Will Be Revelation to Knoxvillians." But the story's second paragraph stole some drama from the headline. The Riviera "is only part of the great expansion plan which has been announced ... by the officers of the Tennessee Enterprises, Inc."

Whether landowner Atkin was a partner in that group is elusive. The two "officers" who spoke on behalf of Tennessee Enterprises in 1920 were Chattanooga businessmen.

"The company already has secured a lease on the property in the rear of the Burwell Building, with an opening onto Gay Street through the building now occupied by the Baltimore Lunch Room. The property which was acquired just about a year ago will be utilized for the construction of another large and modern theatre by this company to cost approximately half a million dollars."

It took longer than expected, and required much more money. For almost eight years, for most of the Roaring Twenties, the Riviera would dominate as Knoxville's largest and finest movie theater.

Tennessee Enterprises set up its headquarters at the Riviera and over the next few years ran that theater as well as older cinemas the Strand, the Queen, and the Majestic, and later the Lyric and the Bijou.

William C. Drumbar was a Chattanooga railroad man who discovered he liked the movie business. He'd moved to Knoxville in 1917 to work with Signal Amusement Company, as manager of the Queen and Strand theaters. By the time the Riviera was completed, he was Tennessee Enterprises' "Manager of Theatres." While he was part of planning the most extravagant theater ever built in East Tennessee, Drumbar kept his home in a room at the old Elks' Lodge, on State Street diagonally across from the work site.

RIVIERA THEATRE · 1921

RIVIERA THEATRE INTERIOR · 1920

In this ca. 1921 photo, the Riviera's signage advertises the romantic comedy "Lessons in Love," starring Constance Talmadge. Completed in 1920 with 1,006 seats, the Riviera was Knoxville's largest and most luxurious cinema before the opening of the Tennessee. Operated by the same company affiliated with Paramount Studios, the two landmark cinemas coexisted half a block from each other for almost half a century, offering both movies and, especially in the early years, frequent live shows. The Riviera's stylish Mediterranean clay-tile awning didn't survive the decades; later photos show a plainer façade. Remodeled after an almost-ruinous fire in 1963, the Riviera was torn down in 1988, with little public notice. Almost 20 years later a new eight-screen multiplex, the Regal Riviera, was built on the same spot.

Theater managers seemed to live very simply in those days; most were young men who lived in modest apartments downtown. They were likely advised to live near their theaters, in case there were problems.

The 1920s' sweeping changes in entertainment technology were perhaps more dramatic than in any decade of the computer era.

Home entertainment arrived in the 1920s, in the form of radio. By the middle of the decade Knoxville had three radio stations, and locals could listen to music, comedy, even drama without leaving their houses. There was even a rumor that there might be something called television.

CONTRACTOR EARL WORSHAM IN "MEN OF AFFAIRS" 1921

Phonographs had been introduced years before but became more common than ever in the 1920s, as even working-class people could listen to jazz crooners, novelty tunes, religious hymns, marching bands — and one previously underappreciated folk style that spawned a few vigorous local practitioners. Never recorded on phonograph records until 1923, it would years later be known as country music.

And motion pictures became more than odd little novelties; the feature film became the norm, more popular than ever before. As the decade began, movies were still silent. The fact that they were usually accompanied by musical or other performers suggested people were looking for more than just flickering images on a screen.

Across the nation, entrepreneurs learned they could tempt people out with an experience they couldn't get at home, by way of astonishing architecture. The 1920s turned out to be the era of the Movie Palace.

It could hardly have been anticipated. It ran contrary to every architectural trend. Around the world, almost all architecture had been getting simpler, with less and less ornamentation. The 1920s was the decade of Bauhaus, the International style, the birth of architectural Modernism, which disdained embellishment, decoration, anything that didn't serve a practical function. Modernism was catching on even in middle-American cities like Knoxville. The simple, big-windowed Daylight Building on Union Avenue, built almost simultaneously with the Tennessee, suggests that contrast. Modernism and movie palace design hardly rubbed shoulders and were almost contrary to one another. Modernist architecture emphasized use of light, with larger and larger windows, sometimes whole walls of them. Cinemas were perhaps the one form of architecture that had no use for natural light at all.

By the mid-1920s, the 600 block of Gay Street made an especially interesting cluster. The project to expand the Burwell and add a huge new theater behind it took out a few Victorian commercial buildings, without obvious regrets. They weren't more than 30 or 40 years old, and in the 1920s there were still hundreds of them. The best-known loss was the once-famous studio of McCrary & Branson. Knoxville's first full-time professional artist, European-trained painter Lloyd Branson had kept his Gay Street studio there until about 1920, when he retired to live his final years quietly in the suburbs of North Knoxville.

GAY STREET BEFORE THE TENNESSEE · 1926

The original frontage of the Burwell, at left, was adjacent to two buildings torn down for the Tennessee Theatre project, which included an expansion of the Burwell. Herbert's Dairy Lunch was on the ground floor of the once-famous McCrary and Branson studio, workplace of photographers and painters, including Lloyd Branson, the European-trained painter who was the first to make a career as a professional artist in Knoxville. Images of this Victorian building were used to advertise the once-busy studio, which had closed before the building was acquired for the Tennessee project. In this 1926 photo, the second floor is plastered with advertisements for the Riviera, half a block away, which also used ground-floor space next door to tout "The Devil's Circus," a romantic drama starring Norma Shearer.

WILLIAM RULE

The 600 block of Gay was an artsy block all around, once also known for piano dealers and voice teachers. Among the businesses forced to move was the Crouch School of Music and the office of locally well-known architect Martin Parmelee. Just down the sidewalk was the stylish new marble-front Journal Arcade, completed in 1924, which housed the newsroom for the feisty morning newspaper, edited, as it had been for half a century, by Union veteran William Rule. Still a sharp-eyed political analyst in his 80s, the white-bearded Rule came to work every day without fail.

This pocket of downtown was seeing a lot of postwar construction. The same block's 1880s Mechanics Bank building got a marble facelift. Behind, on State Street, Knoxville's oldest church, First Presbyterian, underwent the biggest architectural expansion of its history.

Business on the Clinch Avenue side of the theater site was more prosaic: a couple of tailors, a couple of adding-machine and cash-register dealers, an electric contractor, a real estate office, and a small bank. For Knoxville, the construction project's biggest concern might have been the loss of a building facing State. The Davis Manufacturing Company had its headquarters in a building with tall arched windows. The "Try Me" company produced extracts and chemicals, both for recipes and for prescriptions.

Davis moved its aromatic operation to Jackson Avenue. It all had to go, in favor of a grand new theater.

If the Riviera had been an all-local project, the Tennessee, despite its name, would be more exotic, even at the hiring stage. Tennessee Enterprises first enlisted New York architect R.E. Hall, former superintendent of construction of New York's

DEMOLITION ON STATE STREET FOR TENNESSEE THEATRE

famous Rialto, now known as an architect in his own right. Hall was then working on the Florida Theatre in Jacksonville and the Carolina Theatre in Charlotte, both elaborately styled movie palaces completed in 1927.

The mid-1920s was turning out to be an era of big theaters named for states. The name "Tennessee" was apparently an early choice, referred to by that name in the trade press by 1925, and probably just reflected that trend. It's likely a coincidence that it was built one block from the site where the notable state of that name was founded, back in 1796.

During the Roaring Twenties, lots of astonishing million-dollar movie palaces were being built around the country, albeit relatively few in the South. But the trade journals were at least interested. From 1925 to 1928, Hollywood-based *Film Daily* ("The Newspaper of Filmdom") ran about a dozen short articles about the progress of Knoxville's Tennessee Theatre.

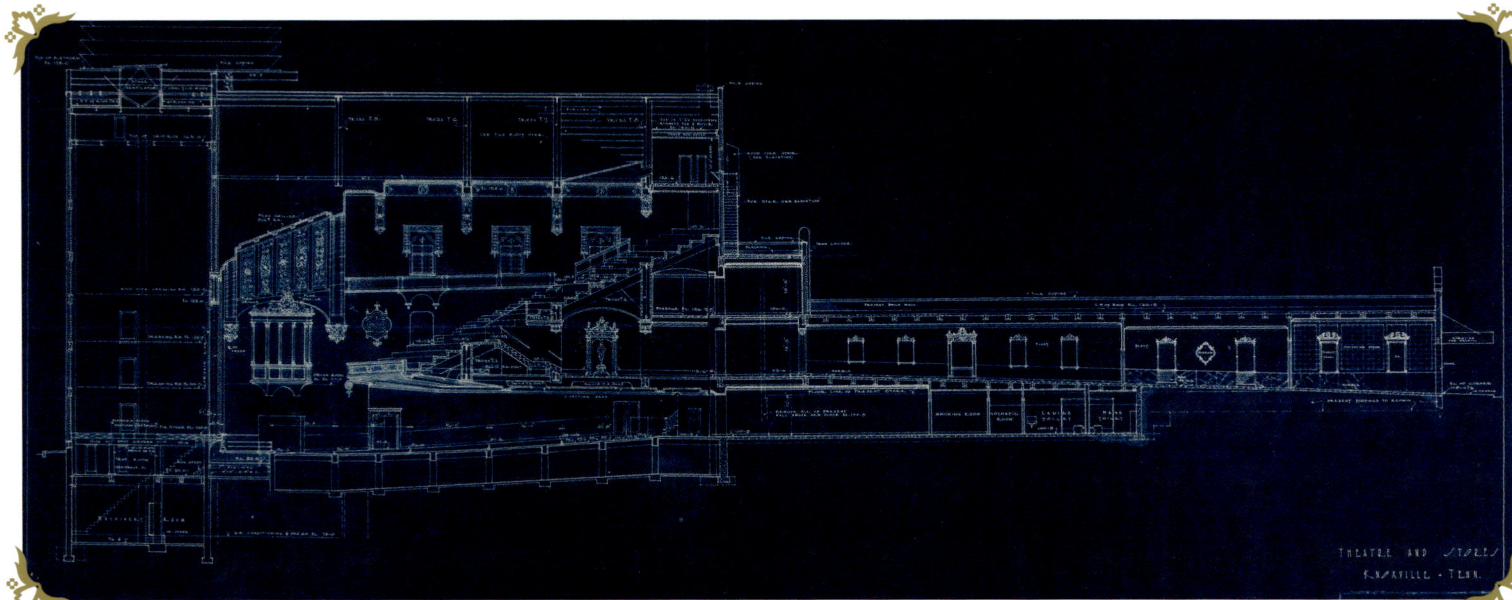

A 1925 ELEVATION DRAWING BY ARCHITECT R.E. HALL, A DESIGN THAT WAS ABANDONED

In late 1925, R.E. Hall met with Tennessee Enterprises and presented a plan of impressive proportions. A modern theater palace seating 2,102 (one source says 2,300), including a deep balcony and loges, the Hall plan would be a standard long, narrow theater, making use of the natural slope of the site. Patrons entering from Gay Street, via an arcade between new store spaces, would walk directly to the capacious balcony, on the same grade. Those who preferred the orchestra floor would have to walk downstairs. One version of the plan also proposed a Clinch Avenue entrance.

An almost magical feat of space usage, the Hall plan would allow for six roomy retail spaces along the Clinch Avenue side, and more on the Gay Street side. Occupied buildings on the site got eviction notices in late 1925. According to *Film Daily*, construction was to begin in March 1926. If Tennessee Enterprises had been ready to go forward with Hall's plan, the Tennessee Theatre might have been completed almost two years before it actually was.

But something about the architect, his design, or perhaps the expected cost of it, was apparently unsatisfying to the project managers. For reasons unrecorded, Tennessee Enterprises let Hall go finish the Carolina and Florida theaters and ended his involvement with the Knoxville project. (Lovers of extravagance may have regretted hearing about Hall's Florida Theatre in Jacksonville, which included grand balconies, fountains, and a rooftop garden. The Florida still exists, though much simplified from Hall's original fantasy.)

GRAVEN & MAYGER'S ALABAMA THEATRE, BIRMINGHAM · 1927

The site was surrounded by fencing as Knoxville, and the movie distribution industry wondered what would happen next. On February 7, 1927, *Film Daily* reported, "Plans for the $1,000,000 Publix-Saenger house which have been deferred for some time are to be resumed, it is understood .... For some time the Gay St. site of the proposed theater has been boarded off."

It was during that delay that Tennessee Enterprises and Publix took a gamble on a lesser-known design duo called Graven & Mayger. They were not exactly like any other theater-design firm in the country.

Anker Sveere Graven and Arthur Guy Mayger were two Chicago architects in their 30s who were just beginning to make a splash. Mayger was born in Deer Lodge, Montana, when it was still the Wild West. A combat veteran of the World War, he was decorated for bravery in action at the Argonne. He had worked prominently for famous theater-architecture firm Rapp & Rapp, who had designed New York's Paramount and other icons of the movie palace form. While working there, Mayger met Graven, who was from Menomonie, Wisconsin. The two came together almost accidentally, and they remained in partnership for only 15 months. But during that short period they did remarkable things.

Their collaboration began when audacious young Detroit architect Charles Agree approached Rapp & Rapp proposing an artistic collaboration on what promised to be a major Detroit landmark, the Hollywood Theatre. The well-established Chicago firm rejected Agree's perhaps impertinent offer, confident that they could get the commission without his help. But young associates Graven and Mayger heard about the discussions and quietly offered to break away from Rapp & Rapp to work with Agree themselves. The ad hoc collaboration earned the job. Though the project was a success, the three-way partnership did not survive it. The Detroit architect found Graven and Mayger to be "drunkards," and simply "no good" as human beings. (Graven, at least, has his defenders. Eighty years later, his son was still taking strong exception to Agree's insults, insisting that the elder Graven was a good man who provided for his family.)

Regardless of personal characterizations, for the next year and three months, Graven and Mayger became one of America's most remarkable theater design firms. Birmingham's Alabama Theatre, one of their early designs completed in 1927, was widely regarded as the most beautiful movie theater in the South.

On July 10, 1927, *Film Daily* ran a headline on the top center of its front page, "Publix in Knoxville" over a very short item: "Publix Theatres will erect a house on Gay Street to cost $1 million." That November, it announced, "Bids are now open on the $1 million Tennessee which will be built by local capital for lease to Tennessee Enterprises, a subsidiary of Publix." If the impetus for the project came from Hollywood, and the design came from Chicago, at least the investment was from Tennessee.

A few weeks later, that trade paper mentioned the architectural firm in charge of the design: "Graven and Nayger of Chicago." Chances are not many noticed the typo. Graven & Mayger weren't well known yet.

The Tennessee's design and construction coincided with a dramatically transitional era in movie history. Plans were on the drawing board in February 1927, when the first feature film ever shot in the region, starring two young Knoxvillians, Helen Mundy and Forrest James, opened at the Riviera. An unusual naturalistic experiment with local actors and on-location

FIRST CONSTRUCTION PHOTO · NOVEMBER 25, 1927

shooting (Mundy was reportedly discovered in a drugstore on Gay Street), *Stark Love* fascinated some national critics and even made some Top 10 lists — but it would be the last major feature film shot in the region for decades.

Meanwhile, as the land was cleared for the Tennessee, some filmmakers were experimenting with recorded soundtracks via Vitaphone technology, basically a phonograph record synchronized with the film. Some primitive "talking pictures" had appeared at Staub's Theatre as early as 1915, apparently using synchronized phonograph records, but the technology improved rapidly in the mid-1920s.

On October 6, 1927, *The Jazz Singer* opened at the Riviera. Though it was mostly silent, the Al Jolson film included several musical numbers, and a little dialogue (notably Jolson's ad-lib, "You ain't heard nothin' yet, folks!").

To build their grand new Knoxville movie palace, Tennessee Enterprises hired the George A. Fuller Company of Chicago. The name of America's skyscraper pioneer was recognizable in Knoxville, and their association with building the Burwell, 20 years earlier, made Fuller seem a natural for the Tennessee.

Despite its reputation for skyscrapers, Fuller did have some theater-building credits, including the Chicago Opera House. The Tennessee Theatre was turning out to be an almost all-Chicago project. Fuller broke ground on November 1, 1927. On Christmas Day, the *News-Sentinel* reported they were pouring concrete.

Graven and Mayger's plan allowed a significant expansion of the Burwell Building in its original style, giving it more frontage on Gay Street. That expansion was news in itself. Maybe Knoxville's once-famous "skyscraper" no longer seemed quite as tall as it once did, as a couple of other downtown buildings had topped it. The expansion would make the skinny building more versatile. Atkin hired Fuller to expand the building they'd built two decades earlier, with an addition above the theater entrance, in accord with the construction already underway.

The importance of the Burwell, designed purely as a practical corner office tower, and the fact that the available space for a theater was mainly on the interior of the block, meant that the Tennessee's extravagance would always be a hidden thing, a

THE JAZZ SINGER · 1927

ORIGINAL GRAVEN & MAYGER BLUEPRINT OF THE BALCONY AND MEZZANINE FOYER

CONSTRUCTION SITE FROM GAY STREET, SHOWING FUTURE ENTRANCE

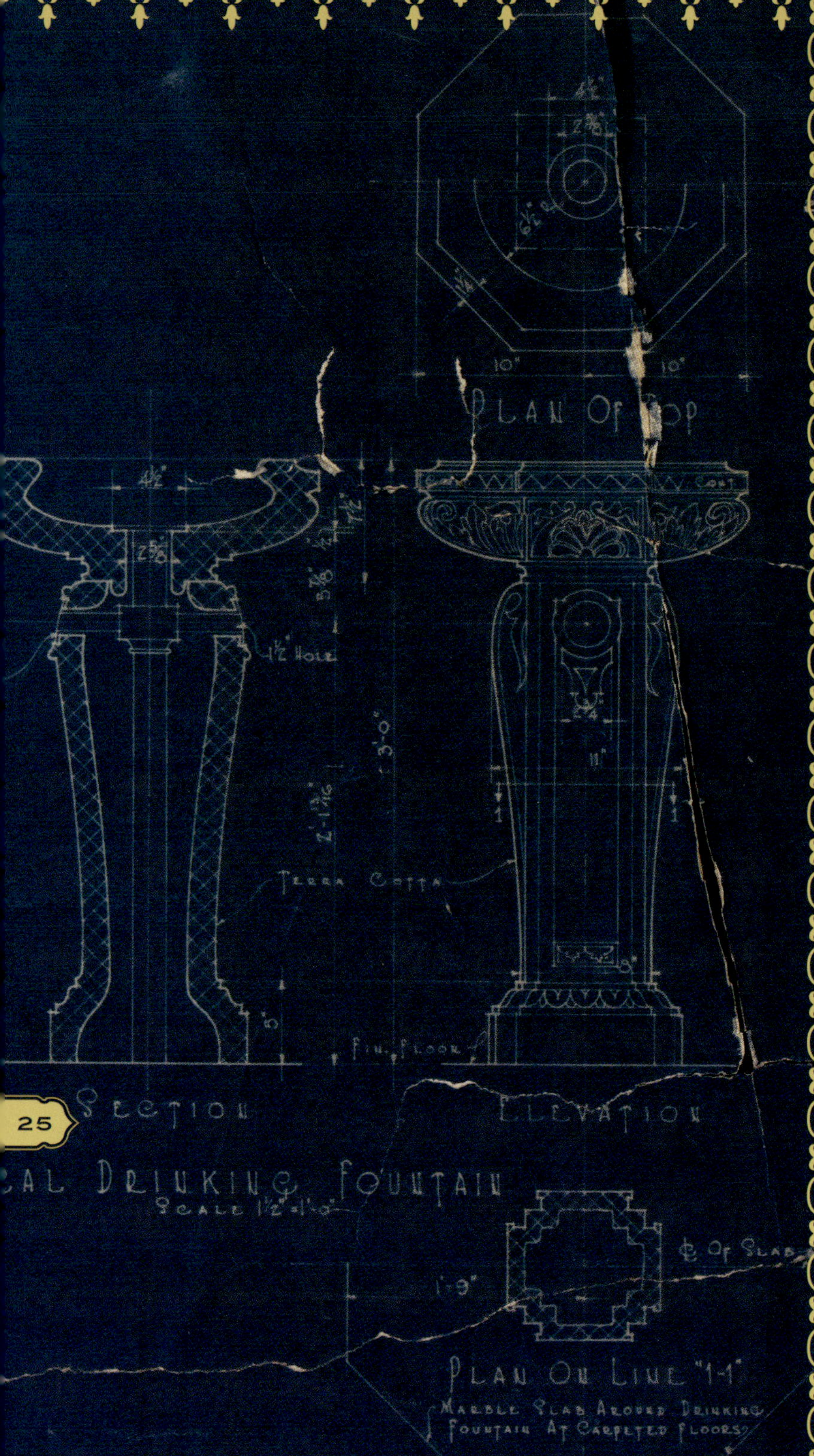

ORIGINAL DETAIL DRAWING OF THE TERRACOTTA DRINKING FOUNTAINS

ORIGINAL DETAIL DRAWING OF EXIT SIGNS FOUND THROUGHOUT THE THEATRE

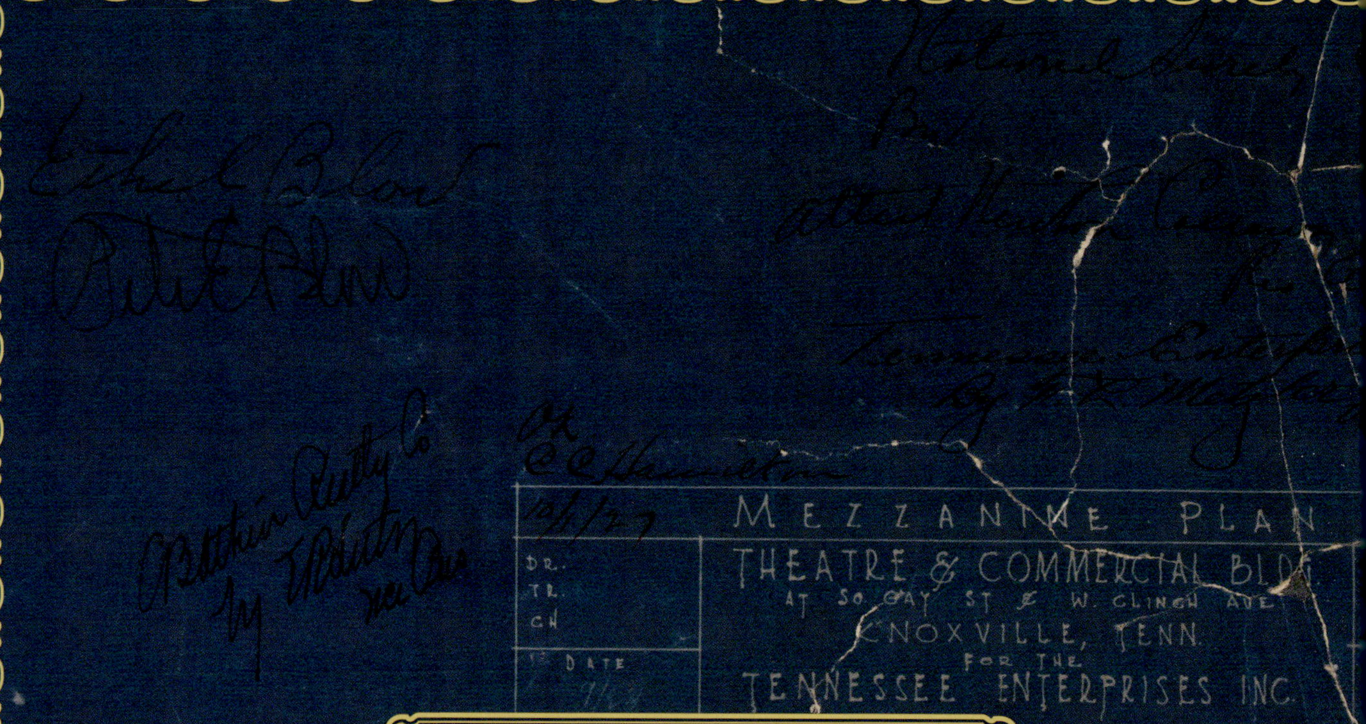

TITLE BLOCK AND SIGNATURES ON ORIGINAL DRAWINGS

STYLE

For decades, the term "Spanish-Moorish" has been used to apply to the Tennessee's exotic style. While not inaccurate, the term might give architectural historians some pause, because it involves an apparent redundancy: all Moorish architecture originated in Spain, and is plausibly Spanish. Moors were the Islamic people of Northern Africa who invaded Spain and remained for generations, developing a distinctive style reflecting both their memories of Arabic architecture and that of Spain.

Moorish Revival, a term more recognizable to movie-theater enthusiasts, applies to the Tennessee Theatre. The word "Spanish" may have been added to the term during the early days, for the benefit of people who didn't know what "Moorish" was. Still, there are some aspects of the Tennessee's interior that may be more Spanish than Moorish.

The Moorish Revival style took the American cinema world by storm in the latter 1920s, perhaps inspired by movies like the 1924 Douglas Fairbanks silent, "The Thief of Bagdad: An Arabian Nights Fantasy." One of the most popular movies of its era, it depicted Arab palaces with Islamic arches, and captured the imagination of mid-Prohibition, Coolidge-era America. It also folded in well with a national Egyptian vogue spawned by the 1922 discovery of King Tutankhamen's tomb.

Whatever the origin, dozens of movie theaters were built in the Arabian Nights Fantasy mode, the Moorish Revival style, all during a very short period. Almost all Moorish Revival theaters in America were built between 1925 and 1930. Those include Birmingham's Alabama Theatre, Atlanta's Fox Theatre, and Knoxville's Tennessee.

In several other Moorish Revival theaters, that style was reflected in the exterior of the theater too. That's not the case with the Tennessee. The arches in the brickwork along its Clinch Avenue side might seem to evoke the Eastern, but could just as easily be construed to reflect the Victorian archwork of some of its neighbors. There's little outside to suggest what's inside.

But part of the Tennessee's charm to the first-time visitor is the sudden transition, walking into an apparently conservative early 20th-century American building and finding oneself in something like an Eastern palace.

The Moorish Revival style was going around, even in Knoxville. First Baptist Church on Main Avenue, completed four years before the Tennessee, has some surprising Eastern elements in its interior design. The 1926 Talahi development (part of what would later be known as Sequoyah Hills) boasted monuments with Egyptian themes. Inventor-industrialist Weston Fulton's bizarre Lyons View mansion, completed the same year as the Tennessee, was distinctly Moorish, including a rooftop minaret.

Of course, some of the Tennessee's design elements are almost random, some resembling Japanese motifs, like the stylized dragons around the ceiling; others strongly suggest French preoccupations, like the fleur-de-lis pattern around the stage. Some have noted vaguely Italian influences here and there—with a little art deco for good measure, especially in the women's room. Perhaps the most perplexing emblems are the slightly wacky cartoon-style geese emblazoned on stone disks on the exterior of the theater, along Clinch Avenue. They look almost as if they waddled out of one of young Mr. Disney's animated shorts.

Concentrating on style may be in vain, because it's not any one thing, and no phrase can really suggest what anyone might expect when first encountering the Tennessee Theatre.

DOGWOOD BLOSSOMS

One of the Tennessee's most abundant motifs, adorning a plaster coil—a "spiral cane" trim, as it's known, in a double row surrounding the proscenium—is distinctly local: more than 100 dogwood blossoms.

That touch is more surprising than some might imagine. In 1928, Knoxville did not celebrate dogwoods in any obvious ways, certainly not with dogwood trails or festivals. By some arborists' accounts, dogwoods were not often planted in yards until the 1930s. The dogwood was an indigenous tree, long familiar to people who knew trees. They grew in the mountains, and their distinctly hard wood was harvested industrially for factory use, especially for textile mill spindles, but dogwoods were not especially cherished in lawns.

Was the dogwood motif unusual in Graven & Mayger designs? As Tennessee Theatre technical director Tim Burns notes, that detail is lacking in Birmingham's Alabama Theatre, though it features a similar spiral cane trim around the proscenium. Burns speculates that the timing of Graven & Mayger's first drawings—July 1927—suggest that they might have been working on it the previous spring, and a site visit, during natural dogwoods' full bloom, may have inspired them.

Is it possible that the design of the theater played a role in popularizing the dogwood? This evocation of dogwood blossoms in such a prominent place, where thousands of people would have the opportunity to sit and contemplate them for hours at a time, may have started something.

secret known only to those who came all the way in. It would offer little suggestion of its glory to the street, but it continues to astonish each new generation as they enter the building.

Graven & Mayger yielded a theater plan sharply different from that of most theaters, much broader than it was long, an extraordinarily unusual transverse oval plan.

Their plan offered fewer seats, less retail space, a shallower balcony and a shallower stage than Hall's 1925 drawings. The stage, in particular, would present a problem for productions for many years to come. What they offered instead was a spectacular space in which almost everybody feels close to the stage. As unusual as it was, the idea of a broad stage, 54 feet (18 yards!) wide, with a broad seating space, had rarely been tried before. The 1921 Chicago Theatre had a stage even broader, but also almost twice as many seats. The width of the Tennessee's stage, in proportion to its total seating, is one of several characteristics that make the theater unusual. And the Tennessee's horizontally stretched oval ceiling may be unique.

Also different for Knoxville was the fact that the fly loft, the area above the stage where curtains and backdrops are controlled and stored, was automatic, not requiring attendants on a bridge.

The duo borrowed another Chicago trick for the construction of the ceiling. Almost 40 years earlier, in the late 1880s, architects Dankmar Adler and Louis Sullivan designed Chicago's Auditorium Theatre pioneering "double shell" construction, with an ornate plaster ceiling that wasn't part of the structure itself, but suspended from the actual roof. The plan allowed for elaborate ornamentation with less concern about cracking, and also improved acoustics. The Tennessee, like most 1920s

CONSTRUCTION WORKERS IN THE MEZZANINE FOYER · SUMMER 1928

movie palaces, employed that technique. At the Tennessee, it rendered an almost surreal effect of a glowing blue dome that appears to suggest another atmosphere, a fantasy sky above and beyond the audience.

The imagery in the interior is a collage of international suggestion, French fleur de lis, English rampant lions, suggestions of Italian balconies, medieval windows, Arabic arches. Such combinations, without any mundane insistence on consistency, was characteristic of the movie palace form and seemed to reflect not only the diversity of movies shown there but also ideals of democratic, multicultural America—and perhaps especially, Chicago.

There's so much Chicago in the theater one might look hard to find any suggestion of Tennessee in this place ostensibly intended to evoke the Moorish architecture of Spain. Were Graven and Mayger thinking about that when they included what appear to be dogwood blossoms, scores of them, molded in the plaster on either side of the stage?

Graven and Mayger promised a much grander lobby than Mr. Hall had, an almost palatial entryway to match a grand era. In days when thousands crushed in to see a new movie during the three days it might be in town, the lobby could accommodate a sizeable ticket-holding audience waiting to be seated for the next feature.

And the Tennessee was air-conditioned. In many cities, theaters were the first buildings to be air-conditioned, because they were by nature windowless places with lots of bodies jammed close together, expected to stay in place for upward of two hours. "Figuratively and actually, the Tennessee Theatre will manufacture its own weather," wrote the *News-Sentinel* just before it opened. "The equipment washes, dries, cools, and then puts just the proper amount of moisture in the air and sends it on out into the theater. If it is summertime, the air will enter the theater from above in cool clean waves, and settle to the breathing zone. The impure air is drawn out thru ducts in the floor, below the breathing zone.... All dust and foreign matter is removed from the air when it passes into the purifying machines, and the air that goes into the theater is much purer than that breathed in the street."

The Tennessee boasted of that amenity with enticements irresistible on the hot sidewalk: "20 Degrees Cooler Inside."

In the winter, the Tennessee was heated with coal, Knoxville's fuel of choice. Coal furnaces left a layer of grime on almost everything in the city, which made the theater's filtration system all the more appealing.

Tennessee Enterprises had sold the Bijou Theatre down the street. By the sales agreement, the new owners agreed to keep the older theater closed until 1931. The Bijou wasn't yet 20 years old, but times were changing so rapidly that it already seemed to belong to a different era. It has long been assumed the no-compete agreement was intended to focus the market on making the Tennessee profitable in its critical first years. Maybe closing one well-known theater might heighten anticipation of a new one. The gesture seems odd, in retrospect, that the smaller, older theater might present any impediment to modern motion-picture palaces. But the Bijou's forced closure occurred two years before the Tennessee opened—even before construction began. At least one researcher has suggested the protection was intended for another theater project never completed. In any case, for five years, including the Tennessee's debut, the Bijou was utterly closed as a theater, stripped of its seats, serving as a fruit stand—and thanks to its large backstage doors, as a parking garage.

"20 DEGREES COOLER"

Air conditioning revolutionized life in the South, and it arrived via movie theaters. Through architecture, dress, and various cooling habits, Southerners had learned to deal with the summer heat. Windows, fans, a front porch, and a pitcher of lemonade made nearly any July tolerable.

But the theater experience does not tolerate windows. Theaters, whether for live drama or movies, required sitting still for long periods in a completely closed room without windows. In the summer, that would have been insufferable and perhaps dangerous. For the first 60-odd years of vaudeville theaters in Knoxville, it went without saying that every theater would close for the summer. Some troupes tried to make up the time with outdoor performances at Chilhowee Park or elsewhere, but for the most part Knoxvillians found other ways to spend their time.

Air conditioning changed all that, offering the theater business a way to add substantially to its season, and to its revenue. Sidewalk signs outside the Tennessee Theatre boasted "20 Degrees Cooler Inside."

The Tennessee has been described as Knoxville's first building to be air-conditioned; whether it was or not, it was the first with a system of ductwork to distribute both heat and cool air throughout the building. Its filtration system, promising cleaner air than the outdoors could offer, was especially important in a city increasingly known for its coal soot. The Tennessee offered an escape from several realities.

A TITLE BLOCK FROM THE ORIGINAL BLUEPRINTS

Graven and Mayger's partnership yielded at least eight (some sources say nine) movie palaces. It was a coincidence of the era that three of them were named for the states where they were located, including the Alabama Theatre in Birmingham and the Minnesota Theatre in Minneapolis. Most of the duo's theaters were in the upper Midwest, four of them in the Detroit area and one, the RKO (Radio Keith Orpheum) Palace, as far east as Rochester, New York. The Alabama and the Tennessee were their only two projects in the South.

Their firm, formed about the time they were hired for the Knoxville project, may have been breaking up by the time the Tennessee was completed. Detroit's Fisher Theatre, their colorfully over-the-top Mayan masterpiece, opened just weeks after the Tennessee, followed by Rochester's RKO Palace that Christmas Day. It was their last.

Anker Graven designed a couple more theaters on his own: the RKO Orpheum, a 2,400-seat art-deco theater later known as the Adler, near the Mississippi River in Davenport, Iowa, and the smaller West Bend Theatre in Wisconsin. Graven was just 41 in October 1932, when he drowned in a boating accident in Little Rice Lake, Minnesota.

Arthur Mayger lived until 1948, without accomplishing anything as famous as his theaters.

For both men, that brief collaboration was the high point of their architectural careers. In Detroit, their distinctive Fisher Theatre design did not survive a 1961 remodeling. Today, Graven & Mayger's only two Southern projects, the Tennessee and the Alabama, are the only largely intact and renovated examples of their collaboration.

The Tennessee Theatre would be the first entity to occupy this whole plot since Reverend Carrick's college, the one that became the University of Tennessee. That school had moved away to "the Hill" in the fall of 1828, almost exactly 100 years before the Tennessee Theatre opened.

CURTAIN

CHAPTER 3

In October 1928, Knoxville had nine movie theaters open every day but Sunday. Even before the Tennessee opened, Gay Street alone hosted six movie theaters, not counting the legally suppressed Bijou. That fall, America was in the midst of a transition to the talkie era. An industry engineered for silents took a couple of years to catch up, and though recorded soundtracks via Vitaphone or similar technologies were becoming standard before the Tennessee opened, most of the movies made in the two years after *The Jazz Singer* are still considered silents. Many or most of those "silents" included music synchronized with the action, sometimes with artificially recorded sound effects, and sometimes a little dialogue. The fact that they included music obviated one of the Tennessee's most boasted advantages before the theater even opened.

The Mighty Wurlitzer — the adjective was part of the brand name — was the pride of the Rudolph Wurlitzer Company of Cincinnati, introduced about a decade before the Tennessee Theatre opened. Improved and refined for motion picture palaces in the 1920s, the Wurlitzer offered a bank of sound-effect bells and whistles, literally, designed to be played to accompany the movie itself. An expensive top-of-the-line model was ordered for the Tennessee. Motion picture technology overtook the Wurlitzer's original function as the Tennessee was under construction. That fact likely caused some headaches for C.B. Atkin and his colleagues in Tennessee Enterprises.

Still, they promoted their expensive organ as a draw in itself. If it wasn't the fate of the Mighty Wurlitzer to accompany new movies, it would be played before and after every evening's presentation, and in the early months of the theater, the organist was always advertised as a star of the show. The Tennessee's first organist was Miss Jean Wilson, and her name appeared on the marquee alongside the earliest films.

Publix ran three regular movie theaters in the 1920s: the Riviera, the Strand, and the Queen. The Queen, just across Gay Street from the Riviera, was a popular theater built just before the World War, and did a pretty lively business. But at the end of September 1928, it offered one more Saturday night showing of Rex Bell in the recent silent *Girl-Shy Cowboy*, then quietly closed forever. There was no ceremony or public regret. Its name simply dropped out of the Publix newspaper ads. Its space became part of an expanded Woolworth's, later to be demolished.

Publix played Gay Street like an organ, closing one stop to open another.

"AN ACRE OF SEATS IN A PALACE OF SPLENDOR" · OCTOBER 1928

TENNESSEE THEATRE, OPENING DAY · OCTOBER 1, 1928

The Tennessee opened that Monday. Charles H. Amos, who'd already been Tennessee Enterprises' "City Supervisor of Theaters" from the Riviera office, was its first manager. He moved his office to the newer, more impressive theater. The Tennessee, the Riviera, the Strand, the Majestic, and the Lyric would all be operated from the Tennessee Theatre's new main office.

For years to come, Knoxville's three primary first-run movie theaters — the Tennessee, the Riviera, and the Strand — thrived on three consecutive blocks of Gay Street.

The *Knoxville News-Sentinel*'s freshman roving columnist, a newcomer from Kentucky named Bert Vincent, got a sneak peek at the Tennessee the week before it opened. He remarked that both the movie's stars and the stage performers "will have to do some lively stepping if they hold the major part of the audience's attention. The theater is a show in itself."

Vincent described one feature that might surprise modern patrons. "On the Clinch Avenue side is a terrace where folk may sit on a summer day until they desire to step back into the auditorium and finish the show." That "terrace" is still there, plainly visible from the sidewalk, but now used as a fire escape. How long it was used as a casual open-air refuge from the theater is unclear.

Vincent described a "smoking room for women" in the basement, but he didn't mention one for men; "reading rooms for men and women"; and a "gymnasium and emergency room ... for the actors and musicians."

"Monday [Oct. 1, 1928] — I went to the new Tennessee Theatre tonight. It opened today. It is so much ahead of the other theatres here that one could hardly compare them to it.
"Thursday night, October 4 — I took Rebecca Smithson to see 'The Docks of New York'.... The Tennessee Theatre is so beautiful that I don't feel like I am in Knoxville when I am there."

FROM THE JOURNAL OF FRANK BACHMAN FAIN

"He asked me to marry him while we were waiting in line on the Theatre's opening day in 1928. I said yes!"

BILLIE VINYARD DALTON

The antique statuary, paintings, and furniture in the lobby and elsewhere, including the remarkable marble statue of a classical goddess on the balcony landing, are genuine, some of it of 19th-century European origin. Although the provenance of these pieces is obscure, it was not unusual for studios, working with buyers, to scout European markets to select objets d'art to decorate their movie palaces at home.

A perhaps lesser but nonetheless eye-catching draw was one that had to be fed daily. In its earliest days, the Tennessee made room for caged canaries, presumably in the lobby.

The *Knoxville Journal*, whose offices were just a few steps away from the Tennessee, ran an unsigned editorial: "The Tennessee — Knoxville's Pride."

"It is a dream," the editorial began. "That expresses briefly and, in a sense, comprehensively, the beauty of Knoxville's new theater, the Tennessee .... It beggars description. It must be seen to be believed. Perhaps one might hazard a lamentable effort at description by saying that the interior is itself one gigantic picture, a masterpiece of architectural skill, a masterpiece of art.

"Even as one enters the concourse, capacious, illuminated with subdued light radiating softly from five immense and costly chandeliers, walls and ceiling artistically decorated, exclamations of wonder, delight and appreciation involuntarily find expression. But description is even more futile when one enters the auditorium, walks over carpets which give forth no sound, gazes upon multicolored lights that adorn the walls and reveal the mural decorations, and ventures a look above to see the most beautiful ceiling imaginable ....

BOOTH THEATRE,
CUMBERLAND AVENUE · 1928

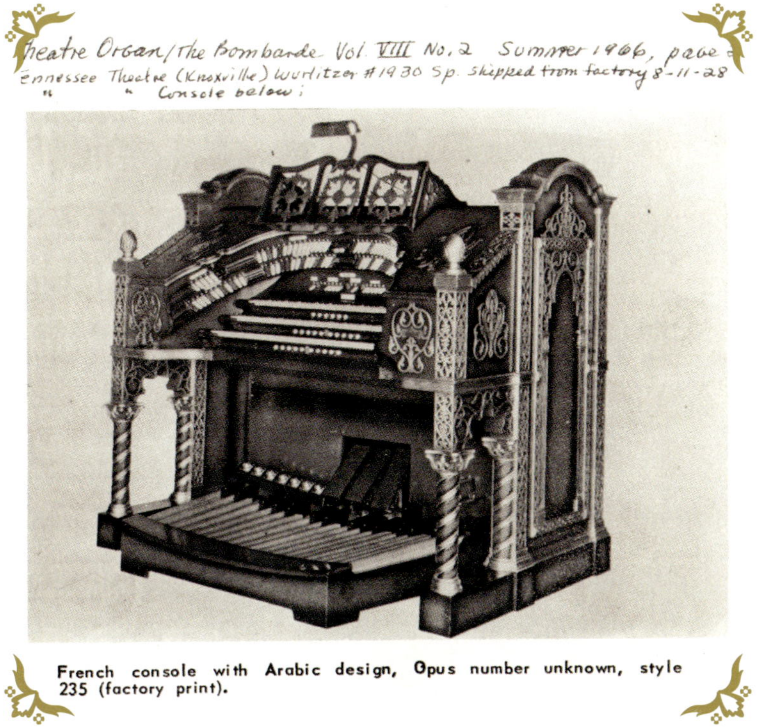

PROMOTIONAL PHOTO OF TENNESSEE'S MIGHTY WURLITZER

"It is the finest theater in the South, barring none. The Alabama, a Publix house at Birmingham, has held that distinction. It must now take second place .... Success to Mr. Amos, manager."

The same editorial page included a shorter welcome for another new cinema that coincidentally opened the same week — the Booth, a small neighborhood theater on western Cumberland Avenue, which is praised as modest, cozy, and homey, in sharp contrast to the Tennessee. Even it includes a rave about the Tennessee: "To step into the Tennessee is to find oneself suddenly transported from a noisy street to the glamour of a metropolitan playhouse."

No.
Tennessee
Knoxville
Graven &

FOUR MARX

PRIVATE

EXIT
EXIT

EXIT
EXIT

THE MOVIE SHOWN ON OPENING DAY

Opening night was a Monday, October 1, 1928. The doors opened to the downtown lunch hour crowd at 12:30, with a show at 1:00. Other shows followed at 3:00, 5:00, 7:00, and 9:00. It's likely that almost 10,000 people were seated at the Tennessee that first day.

Tennessee Enterprises' advertising was ecstatic. "Everybody happy? You bet! The new Tennessee opens today!"

That matinée price was 40 cents for adults, a dime for children. Evening prices were 60 cents for adults, 15 cents for children. Those prices made it Knoxville's most expensive theater.

The first feature film shown that Monday was *The Fleet's In*, the latest movie featuring the previous year's star of *It*, the eye-opening movie about sex appeal. At 23, Clara Bow was also famous for her role in the war film that won the first-ever Oscar for Best Picture, *Wings*. Though it came with a Vitaphone musical soundtrack, *The Fleet's In* was a silent film about a star-crossed romance between a sailor and a dime-store clerk, partly set at San Francisco's famous Roseland dance hall. It was shot only three months before it was shown at the Tennessee.

And today it's considered a "lost film." Even major feature films were considered to have little or no value to the studio after they were no longer making money. When they weren't just forgotten, they were melted for their silver content. Only a minority of films made in the 1920s have survived intact. Early films with soundtracks seem to have fared worse than pure silents.

It's likely that most who watched that first movie came to see the theater itself, and to hear Jean Wilson play the wonderful new Wurlitzer. Exactly what she played is not recorded.

That first night included a newsreel, perhaps something about September's devastating Florida hurricane, the upcoming World Series pitting Ruth and Gehrig's Yankees against the Cardinals, or the Herbert Hoover vs. Al Smith presidential campaign; the election was just a month away. One of the most interesting features of that evening was the first of many nightly appearances by Don Pedro and His Melody Boys, presenting a program called "Joy Bells."

Pedro, whose origin is not clear, was familiar to Knoxville audiences. A year or so before he'd been organist at the Riviera. With the Melody Boys, though, he seems to have been leader

CLARA BOW

"THE IT GIRL"

JEAN WILSON

THE TENNESSEE'S FIRST ORGANIST

This newspaper advertisement for the Tennessee's opening night testifies to the exuberance of its era and suggests the variety of entertainment Tennessee patrons expected during the theater's first year or so. For at least eight months, every night at the Tennessee featured the jazz band Don Pedro and His Melody Boys, a live organist "at the Golden-Voiced Wurlitzer," and a feature film, plus several short subjects, including cartoons. "And wait until you see the theatre!" The Tennessee's first film, "The Fleet's In," was a popular silent drama starring major starlet Clara Bow, but like many films from that era, it's now considered lost.

SEPTEMBER 30, 1928

of a jazz band that played in the pit. Likely working on a three-month contract, Don Pedro and His Melody Boys would play with every movie, with a different musical theme, until January. For the Tennessee's second feature film, *The Docks of New York*, the band's theme was "Jazz Ahoy!" Later that first month, the theme was "Rhapsody in Rhythm," obviously a riff on Gershwin's recent classic.

The next-day ad touted the Tennessee as the talk of the town. "They talk about the beautiful lobby, the handsome foyer, the magnificent auditorium, 'An acre of seats in a palace of splendor.'"

The last line was in quotations, but unattributed. That felicitous phrase was used for several other Paramount movie palaces that opened in 1928, from Pittsburgh to Seattle — and has appeared as the title of more than one theater's history — but it fit the Tennessee just as well.

It's curious that the first two movies ever shown at the Tennessee had similar plots: lonely sailors falling in love with harbor women perceived to be prostitutes. In its first few years, the Tennessee's feature films were searing dramas about adultery, prostitution, alcoholism, blackmail, murder. During the theater's first month, Tennessee patrons witnessed Joan Crawford's movie about alcoholism and illicit love, *Our Dancing Daughters*, and Lon Chaney's violent crime drama, *While the City Sleeps*. What comedies and fantasy films the Tennessee showed were mostly very short. The feature-length "family film" seems to have been a thing of the future. Children were permitted at the Tennessee, but probably didn't find much of interest in a typical movie of the late 1920s.

By the cinema business plan of the Tennessee's first decade, a new Hollywood movie arrived, usually a week or two after its major big-city release, and played for exactly three days. Some

LOBBY DISPLAY BY JOE PARROTT · SEPTEMBER 1930

might return to a smaller "second-run" theater down the street, but they wouldn't be played again at the Tennessee.

The theater was hardly three months old when it showed the big new MGM drama, *A Woman of Affairs.* The Knoxville crowds went for the big stars on the marquee, John Gilbert and Greta Garbo (Ad copy read: "They're Together Again!!! The Greatest Lovers of the Screen Now! WILD DESIRE ... burning lips ... racing hearts ... pounding pulses ....").

Beneath all that Paramount hyperbole in the Tennessee's ad was one line aimed at the local market: "Directed by Knoxville's Own CLARENCE BROWN." It had been 18 years since the North Knoxville resident graduated from UT with a double major in engineering, but perhaps some remembered when Brown, Garbo's favorite director, was a familiar face on Gay Street, a precocious little kid in short pants who enjoyed giving dramatic presentations.

The Tennessee played more than 100 feature films a year, almost all of them less than six weeks old. Hollywood's output was such that management was rarely tempted to hold a movie over or replay one, regardless of its popularity. Customers might have only one chance to see any given movie, and it was during the three-night window when it was at the Tennessee. That's why the theater needed almost 2,000 seats.

Studios played them up big, with sidewalk advertising and lobby displays. Pictures of large-set creations and performers in tuxedos seem to suggest a world premiere, when all they're promoting is a three-day showing of one movie in a mid-market theater.

Unlike modern cinema operators, the Tennessee enlisted a full-time artist to create posters and lobby displays for each movie. Just 23, artist Joe Parrott established a studio backstage,

A LOBBY DISPLAY BY JOE PARROTT

JOE PARROT

CA. 1929

DETAIL OF LOBBY DISPLAY BY JOE PARROT · AUGUST 1929

alongside dressing rooms. He was so exhausted from preparing for the theater's grand opening that the night before the big day he slept in the carpeted aisles. For the next four years Parrott created some extraordinary displays, some as big as the facades of buildings, to startle, delight, and entice theater patrons. The large architecturally scaled pieces were cut out of a rigid cardboard material with a jigsaw, often with intricate detail. His unusual work got the attention of a journalist who wrote about the sign-painting industry. "The class of work that he is turning out is as good as the best I have seen in any city," wrote J.H. Ziegler, in an illustrated profile titled "Joe Parrott: Knoxville's Own Poster Artist," in the national trade monthly *Signs of the Times*. "The lobby of the Tennessee is very large, and Joe is kept very busy, with his one assistant, Ted Burnett, to keep it filled with posters and shadow boxes ... he is a real artist when it comes to handling colors."

Ziegler even quoted Duke Wellington, the New York-based art director for the whole Publix chain, declaring Parrott's work at the Tennessee was "as modern and artistic as any work I have seen anywhere."

Parrott told Ziegler his only training was from Knoxville High School — and from a Knoxville artist named Robert Lindsay Mason. A prominent promoter of the new Great Smoky Mountains National Park, Mason was a professional artist who had studied in Philadelphia with Howard Pyle and Maxfield Parrish, two of the most celebrated illustrators of the era. He ran a small private art school on East Church Avenue, where Parrott seems to have learned a few tricks.

Parrott was also drummer for Knoxville's most successful and widely traveled jazz band, Maynard Baird and his Southern Serenaders. The small orchestra were radio stars who recorded a few singles and had fans throughout the urban north. The Serenaders had other Gay Street cinema connections; bandleader Baird had been projectionist at the Majestic, and the band was known for their late-night concerts at the Riviera.

During the first several months of the Tennessee Theatre, there was no such thing as just a movie. Every movie showing was always accompanied by a live show, and at the Tennessee it was almost always a combination of local talent, including the regular organist and a jazz band, and a traveling vaudeville-style performer — a singer, a dancer, a comic, a magician, sometimes an acrobat — sometimes one with a reputation. The early live traveling performers were mostly associated with the well-known Keith Vaudeville circuit.

One of the Tennessee's first vaudeville performers happened to be one that mixed theater with front-page police news. The previous June, an aspiring 12-year-old actress named Pinkie Lee Koehn had appeared in a local comedy silent called *Too Much Flapper*. Just before the film's debut at the Riviera, Pinkie Lee vanished.

During the Tennessee's second week as a theater, renowned Kansas psychic Gene Dennis did repeated shows at the Tennessee, answering questions from the audience.

Pinkie Lee's frantic mother came to the theater just to ask where her daughter was. "Your little girl is dead," Dennis told her, before a rapt audience, adding some detail that Pinkie Lee was buried by a waterfall with a rainbow mist. It began a rumor that the girl was buried at the Smokies' Rainbow Falls.

THURS.-FRI.-SAT.
For the First Time in the History of Knoxville
RADIO-KEITH-ORPHEUM
Vaudebille
Direct from the Keith's Georgia Theatre, Atlanta
And What an Opening Show!!
ANATOLE FRIEDLAND
and His
Night Club Revue
Hey, Hey — Wot a Nite!
No Cover Charges! No Hangovers!
with
Twenty Exceptionally Talented Artists and a Dazzling Array of Broadway Beauties
Bringing New York's Night Life to Knoxville
— plus —
GEORGE SIDNEY
— and —
JEAN HERSHOLT
in a Screamingly Funny Talking Comedy
"GIVE AND TAKE"

MON.-TUES.-WED.
"DICK"
Barthelmess
As the Toughest Two Fisted Sailor on the Seven Seas
— in —
"SCARLET SEAS"
with BETTY COMPTON
— plus —
Highly Entertaining Sound Presentations
— and —
COLLEGIANS No. 5
Hear HARRIS WATERS
"The Jesse Crawford of the South"
at the Tennessee Organ

Tennessee
THEATRE

NEWSPAPER AD · JANUARY 1929

Hardly two weeks later, Pinkie Lee Koehn was found safe, living with a family in Asheville. She'd just run away from home, she said, for the experience of it. By then the vaudeville psychic had moved on, and somehow maintained her reputation for uncanny accuracy. Nine years later Dennis got in the national news when George Putnam appealed to her about his missing wife, whose name was Amelia Earhart.

Psychic Gene Dennis died young, but Pinkie Lee, later a South Knoxville grocer, lived to the age of 94.

Individual acts would perform every night for three nights in a row, typically, and move on, perhaps never to return. Most of those performers are obscure now, but a few who trod the boards at the Tennessee in its first year are minor legends, some with cult followings even in the 21st century.

That first December saw one of vaudeville's stars, the singer-violinist known as Miss Patricola, who'd been top-billed at Manhattan's Palace Theatre several times. The magician known as Tampa, who billed himself as "England's Court Magician," was long associated with the legendary Howard Thurston and has been the subject of a biography; he performed at the Tennessee for three nights in January 1929. A big revue in March featured more than one performer who would later have screen credits: that night's star, James Burke, would later be a familiar character actor in movies from *The Maltese Falcon to Beau Geste.* Also in that troupe was Paul Jung, a circus performer so well known he played himself in Cecil B. DeMille's *The Greatest Show on Earth* — 23 years after his turn on the Tennessee's stage. Vaudeville tours were how ambitious actors got their starts, and we'll probably never know the names of all the future movie stars who appeared anonymously with a troupe at the Tennessee.

LOU TELLEGEN

For three nights in late March of that year, Dutch-born actor Lou Tellegen, the tall, handsome former matinée idol, once Sarah Bernhardt's leading man on both stage and screen, and one whose muscular frame and classical good looks had earned him work as a model for Rodin sculptures, somehow appeared at the Tennessee in a skit called "Drinks for Three." His co-star here was Eve Casanova, a Broadway actress who later became

KNOXVILLE IN 1928

The day the Tennessee Theatre opened, Knoxvillians had no clue they were at the very end of a long boom era in the city's history, a 60-year period of exciting growth and change. Though still tightly defined geographically, Knoxville did not yet include outlying suburban areas like Bearden, South Knoxville, and Fountain City, but still supported a population of about 100,000, most of it linked by an exemplary system of electric streetcars. Knoxville had two busy passenger-train stations and two daily newspapers that maintained a politically partisan rivalry.

Until just two months before the opening of the Tennessee, the morning Journal was edited by a Civil War veteran, former Union captain William Rule, who died that summer at age 89. In 1928, a few Civil War veterans of both sides still walked on Gay Street, and perhaps visited movie theaters.

The University of Tennessee was becoming a significant part of the city's economy, but in 1928 most Knoxvillians had never found cause to visit its small campus, still concentrated on The Hill, without public auditoriums or other facilities for visitors. Young football coach Robert Neyland was making the Vols a national contender for the first time, but Knoxville's favorite sport was baseball. Pro baseball, including Knoxville's own minor-league team, recently renamed the Smokies, got more attention in the sports pages than all college sports put together.

The Tennessee Valley Authority did not exist, and the undammed Tennessee River flooded regularly, often wreaking havoc on poorly planned farmland. Thousands of acres in the Knoxville area, stripped of their topsoil, were muddy and barren red clay. Ft. Loudoun Lake, Norris Lake, Douglas, Watts Bar—none of those existed. When locals referred to "the lake," they were usually referring to either of the large ponds in Chilhowee Park or Fountain City.

The Great Smoky Mountains were always there in the distance, visible on days when the coal smoke wasn't too bad, but most Knoxvillians had never seen the mountains up close. A national park project was well underway, and a few daring souls had made the trip up to see the Smokies in person, but the new network of roads was still sketchy, and most Knoxvillians didn't have cars anyway.

Knoxville had an airport, already named McGhee Tyson, but it mainly consisted of a field on Sutherland Avenue. It did not yet support significant passenger traffic, and most of its use was from daring hobbyists.

The Tennessee was completed during a year of national prohibition, when it was against the law even to sell a glass of beer. Prohibition lasted longer in Knoxville than it did nationally. In fact, for the Tennessee Theatre's first 44 years, liquor and even wine by the drink were illegal in Knoxville.

Knoxville always seemed to have plenty to keep itself busy. Three mainstream radio stations brought both local live music and national dramatic and musical programs to local homes. Jazz was the most popular form of music in Knoxville, but a few locals were experimenting with a new form of folk music then called Hillbilly.

continues on next page...

The city had nine movie theaters in 1928, and even before the Tennessee, six of them were on Gay Street.

There was another exciting new project down the street, the Andrew Johnson Hotel, at 17 stories the tallest building ever built in East Tennessee, a title it would hold for almost half a century—as well as another stylish new skyscraper, the Medical Arts Building. There were plans for a new Henley Street Bridge, and a new federal post office building, and a grand new cathedral-like Methodist church. More in line with international modernist architecture of the period was the Daylight Building on Union Avenue, a simpler building erected about the same time as the Tennessee, named for its then-unusual expanses of glass windows. It was followed, just afterward and just across the street, by the taller office building then called the New Sprankle Building, later better known as the Pembroke. Near those, one more mid-sized movie theater, called the Roxy, was completed less than two years after the Tennessee. It would be the last movie theater built in downtown Knoxville until the 21st century.

In fact, after the pocket building boom that included the Tennessee Theatre, very few new buildings of any kind were built downtown before the 1960s. It was a last period of exuberance during an optimistic era with no expectation of a Great Depression.

The years to come would bring many welcome changes to Knoxville, but in the three decades after the completion of the Tennessee Theatre, the city would not grow in population at all, and what population it did keep was sprawling toward the suburbs. Through it all, somehow, the Tennessee Theatre remained popular.

JEAN WILSON AS THE TENNESSEE'S BANDLEADER

his fourth wife. The 47-year-old Tellegen was no longer an international heartthrob when he performed at the Tennessee, about five years before his lurid suicide.

HADJI ALI

GENE AUSTIN

"Koran, the Marvelous Mentalist" did whatever he did on the Tennessee's stage in early 1929. But perhaps that first season's strangest performer was Hadji Ali, a bizarre master of "controlled regurgitation" who had performed for Tsar Nicholas II and later allowed his act to be recorded for a Laurel and Hardy film. Known for his ability to expel both objects, like metal balls, and long streams of water from his stomach, he performed at the Tennessee from February 28 to March 2, 1929.

The Tennessee had opened just in time to witness the end of vaudeville, and it was symptomatic of the rapidly changing business that in 1929, before the Tennessee was fully a year old, the live component of its variety shows was already diminishing. A theater orchestra accompanied every movie night of the Tennessee's first seven months, often conducted by organist Jean Wilson. They sometimes performed recent Broadway hits, and on one occasion in early April 1929 even took on "Offenbach's Orpheus"—probably just the overture of Jacques Offenbach's famous opera *Orpheus in the Underworld*. Whatever it was, it may have been the first classical performance in the Tennessee's history.

That house band apparently was no longer a regular thing after the theater's first seven months. A chronicler noted "Last Appearance of Vaudeville Orchestra" on April 27, 1929. But live music remained a semi-regular treat. Popular Jazz Age crooner Gene Austin appeared in late May, accompanied by organist Harry Waters, singing "Wedding Bells Are Breaking Up That Old Gang of Mine"—one of the big hits of 1929—and "Sweetheart of All My Dreams." Bandleader-composer Nat Shilkret, popular Victor recording artist and Austin's sometime collaborator, also appeared at the Tennessee the same week. (The Texas-born Austin, known as the Voice of the Southland, performed at the Tennessee on at least one other occasion, four years later—a two-and-a-half-hour show in which he headed a cast of 50 and sang "My Blue Heaven," "Ramona," and "Broadway Rhapsody.")

Jim Crow laws mandated that theater audiences be segregated. In a few Southern theaters, like the Bijou, a balcony was reserved for black audiences, but that was never the case at the Tennessee. It appears that almost all of the performers at the Tennessee were white, too, but there may have been exceptions. A November 1928 show called "The New York Revue," if it's the same one touring by that name at that time, included black performers like Trixie Smith, a dancer and vocalist who made jazz recordings with Louis Armstrong.

In February 1929, as a short to accompany the Garbo silent *Wild Orchids*, the Tennessee showed a 21-minute-long romantic comedy about upscale blacks in a jazz nightclub setting, called *The Melancholy Dame*. Though directed by Swedish immigrant Arvid Gillstrom, it's sometimes described as "the first black talkie." On a couple of occasions that year, the theater advertised a short film with an "All Negro Cast." That October, the Tennessee advertised "Mamie Smith in Jailhouse Blues," a one-reeler featuring a performance by that already-famous blues singer from Cincinnati.

But they were presumably seen only by whites. There were few public complaints about movie-house segregation at the time.

GEM THEATRE, VINE AND CENTRAL · CA. 1930

In the South, and in fact in most of America, any other policy would have been surprising. In Knoxville, the black community was proud of its own theater, the Gem, a large theater about five blocks from the Tennessee on Vine Avenue, which showed movies every night and often featured major jazz and blues artists live onstage.

Feature films lured audiences to the Tennessee with familiar names from the silent era like Douglas Fairbanks (Sr.), Mary Pickford, Lon Chaney (Sr.) and Wallace Beery, but that first year, the theater also introduced Knoxville audiences to new stars of the budding sound era, like Gary Cooper. A recent Laurel and Hardy silent, *That's My Wife*, showed in late June 1929; with the arrival of sound, that duo would soon be much better known.

Sound came to movies by degrees, first with Vitaphone musical soundtracks, sometimes with selected sound effects, sometimes with limited bits of recorded dialogue, and eventually "all talking."

Because sound crept into films so gradually, it's hard to know what to call the Tennessee's first "talkie." On January 28, 1929, the Tennessee showed the William Powell thriller *Interference*, Paramount's first all-talking movie.

On February 11, 1929, the theater showed the early Our Gang comedy short *The Spanking Age*, advertised with the word "Sound." (Despite the title, it was well before the "Spanky" era; the star of that short was the tomboy Mary Ann.)

A few weeks later, on March 7, the Tennessee showed *Strange Cargo*, advertising it as an "All Talking Picture." Living up to its title, it's a weird murder mystery set on a yacht. (Once believed lost, it's rarely seen today.)

Just three days later, the Tennessee showed President Herbert Hoover's inaugural speech, with sound, barely a week after it was recorded in Washington.

GOLDEN AGE

Paramount and the people of Tennessee Enterprises could hardly have guessed their project on Gay Street would align almost exactly with the approximately 35-year period remembered as Hollywood's Golden Age. The people who built the Tennessee Theatre and first occupied its seats had probably never heard of Cary Grant, or Katharine Hepburn, or Clark Gable, or Bette Davis, or John Wayne, or Jimmy Stewart, or Boris Karloff, or Fred Astaire, or Ginger Rogers, or Bob Hope, or Humphrey Bogart. These were all careers that would rise, flourish, and peak during the Tennessee's era.

The Tennessee even showed a few color films, like *The Love Charm*, a 1928 silent short set in the South Pacific. Color film technology — Technicolor — existed in the 1920s but was expensive, and was generally put to use for the spectacle of it or in guaranteed blockbusters. For about 30 years after the first color film showing, most films shown at the Tennessee would be in black and white.

The Marx Brothers' very first movie, *The Cocoanuts*, debuted at the Tennessee on August 2, 1929, one day before its official national release date. Perhaps someone in the audience recognized the manic troupe that had performed live onstage at the Bijou 16 years earlier.

Joe Parrott's astonishing lobby display for that movie towered over the lobby doors. Unlike most of his work, which awed visitors for a few days and was then thrown away, a photograph of the Cocoanuts display illustrated the national monthly *Signs of the Times* magazine profile. Though the movie is known for its role in launching the cinema career of that not-yet-legendary comedy team, he used the studio's surprising pitch for The Cocoanuts: "Screen's First Musical Extravaganza."

One year later, the Marx Brothers' second film, the more-polished *Animal Crackers* (that farcical musical featured the signature "Hooray for Captain Spaulding!" tune), showed how far cinema technology had come in a short time, especially in regard to sound.

Despite the infancy of sound technology, many of the Tennessee's early offerings were musicals. On its first Valentine's Day, the

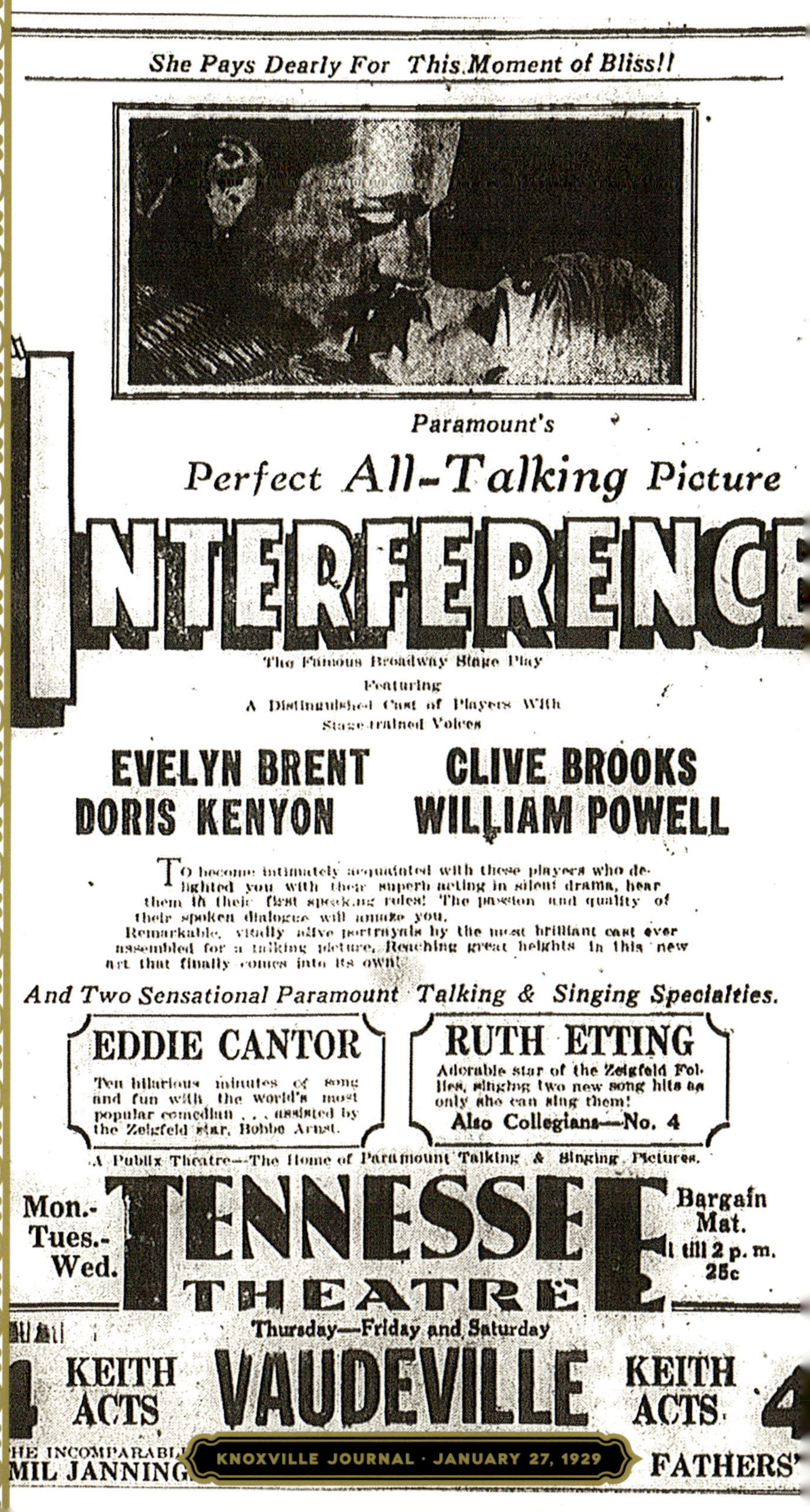

KNOXVILLE JOURNAL · JANUARY 27, 1929

Tennessee showed a short about dancer Ruby Keeler, who was then just 18. She'd be a major star in Hollywood musicals to come.

A novelty film about Rodgers and Hart, the Broadway songwriting team whose busiest years were still ahead of them, showed on July 15, 1929, followed a couple of weeks later by Rudy Vallee's *Radio Rhythm*, another novelty short featuring the popular singer stepping out of a radio speaker to sing a few numbers. It was an early music video.

The animated series called Paramount Screen Songs promoted popular music, inviting audiences to "follow the bouncing ball" and sing along, often with cartoons by Max Fleisher, before his "Popeye" fame. They included "Oh! You Beautiful Doll," "Chinatown My Chinatown," "I Wonder Who's Kissing Her Now," and "Glow Worm."

Music historians are likely to think of Knoxville in the late 1920s and '30s in terms of country music, which was being broadcast live by important early performers in the studios of radio stations WNOX and WROL, both located on Gay Street. The years 1929 and 1930 also witnessed Knoxville's only experiments with commercial recording, when the Brunswick label set up a studio at the St. James Hotel on Wall Avenue. About half of what those sessions produced might be called country or folk.

The Tennessee's early years suggest very little country music or country-style culture, however. For some, maybe, locals saw it as a place to get away from that, to feel sophisticated, dressed up, and well-traveled. In the late '20s, country music was still a sort of outfield novelty, not broadly popular yet. Jazz ruled the day, even in Knoxville.

One exception was the bill on March 14, 1929 — "Lasses White and Darkey: Delineations as you like them" — a comedy duo act likely questionable by modern standards, probably featuring the same Lasses White who was a minor star on the early Grand Ole Opry. The same evening presented a forgotten duo, Summers and Hunt, described as "rural eccentrics." It made quite a contrast with the feature film that evening, Cecil B. DeMille's *The Godless Girl*, a grimly serious film about atheism.

One of the first Disney films ever shown at the Tennessee was the 1929 Mickey Mouse cartoon, *Opry House*, but it had nothing to do with Nashville's Ryman Auditorium or country music. It

KNOXVILLE JOURNAL · MARCH 7, 1929

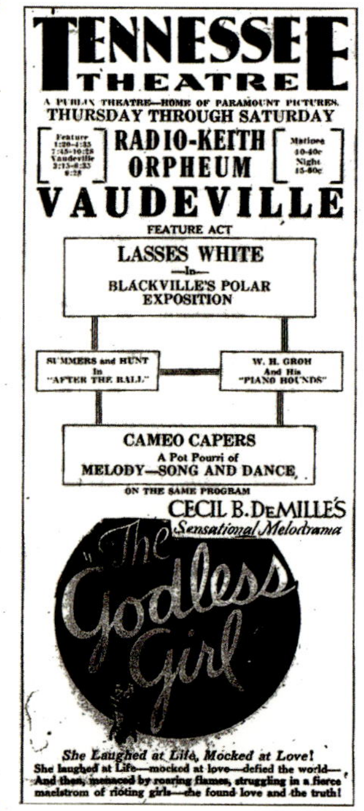

KNOXVILLE JOURNAL
MARCH 14, 1929

The Tennessee's resident artist Joe Parrott, whose studios were alongside dressing rooms backstage, earned national fame within his trade for his creative lobby displays. The photograph, taken from within the lobby looking toward the street, advertises "The Cocoanuts," one of the big movies of the Tennessee's first year. Although Paramount touted it as "the Screen's First Musical Extravaganza," the early sound movie is today more often recalled as the Marx Brothers' first comedy. "On With the Show" and "Charming Sinners" (which starred William Powell before his Thin Man fame) were other Paramount features of 1929. Parrott's unusual pinwheel display, at right, references several other new movies, including "Welcome Danger," featuring comedian Harold Lloyd in "His First Talking Picture."

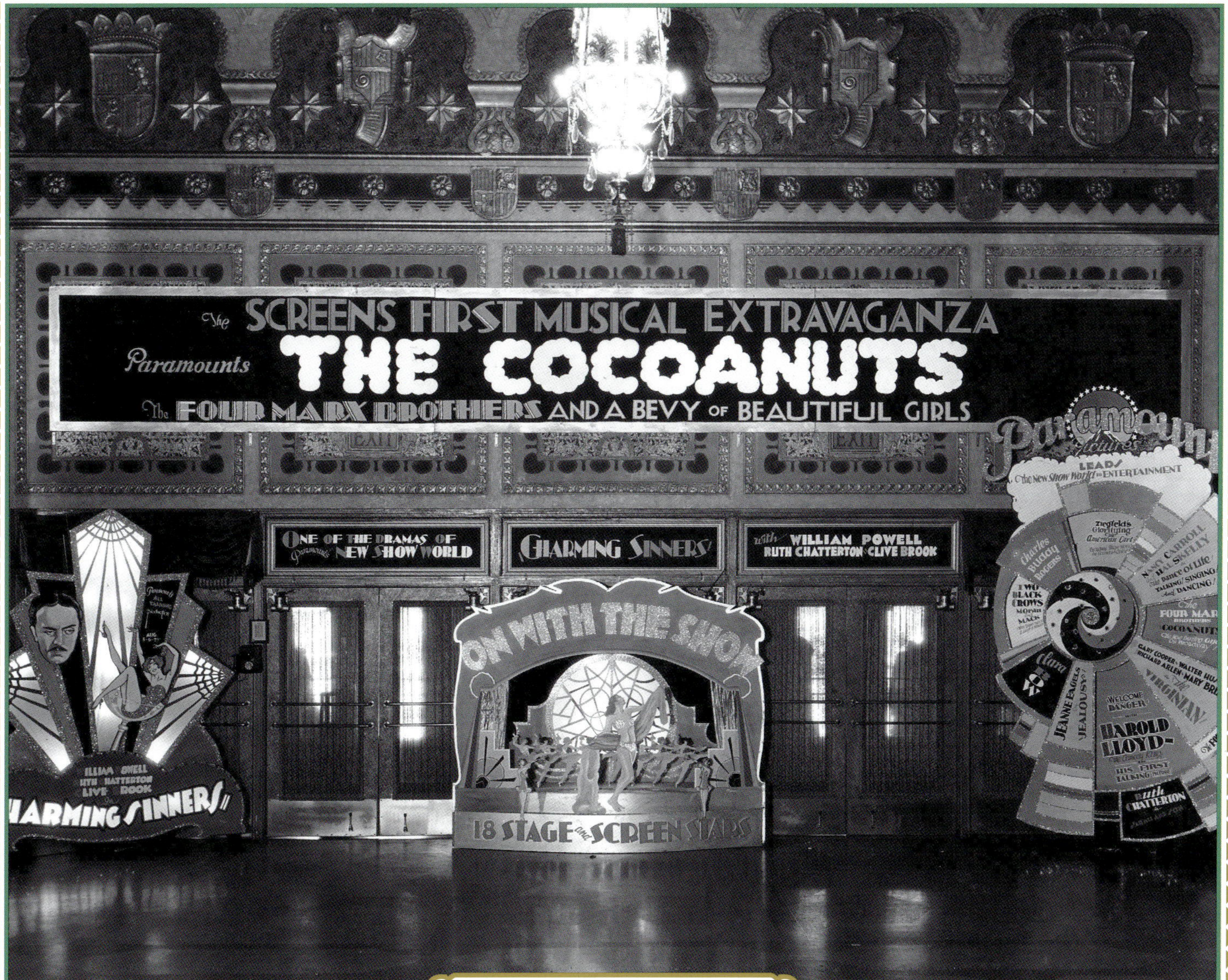

LOBBY DISPLAY FOR THE COCOANUTS

UT FOOTBALL ON THE BIG SCREEN

VOLUNTEERS

Developing in Knoxville in the late twenties was a new enthusiasm for college football. When the Tennessee opened, football had limited appeal in a city that in those days turned out in larger numbers for minor-league baseball. In September 1930, the movie theater commenced a series of films about Notre Dame coach Knute Rockne. Seeing football on the big screen may have given local fans ideas. On November 17 – 19, 1930, after a couple of months of the Rockne films, the Tennessee showed "Pictures of the Vol-Vandy Game". A quarter-century before the first televised games, hundreds, perhaps thousands, of East Tennesseans likely saw their first moving images of Volunteer football in this big room.

depicted Mickey trying, with mixed success, to put on a classical music concert in a small vaudeville theater. Just months old as a creation, Mickey Mouse was still new to theater audiences. Walt Disney was only 27 when his early films were delighting crowds at the Tennessee Theatre.

George Stanley and his Georgia Crackers performed live onstage at the Tennessee in February 1931. The group of banjo-playing "Hill Billies" was definitely a country music act and may suggest an awakening to the style in mainstream Knoxville. But the Georgia Crackers' authenticity as genuine mountaineers has to be footnoted by the fact that before they ever played at the Tennessee, they had honed their act on New York's Broadway.

Four members of the vaudeville troupe known as the Georgia Crackers, who'll entertain patrons from the stage of the Tennessee theatre the last half of the week.

KNOXVILLE JOURNAL · FEBRUARY 22, 1931

In its first year the Tennessee had shown a wide variety of movies, silent movies, sound movies, color movies, animated movies, all-black-cast movies, movies directed by women. But it had never shown a movie that was more than six weeks old.

On November 4, 1929, the Tennessee crossed that line, presenting one sort of movie it had never shown before: an old one. The Dixie Gem Coal Co. sponsored a favorite from eight years earlier, *Peck's Bad Boy*, starring 7-year-old Jackie Coogan. They may have gotten some encouragement from Paramount to do so. No longer the cute little kid who'd charmed Charlie Chaplin, and at 15 no longer one of Hollywood's busier child actors, Coogan had the title role of a big new Paramount movie, the first sound version of *Tom Sawyer*, then in production.

One of the first family-friendly feature films ever shown at the Tennessee, *Tom Sawyer* would appear on its big screen one year later.

The Tennessee showed an even older oldie in March 1930, as a novelty. As the advertisement ran, the Tennessee would show "*The Great Train Robbery*, a Picture Produced by Thomas Edison in 1903 – 27 years ago!" It was hard to imagine a movie so old.

It may say something about the entertainment business that no individual represented the Tennessee for very long. After his moment of glory hosting the opening of the Tennessee, manager Charles Amos soon found himself in charge of a smaller theater in Asheville. For a while, the Tennessee seemed to have a new manager every few months.

William Drumbar, who had worked to plan the Tennessee, only to be transferred to Charlotte before it opened, returned to take an office at the theater as city manager for Tennessee Enterprises in 1930. He married a local girl and was soon off to Dallas to manage more Publix theaters there. Then he'd be back in Knoxville, associated with the Bijou and half a dozen other theaters, for the last 25 years of his life.

One of the Tennessee's early managers earned a few minutes of national fame. In April 1930, *Motion Picture News* called out the Tennessee's manager, William Brock, as a "live-wire showman" for his creative lobby displays photographed for the article — specifically of *Sons of the Gods*, an early Constance Bennett movie, and *Anna Christie*, one of Clarence Brown's several pictures with Garbo. "There is not only individuality, but extreme beauty in this group of lobby displays, which were designed and executed by W.M. Brock, manager of the Tennessee Theatre ...."

Several of the Tennessee's early successive managers, including Brock, lived in the Terry Apartments in Maplehurst, on the southwestern corner of downtown. Of course, Brock was soon gone too. He made one appearance in the Knoxville City Directory, and then vanished. In those days, career theater managers, successful or not, were from elsewhere, on their way elsewhere. In that regard they were almost like performers.

The Tennessee Theatre had opened just in time to witness the final decline of vaudeville, the city's most popular entertainment for half a century. Talkies satisfied some of the demand for spoken comedy and music, which were the heart and soul of vaudeville. The Depression, starting with the Crash of October 1929, didn't help. It was cheaper to run movies and cartoons than to pay stage performers, and by 1930 people were demanding cheap. Thanks to movies, and the plaster illusions of the movie palaces, Americans had never been treated so royally for so little money.

Signa Serene, "the Danish Psychic," performed a six-nighter on stage in early December 1930. Billy Beard, the minstrel performer billed as "The Party from the South," appeared onstage in February 1931. Though live performances like these would offer occasional attractions for more than a decade to come, the theater's advertisements suggest that in the '30s, most evenings were devoted entirely to movies — and, of course, introductory tunes on the Wurlitzer. But there was quite a variety of movies, every night: newsreels both local and national, travelogues, cartoons, musical shorts, tribute films of various kinds.

The Tennessee showed about 100 feature films a year, and three or four times as many shorts. If one were to watch all the movies shown at the Tennessee in one year — say, 1930 — on the basis of a full-time job, it would take about two months. Movie fans had to stay alert, because each new release was shown for only three days, and as was the case with half of the new movies that arrived, they were shown only Monday, Tuesday, and Wednesday. One who went out only on weekends missed about half of Hollywood's output. Of course, many of the more successful films did come back around in second runs, in smaller theaters. But to catch any movie at the Tennessee, you had to be there the three days it showed.

The theater reflected the development of much of American popular culture: Gary Cooper and Fay Wray in *The Texan*, Al Jolson in Mammy, Marlene Dietrich in *The Blue Angel*, Will Rogers in *A Connecticut Yankee* — and *The Big Trail*, starring, in his first big role, the 23-year-old John Wayne.

"I can remember it like it was yesterday!" Frank remembers one Saturday evening in the late 1920s waiting in the lobby at the Tennessee with his parents, Hobart and Annabel Johnson, and his twin brother, Dick... "when in comes the University of Tennessee football team. Our father spoke to Dick and me and pointed out Bobby Dodd — an exciting experience for two 7-year-old boys!"

FRANK R. JOHNSON

TENNESSEE
ON THE HAPPY LAWSON
STAGE FRANK LEDGERWOOD
WILLIAM HAINES JOAN CRAWFORD
THE DUKE STEPS OUT THEY TALK
William HAINES
MR. AND MRS. HAPPY LAWSON
A NOVELTY OFFERING
William Haines
The Duke Steps Out
Special Stage Attractions

MARCH 1929

WILD ORCHIDS · 1929

THE BLUE ANGEL · 1930

THE TEXAN · 1930

ANIMAL CRACKERS · 1930

THE GODLESS GIRL · 1929

A WOMAN OF AFFAIRS · 1928

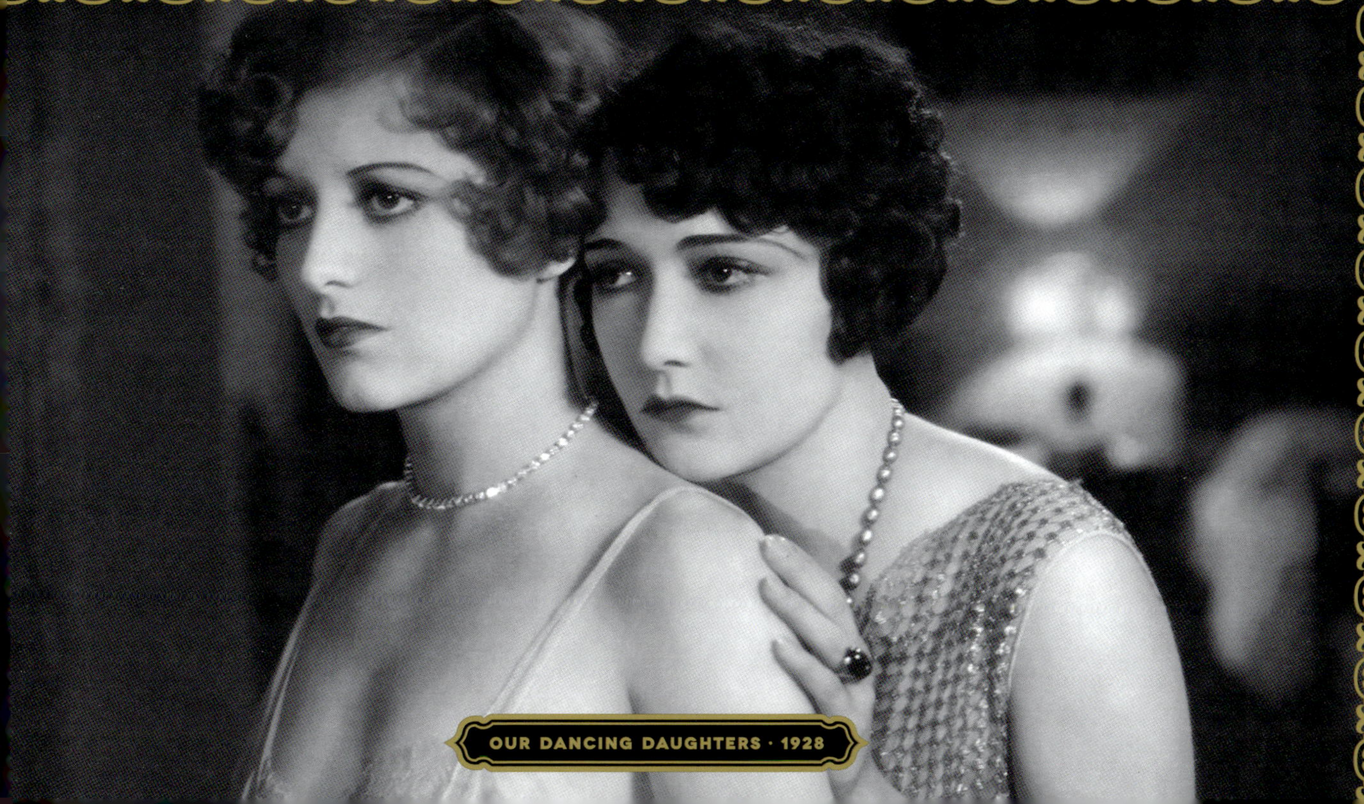

OUR DANCING DAUGHTERS · 1928

CITY LIGHTS · 1931

In January 1931, the Tennessee showed the weird horror film *The Bat Whispers*, often cited as an inspiration for the Batman comic-book character. There was something in the air. Bela Lugosi's *Dracula* opened just a few weeks later, on March 2.

And on April 27 – 29, 1931, the Tennessee, which had shown close to 200 talkie features in a row, suddenly allowed one more silent: Charlie Chaplin's surprising masterpiece *City Lights*.

An organist played regularly, if only occasionally mentioned by name on the marquee. One of the Tennessee's early regular organists has a name that leaps out of lists. At the Wurlitzer's bench for several weeks in late 1930 and early '31 was the one and only C. Sharpe Minor. The Louisiana-born organist had first made his mark in San Francisco in 1917, later gravitating to Los Angeles, where he became known as the Wizard of the Wurlitzer for his trick effects, "lightning speed," and novelty arrangements. But records indicate that by 1930 he owed several people on the West Coast a lot of money, and there was a warrant for his arrest. When he took the job as organist at the Tennessee, he may have been on the lam.

The Publix chain went bankrupt, a victim of the Depression and complex power maneuvers in the movie business. Its regional organization, Tennessee Enterprises, which had planned the Tennessee, evaporated when the theater was hardly three years old. Another regional company, an Atlanta-based company known as Valatenga Theatre Corp., took over management of the Tennessee, just as it was trying out a new motto: "Show Place of the Tennessee Valley."

Companies went bankrupt, but most citizens could afford a few dimes for an escape from the grim realities of the Depression. Not

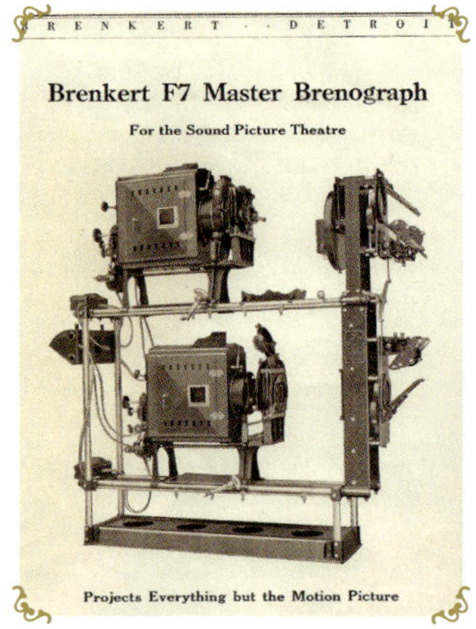

The Tennessee's projection booth was equipped with a Brenograph projector that was used to display special effects onto the stage and screen. It had multiple lens and mirrors to project both animated and static images. A common use was to create a border of moving effects, such as clouds, around the preview trailers and news reels. The Brenograph was also used to project song lyrics for the organ interludes. The Brenograph was used at the Tennessee until the mid-1960s. At left are two of the actual Brenograph slides that were used at the Tennessee.

ORGANIST GRACE JUSTIS · DECEMBER 1928

every movie was a sellout, but the Tennessee typically entertained a few hundred paying customers at a time, all day from when it opened around noon to when it closed around midnight, six days a week. (For the theater's first 19 years, state and local blue laws decreed that movies never be shown on Sunday.)

One casualty of the end of the Publix era was the Tennessee's famous staff artist. Joe Parrott left the theater in 1932 and for many years thereafter ran a commercial art studio just across Gay Street. His departure coincided with the end of the extravagant, architecturally scaled lobby display.

Wallace remembers his first visit to the Tennessee when his mother took him to the theatre to celebrate his sixth birthday.

"WHEN THE CURTAINS CLOSED AND THAT BEAUTIFUL RED AND GOLD WURLITZER ORGAN CONSOLE ROSE MAJESTICALLY IN THE SPOTLIGHT, PLAYING MUSIC THAT FILLED THE THEATRE, LITTLE WALLACE THOUGHT HE HAD DIED AND GONE TO HEAVEN!"

WALLACE W. BAUMANN

ON STAGE AND SCREEN

CHAPTER 4

On May 19, 1931, Clay Brown Atkin died, at age 66. Born before the city had any real theater or regular live entertainment other than horse races and cockfights, he'd seen the growth and flourishing of vaudeville, the dawn of motion pictures, the beginning of radio, and even the beginning of sound movies.

When he died he had a legacy he didn't know about. The Atkins family of Union County was not related to the Atkin family of Knoxville. But in 1924, when a poor farmer's wife bore a son, she'd seen the trucks marked C.B. Atkin and wanted her son to be as successful as that Mr. Atkin, whoever he was. She didn't know what C.B. stood for, but the first names she could think of were Chester and Burton. That's the story this C.B. Atkins told for the rest of his long life about the origin of his name. The world would know him as Chet Atkins, the guitar wizard who expanded the definition of what people could expect from "country" music. In years to come, on a certain special occasion, he would perform to a packed house at the Tennessee Theatre.

Although country music was rare in the early years of the motion-picture palace, the Tennessee did play a surprising role in the development of that form. Maynardville-born, Knoxville-bred Roy Acuff, who'd learned fiddle from a mechanic in Fountain City, performed with a trio during irregular talent shows held on the Tennessee's stage between movies. His group, in those days just before he formed the Tennessee Crackerjacks, was known as the Three Rolling Stones — it included Acuff, his brother "Spot," and bassist Red Jones. They performed at the Tennessee in the fall of 1932. Acuff, who would become the Grand Ole Opry's first national star and go on to be one of the most famous and influential figures in the history of country music in Nashville, likely performed before his first auditorium audience at the Tennessee Theatre.

Thanks to its affiliation with Paramount, the Tennessee introduced a new cartoon character to the region. Promoted with bigger display ads than most feature films merited, Popeye the Sailor Man ("The funniest character in pictures!"), first hit the Tennessee's screen in 1933. The theater kept showing Mickey Mouse films, but Popeye was management's favorite.

With the cooperation of the *Knoxville Journal*, the morning newspaper with which the Tennessee had a cozy relationship, the Tennessee started a popular tradition, the Popeye Club. Every Saturday morning at 9:00, the theater would present a variety presentation for kids, with a kid-friendly feature film,

SKIPPY
TENNESSEE
COME ON BE A KID AGAIN WITH "SKIPPY" JACKIE COOPER
ITZI GREEN BOBBY COOGAN JACKIE SEARL JOHNNY WINTERS
TOM SAWYER DELIGHTED YO HERES GREATER JOY
ITZI GREEN
JACKIE COOPER
SKIPPY
JACKIE SEARL
ROBERT COOGAN
Come!
BE A KID AGAIN
with
MITZI GREEN
JACKIE COOPER
SKIPPY
Come!
BE A KID AGAIN
with
MITZI GREEN
JACKIE COOPER
KIPPY

APRIL 1931

CHET ATKINS, CENTER, WITH FIDDLE

a comedy short of the "Three Stooges" variety, a cartoon, and a local talent show called "Stars of Tomorrow." There were always door prizes and a small birthday cake for "members" who walked across the stage to receive the honor. Enough kids came to the Tennessee every Saturday that it was always somebody's birthday. Popeye Club members proudly carried ID cards with their own stamped membership number.

It was much appreciated by the kids (some of them loyal to the Popeye Club in a rivalry with the corresponding Bugs Bunny Club at the Bijou) — as well as their parents, who appreciated the chance to do some Saturday shopping without kids in tow.

Vaudeville declined in frequency, but those shows that did arrive on the Tennessee's stage were sometimes extraordinary.

Iconic cowboy Tom Mix, tall-hatted legend of both silent and talking Westerns, was "gallant, youthful, and vigorous despite his rather considerable load of years," a reporter remarked, when he arrived at the Tennessee Theatre in November 1933. Mix was 53 but still a convincing action hero; he'd made 10 movies in the previous two years.

With him was his fifth wife, Mabel; his famous horse, Tony; and a small rodeo circus. The "Tom Mix Round Up" is hard to picture on the Tennessee's then-modest stage: a "thundering herd of fine horses and dare-devil riders, ropers, and shooters. Tony, the horse, will be among those present on the Tennessee's stage." (Whether it was the original Tony from the silent era is doubtful. That Tony, then in his mid-20s, had formally "retired" to a place of honor at the Mix Ranch in California just four months earlier. Mix sometimes toured with a horse he called Tony Jr.)

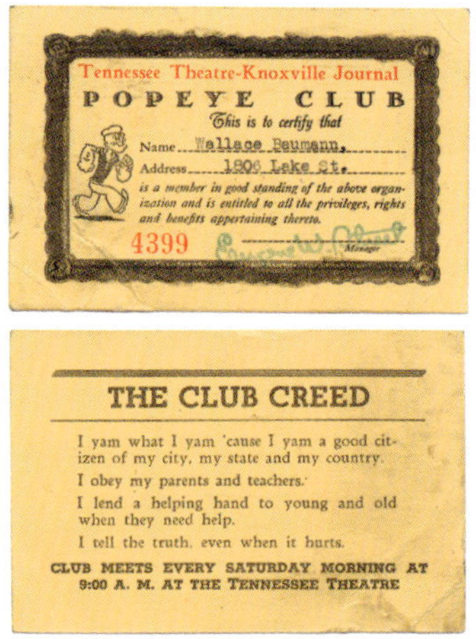

THE POPEYE CLUB MEMBERSHIP CARD

TOM MIX

In addition, there was an aspect called "Sky Ridin'," an aerial acrobatic routine including Mrs. Mix and her sister, Irma Ward, "Empress of the Air."

A *Knoxville Journal* reporter caught up with Mix: "The tiny dressing room he occupied backstage at the Tennessee Theatre fitted his brawny frame as snugly as did the skin-tight, gaudily decorated white cow-puncher outfit he wore." Mix remarked, "This old town seems to have grown up overnight." He spoke of a previous trip to Knoxville, during the Appalachian Exposition of 1910, during which he said he spent much of his time hanging out nights at the Elks Club ("We had some fine times there") and touring the city with Teddy Roosevelt. "I ran around with him quite a lot," he said. "This always was the best town in the South," he said, "and I'm not saying that just because I'm here right now, either. You've got the world in your lap here. With the TVA, and what it means, if Knoxville takes things right and does its bit, this city can have anything it wants."

KNOXVILLE JOURNAL
NOVEMBER 15, 1933

ROY ACUFF, LEFT, PERFORMING ON WNOX

THE STRAND THEATRE, GAY STREET · 1933

The Tom Mix Round Up performed eight shows at the Tennessee, in two days — between showings of an unrelated Ginger Rodgers movie, *Rafter Romance* — during which Mix made time to speak to the local Kiwanis Club.

The logistics of that visit have puzzled stagehands since. Because of the limitations of the backstage area, Mix would have had to lead Tony and his peers all the way through the lobby and somehow canter up the narrow steps at the sides of the stage. Despite some skepticism, equestrians attest that with a well-trained horse, it's possible. Records of how many horses were on stage (there were at least two) and exactly what they did are elusive.

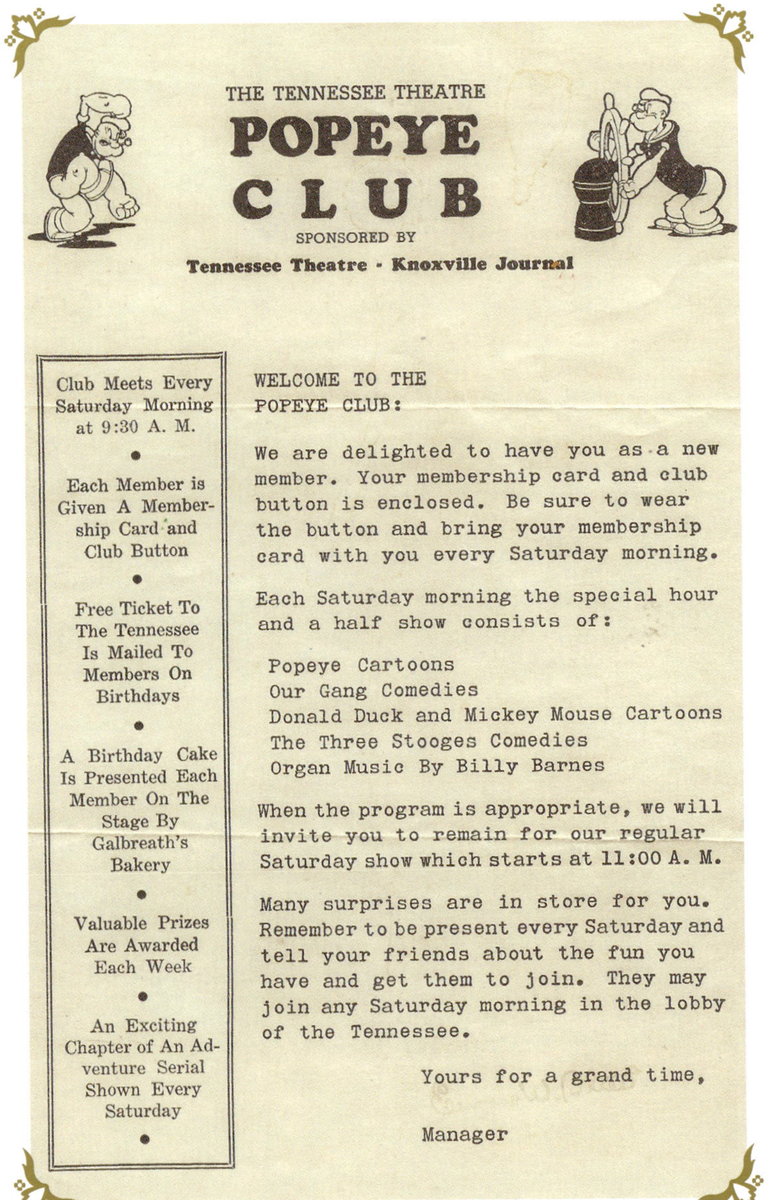

THE TENNESSEE THEATRE

POPEYE CLUB

SPONSORED BY

Tennessee Theatre - Knoxville Journal

Club Meets Every Saturday Morning at 9:30 A. M.

•

Each Member is Given A Membership Card and Club Button

•

Free Ticket To The Tennessee Is Mailed To Members On Birthdays

•

A Birthday Cake Is Presented Each Member On The Stage By Galbreath's Bakery

•

Valuable Prizes Are Awarded Each Week

•

An Exciting Chapter of An Adventure Serial Shown Every Saturday

•

WELCOME TO THE POPEYE CLUB:

We are delighted to have you as a new member. Your membership card and club button is enclosed. Be sure to wear the button and bring your membership card with you every Saturday morning.

Each Saturday morning the special hour and a half show consists of:

Popeye Cartoons
Our Gang Comedies
Donald Duck and Mickey Mouse Cartoons
The Three Stooges Comedies
Organ Music By Billy Barnes

When the program is appropriate, we will invite you to remain for our regular Saturday show which starts at 11:00 A. M.

Many surprises are in store for you. Remember to be present every Saturday and tell your friends about the fun you have and get them to join. They may join any Saturday morning in the lobby of the Tennessee.

Yours for a grand time,

Manager

POPEYE CLUB MEMBERSHIP LETTER

Later that month, perhaps after a thorough cleaning, the same stage made way for a very different act: Nick Lucas, "the grandfather of the jazz guitar," best known for his 1929 hit, "Tiptoe Through the Tulips."

In early 1934, just after the holidays, a "burlesque" vaudeville troupe called The Marcus Show, which had been making the rounds since the early '20s offered a late-night "Midnight Frolic" presentation called *La Vie Paree*. Though unheralded at the time, one of its dancers was a 23-year-old unknown named Danny Kaye.

Spring and summer of '34 saw the Knoxville debut of some classic movies: *It Happened One Night, Tarzan and His Mate, Little Miss Marker, The Thin Man. Treasure Island* arrived in October. On November 14, the Tennessee presented *One Night of Love*, the early operatic Hollywood musical for which East Tennessee soprano Grace Moore would be nominated for a Best Actress Oscar. Years later her legacy would be the occasion for one of the highest-profile events ever held in this big room.

Bandleader Ray Teal, who would later be better known as a movie and television actor, played a three-night stand with his band, the Floridians, that July. In October, Henry Santrey, a dance-band conductor who had made some recordings back in the early '20s, brought his new band, the Soldiers of Fortune, and singer-dancer Loretta Gray.

And late that November, the Tennessee greeted perhaps its most controversial show, Earl Carroll's Vanities. Known as the "Flesh Peddler" and "Troubadour of the Nude," Carroll was famous for assembling dozens of beautiful women dancing while wearing

NOVEMBER 14, 1934

GRACE MOORE

as little as possible, along with particularly zany comedians. He promised "The Most Beautiful Girls in the World" and "1,000 Laughs."

Ken Murray, the headliner, was a show-biz stalwart whose later bizarre bird movie, *Bill & Coo*, would win a special Oscar; he was later a familiar comic face on 1950s television and was still appearing in major movies into the 1970s. Chaz Chase, who made a hilarious act of ingesting random objects, became a familiar comedian on movies and TV, performing for half a century — long enough, in fact, to appear on *Late Night With David Letterman*. The *Knoxville Journal* called the Vanities a "flesh and blood extravaganza" that challenged our moviegoing habits. But any old-movie fan transported back to watch that show would be repeatedly distracted by familiar faces. The Vanities' known performers have more than 100 movie credits between them.

Songs included the up-tempo Harlem hit "Savage Rhythm," as well as "Cocktails for Two." That celebration of the end of Prohibition, a future standard, recorded by Bing Crosby, Duke Ellington, Tommy Dorsey and others, was brand-new, written that year, and originated with the Vanities show. Those who attended were among the first Americans to hear "Cocktails for Two" performed live. Alas, a year after national Prohibition was repealed, cocktails were still illegal in Knoxville.

The Vanities presented two shows that Thursday, matinée and evening, with reserved seats ranging from 83 cents to $2.75, much more expensive than any movie ticket. It was the Vanities' 10th production, but their first-ever Southern tour, maybe to promote their new movie, *Murder at the Vanities* — although it had already shown at the Tennessee six months earlier.

Corinne recalls Saturday mornings in the late 1930s and 40s and no school! She and her friends would hop the Broadway Avenue bus to the Tennessee for the Popeye Club. "A huge cheer would go up as the magnificent Wurlitzer organ arose from the orchestra pit with the music in full swing."

CORINNE PALKO

"They would stand me on a box in order to reach the microphone." Helen remembers singing over WNOX radio and on stage at the Tennessee Theatre in 1940 at the Popeye Club when she was only 3 or 4 years old.

HELEN BEELER PARRIS

KNOXVILLE JOURNAL · NOVEMBER 24, 1935

The show represented an audience experiment by Tennessee manager Harry Hardy, whose five years at the Tennessee made him the theater's longest-tenured manager before World War II. No manager was more personally associated with the theater during its early years, and Hardy became a spokesman for the business in general, loudly denouncing a proposed state amusement tax.

He pushed several big shows over the next couple of years. Before Hardy, the Tennessee had seen an interesting diet of vaudeville. After Hardy, the theater hosted lots of memorable movie promotions, including gala regional and world premieres. But it was mainly during Hardy's tenure that the Tennessee hosted, with varying success, real Broadway shows and big song-and-dance extravaganzas, with dozens of performers in a single night.

Just after the Vanities, Hardy brought Bert Lown and his Baltimore Hotel Orchestra; Lown became famous, years ago, for writing and introducing the jazz standard, "Bye, Bye Blues."

The Tennessee observed the holidays not by closing, but by offering special events. There was always a special Christmas Day show, sometimes with a visiting organist, like Jimmy Beers, up from Atlanta's Fox. On New Year's Eve, the Tennessee threw a "watch party." New Year's Eve 1934 offered a "Midnight Prevue" of a new movie, *The Gay Divorcee*, the first movie in which Fred Astaire and Ginger Rogers appeared together as headliners. It introduced Cole Porter's "Night and Day" and the incredibly long (17-minute) dance number, "The Continental."

For two nights in late January 1935, the Tennessee presented Husk O'Hare and his Genial Gentlemen of the Air, featuring radio star O'Hare, the jazz bandleader from Chicago who rarely performed live concerts. Perhaps to make it easier for himself, he brought a variety show of singing, dancing, and comedy acts: "one solid hour of fast, furious, dazzling entertainment." The movie those nights was W.C. Fields's *It's a Gift*.

What was heralded as "the Biggest Attraction Ever Beheld in Knoxville" arrived on the stage of the Tennessee Theatre at 8:30 p.m. on Friday, February 22, 1935. The legendary Ziegfeld Follies was on a limited national tour of 40 cities. For 27 years the Follies had been vaudeville's greatest legend, famous for its combination of singers, dancers, comedians, and platoons of beautiful dancing girls. One of Ziegfeld's biggest stars from its early days was Fanny Brice, the pop singer and brilliantly irreverent comedienne. She'd started with the Follies as a teenager in 1910 and became the performer most associated with the show.

FANNY BRICE

Florenz Ziegfeld had died in 1932. By some strict accounts of its history, the real Ziegfeld Follies ended then. Several of Ziegfeld's famous stars, like W.C. Fields, Eddie Cantor, and Will Rogers, were no longer part of the show. When Ziegfeld's widow, Billie Burke, launched a New York revival of the Follies, she got Brice to be part of it, and it was a hit on Broadway in 1934. The tour reputedly brought the Follies to the South for the first time in its history. Knoxville advertising was adamant that this was "Not a 'Road' or a Number Two outfit trading on its Big City reputation, but the One, Only, and Original." Fanny Brice, advertised as the chief attraction, was a very big part of the show.

"The organ music was grand and the theatre cool, just like the mountains." Dorothy, who lived in the Elkmont area of the Smoky Mountains in the early 1930s remembers a Mrs. John Richards of Knoxville befriended her and brought her down from the mountains to the Tennessee Theatre one day to see "Mutiny on the Bounty," starring Clark Gable, Franchot Tone, and Charles Laughton. "She introduced me as her mountain friend," Dorothy recalls.

DOROTHY TRAMMELL

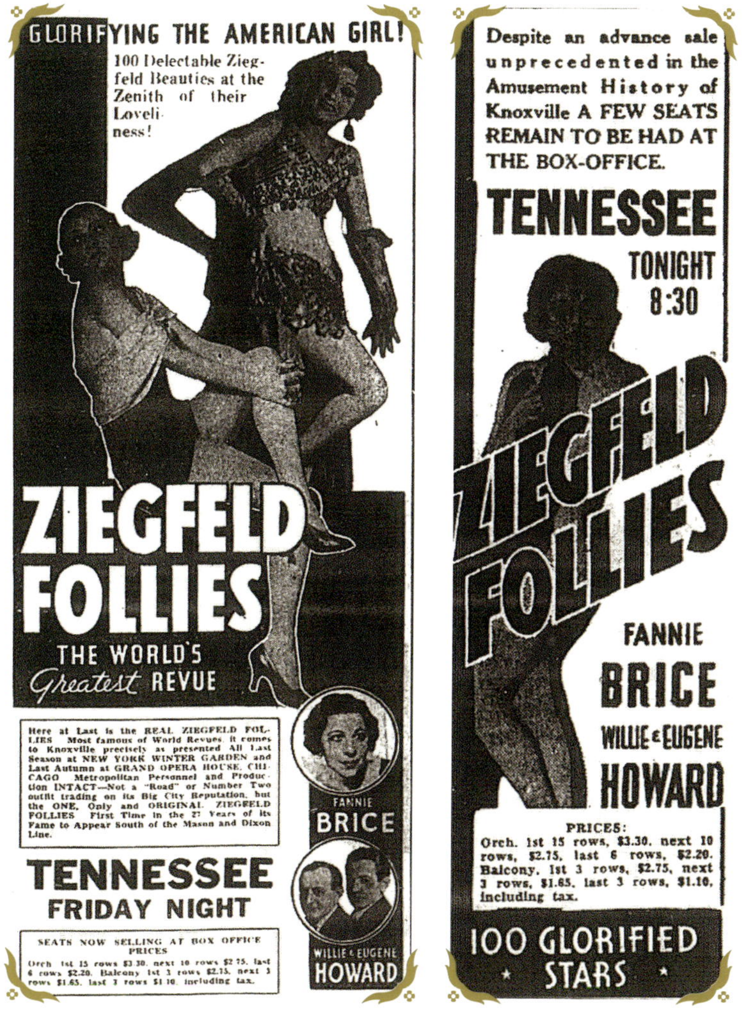

KNOXVILLE JOURNAL · FEBRUARY 17 AND 22, 1935

It's perhaps unlikely producer Burke herself—who'd performed in other theaters on Gay Street back in vaudeville days and who, four years later, would be better known to many as Glynda, the Good Witch of the North—was backstage. But the big show packed the house, with 100 buying standing-room-only tickets, in back. At 43, Brice was still an energetic performer, going through seven separate acts at the Tennessee, including a bizarre parody of evangelist Amy Semple MacPherson as "Soul-Saving Sadie" (with a Yiddish accent!); a skit called "Sailor Behave"; "Sarah the Sunshine Girl," a sendup of nudism; the "Baby Snooks" routine, which would evolve into a popular radio show; and a burlesque of Sally Rand's famously risqué fan dance. (Rand herself appeared, in the flesh, at the Lyric less than a year later.)

And that wasn't all. On stage were reputedly 100 performers in all, including the famous Ziegfeld dancing girls. The stars, according to the Journal's locally well-known theater critic Malcolm Miller, were Brice, singer Leone Sousa, and comedians Willie and Eugene Howard, who both had minor Hollywood careers ahead of them. One of two teenaged girls Miller described as "clever little dancers" was June Preisser. A few years later she'd be a familiar young actress on the big screen in some major Rooney-Garland movies like *Babes in Arms*.

A few members of the chorus, unmentioned at the Tennessee but known to be touring with the show, would later be well known in film and television, including 25-year-old Eve Arden, shortly before she was well-known as a comedic supporting actress in Hollywood (almost 20 years before she was "Our Miss Brooks" in one of TV's first sitcoms, and more than 40 years before she was Principal McGhee in *Grease*). Another performer associated with the show was Buddy Ebsen, then best known as a dancer. Ebsen started with that show but by 1935 was getting other offers; it's less certain he followed the whole tour, as Arden did.

The tour ended four weeks later in New Haven, Connecticut, so popular it prompted a commercial live recording. The Follies was revived one more time, the following year, with Brice and a new rising star named Bob Hope. Later, a few popular movie homages to the Ziegfeld legend reunited some surviving stars. But Tennessee Theatre patrons were among the last Americans to see Ziegfeld Follies on the road.

KNOXVILLE JOURNAL · MARCH 24, 1935

What was likely the Tennessee's first full Broadway show arrived just a month later. Maxwell Anderson's play *Mary of Scotland*, a searing account of forbidden love, murder, and vengeance written in luminous blank verse, had closed on Broadway just the year before. It was a whistle-stop production, one performance, probably with simple sets for its seven scenes, but it was the real thing, directed by New York Theater Guild stalwart Theresa Helburn and featuring 25 actors, including, in the title role, the one and only Helen Hayes. The play was so popular that even as it was playing at the Tennessee it was being turned into a major Hollywood movie (starring Katharine Hepburn and Frederick March, and directed by John Ford). Dubbed "First Lady of the American Theatre," Hayes, then 34, was keeping one foot in Broadway and another in Hollywood, where she had recently worked for Clarence Brown. The cast brought to the Tennessee also included well-known Broadway actors Pauline Frederick as Queen Elizabeth Tudor and Philip Merivale as James Hepburn.

MARY OF SCOTLAND

HELEN HAYES

TENNESSEE THEATRE USHER

UNDER THE MARQUEE · JUNE 1935

Frederick, who was also a major Hollywood actress of the silent era — she'd starred in Clarence Brown's 1925 classic, *Smouldering Fires* — was almost as famous as Hayes in 1935, but she was near the end of a career soon to be curtailed by illness.

It was a near-sellout, standing-room only for the single show, the largest Knoxville audience ever to see a serious drama indoors.

"Helen Hayes cast an enchanting spell, with a beauty of enunciation and a cadence of expression seldom heard on the stage today," wrote critic Malcolm Miller. "Her denunciation of Queen Elizabeth was one of the greatest scenes I have ever witnessed." But Miller, who would unexpectedly find himself manager of the theater a few years later, brought up some acoustical problems. Pauline Frederick's voice, he said, was the only one he could thoroughly hear. It was Frederick who declaimed: "We live in a world of shadows, my lord. We are not what we are, but what is said of us, and what we read in others' eyes."

The play received "deafening applause" and the players answered six curtain calls.

According to a long-passed-down legend, Hayes declared she wouldn't return to Knoxville until the city had a proper theater for drama. In her only published interview during her short visit, though, she was gracious and polite, admitting only that she was intimidated by the size of the Tennessee when she first stepped out on stage. Broadway's Alvin Theatre, which launched the play, was less than three-quarters the size.

"We were delighted with the response," Hayes said. "Was it really all right? I was scared to death by the size of the house until we became accustomed to it. Most theaters we play are much smaller than this one."

She could have found things to complain about. Dressing rooms were rarely luxurious, even on Broadway, but the Tennessee's up-and-down warren of cubicles remained a distinctive problem, one little known to the public at large. That architectural flaw would not be substantially improved for another 70 years.

Despite the brevity of the day trip, Hayes made some time to look around, but was quoted mentioning only one site: the Main Street home of the late C.B. Atkin. "I've been around the country quite a bit," she said, "but I haven't seen many places I liked as well as that one." The modified antebellum mansion was torn down, for parking, a few years later.

When Hayes left the stage, close to midnight, she was mobbed by waiting fans. "You're so sweet," an elderly woman declared.

Hours after the Broadway legends left the stage, different crowds were in the same room, guffawing at the hog-calling scene in the matinée of Will Rogers' latest movie, *Life Begins at 40.*

Bandleader Ray Teal returned in April with vaudeville comedian Ben Blue, who many years later would be familiar on television.

That September, Major (Edward) Bowes himself, manager of New York's Capitol Theatre and host of America's most popular radio talent show, arrived with a show called "NBC Presents Major Bowes Amateur Show on the Stage." Bowes, who popularized the gong, which he employed mercilessly with sub-par performances, also popularized—that year—a 19-year old singer from New Jersey named Frank Sinatra. Bowes played key roles in the early careers of Beverly Sills, Robert Merrill, and Lily Pons. What he found in Knoxville, early in the history of his show, we can only guess.

A variety show that would prove even more durable than the Follies appeared at the Tennessee on October 2, 1935. The "midnight show"—to start at 11 p.m., after the last showing of the Claudette Colbert comedy, *She Married Her Boss*—was a peculiar live stage show hardly heralded in the papers. Journal movie critic Sam Adkin, in the 12th paragraph of a column about the week's movies, dismissed it as a "hillbilly potpourri.... It will be a cross between vaudeville and a barn dance, without the dancing."

KNOXVILLE JOURNAL · NOVEMBER 17, 1935

It was a rare touring version of the Grand Ole Opry, in its only known Knoxville visit. Featured was its first big star, irrepressible banjoist Uncle Dave Macon, five days before his 65th birthday; Alabama's Delmore Brothers, the guitar-playing harmonists at the height of their national popularity; the Gully Jumpers, pioneer Nashville recording artists; and noted fiddler Sid Harkreeder. The MC was Curt Poulton, an Opry vocalist himself. The Wednesday night show may not have been broadcast

KNOXVILLE JOURNAL
SEPTEMBER 4, 1935

live, but it was the Tennessee Theatre's first known all-country show, and it was a late-night doozy. As impressive as were the performers on stage, it's interesting to speculate what Gay Street denizens were in the audience — perhaps the young fiddler who would be the Opry's next big star, Roy Acuff.

Despite its obvious regional appeal, that rare Opry night may have been the last all-country show at the Tennessee for a half-century to come. For the time being, Tennessee patrons preferred the exotic. A road production of the Broadway racetrack comedy *Three Men on a Horse* was staged that November. The show featured no stars already famous in 1935, but several cast members, including Chester Clute in the leading role (Miller described his performance as a "wow") and Grandon Rhodes, would become recognizable character actors in movies and television. Robert F. Griffith, who had a small role in the show, would 25 years later be one of Broadway's most successful producers, leading musicals like *The Pajama Game*, *Damn Yankees*, and *West Side Story*. One of the leading roles at the Tennessee belonged to Sheldon Leonard, who Miller wrote "carried the weight of the underworld with smooth authority." Later a familiar movie character actor, usually as a tough guy, Leonard would become one of the most influential TV executives of the 1960s, executive producer of *The Dick Van Dyke Show*, *The Andy Griffith Show*, and *I Spy*.

FIFI D'ORSAY

Perhaps poignantly, the *Journal* announced *Three Men* as "the first road show of the season." In fact it was likely the last full-scale Broadway play presented at the Tennessee for almost half a century. Whether it was obvious or not at the end of that remarkable year, the Tennessee's big-show era was fading, but it wasn't over yet.

EARL CARROLL WITH HIS VANITIES

Fifi D'Orsay was the nubile singer-dancer known as "the ou-la-la girl of film" and "the French bombshell from Gay Paree" (she was actually from Canada), and quite a sensation when she appeared with the boundary-challenging Earl Carroll's Vanities on November 25, 1935. She was the show's best-known performer, but she wasn't the headliner — that honor went to the wacky comedy duo of Clark & McCullough, known for their movie shorts. Still, D'Orsay was the one pictured on the front page of the *Journal* that day. Smitten *Journal* reporter Gordon Gaskill got an interview with her over a steak dinner. He wrote, "think of her as a sort of champagne, bubbly with spirits and laughter, impish, sly, alluring, coquettish, human, feminine, charming ...."

He spoke with her about accusations of communism and "the Charlotte Affair," an incident in which, during an Actors Equity wage dispute, an actor interrupted a performance and was fired. It was first announced that D'Orsay, who tried to intervene after a manager had yanked comedian Paul McCullough out of a Pullman sleeper bunk and beaten him, would leave the show, but the announcement was amended that she would remain for two more weeks — hence she was still with the show when it arrived at the Tennessee.

Critic Malcolm Miller reviewed the show, especially impressed with comic tap-dancer Buster West, at the height of his movie-short fame; Lucille Page, the future movie actress; comedian McCullough; and tiny, energetic Violet Carlson, who "was a panic through the show." (Carlson would, 30 years later, play cute old ladies on TV's *Batman*.) D'Orsay, he thought, was wasted on the show. "D'Orsay labored courageously with an impossible and thankless part. She has an abundance of talent and personality, but no name is big enough to get away with the kind of tripe she had to dish out. They done the mademoiselle wrong."

Furthermore, Miller had a question about Carroll's pride. "Earl Carroll's slogan, 'Through these portals pass the most beautiful girls in the world,' is not open to debate," Miller wrote in the *Journal*. "Evidently they passed through and did not return for the Knoxville engagement."

Just three days later, the Tennessee kept the exotic spirit aglow with Earl Taylor's "Oo-la-la Continental," a Thanksgiving night extravaganza — and another 11 p.m. show — featuring, among others, "40 French models." There were also animal acts. One attraction was "Connie Cella and her chow, Chang."

It's remarkable how much these extravaganzas were part of the Tennessee's fare during the Great Depression, and most of them did well. As Taylor remarked, "There is no Depression if you have what the public wants."

It was show business, and much about putting on a happy face. At the end of that Vanities tour, headliner Paul McCullough, the center of the labor controversy and one of Miller's favorites, checked into a Massachusetts sanitarium for severe depression. Upon his release, just four months after the Knoxville show, the comedian killed himself.

Surveying all the razzle-dazzle extravaganzas of the mid-1930s, it might be easy to forget that the Tennessee was, mainly, a movie theater. Weeks and even months passed with nothing but movies and Wurlitzer tunes.

The 1935 movie *Ah, Wilderness!* is a not-quite-forgotten oddity in Hollywood history. Eugene O'Neill's only comedy became a movie starring Lionel Barrymore, Wallace Beery, and the 15-year-old Mickey Rooney. When it showed at the Tennessee, a group of Knoxville High School alumni, all of them in their late 40s, attended together, an occasion covered in the newspapers. They came together because their old classmate had directed the movie. By then, director Clarence Brown, who'd grown up in North Knoxville, was one of Hollywood's most successful directors. He'd graduated from UT with two engineering degrees, got interested in cinematography, and during the silent era became famous in Hollywood for his innovations in light and motion.

But the rumor was that his old classmates might recognize a few things in this one. Although the MGM movie was based in New England, and — unlike most Hollywood movies of the era — was largely shot on location in Massachusetts, Brown based some architectural details and incidental characters on his old classmates at Knoxville High School, when it was located at

KNOXVILLE JOURNAL
NOVEMBER 27, 1935

LOVE'S SOUNDTRACK

The musical choices at the Easterday double wedding of 1936 may testify to the power of movies. Many pastors still objected to the use of Wagner's "Bridal Chorus" in weddings, due to its pagan elements. And opera fans knew that the wedding it celebrated, in Lohengrin, turned out extremely badly, with several members of the wedding party, including the abandoned bride, dead. By 1936, however, the song had accompanied dozens of happy weddings in motion pictures. And the 1901 pop song "I Love You Truly" wouldn't necessarily be a tune young people would recognize — except for the fact that it had appeared in 10 major motion pictures since 1929.

In fact, the 86-year-old operatic aria and the 35-year-old pop song had been paired in more than one recent movie, like "We're Rich Again" in 1934. For better or worse, the two tunes became common in the soundtracks of American weddings.

JUNE BRIDE SECTION

The Knoxville Sunday Journal

Tennessee Valley's Greatest Newspaper

FIRST IN PRESTIGE — KNOXVILLE, TENN., SUNDAY, MAY 31, 1936 — MOST NEWS FIRST

KNOXVILLE JOURNAL-TENNESSEE THEATRE STAGE WEDDING

Mr. and Mrs. William Norman

Invite You to be Present

Lula Myrtle

Mr. Claude Raymond Easterday

Wednesday Evening Nine O'Clock June Third

Tennessee Theatre

Mr. and Mrs. John S. Hall

Invite You to be Present

Mary Alice

Mr. Ben Howard Easterday

Wednesday Evening Nine O'Clock June Third

Tennessee Theatre

Tennessee Theatre

Presents Its

DOUBLE WEDDING

On the Stage--9:00 P. M.

WEDNESDAY -- JUNE 3rd.

KNOXVILLE JOURNAL · MAY 31, 1936

Bridal Couples Who Will This Coming Wednesday Become Part Of The Marital Life Of Knoxville

MISS MARY ALICE HALL — MISS LULA MYRTLE NORMAN

Miss Hall will become the bride of Ben Howard Easterday, and Miss Norman will become the bride of Claude Raymond Easterday at a double wedding ceremony, sponsored by The Knoxville Journal and the management of the Tennessee theatre, on the stage of the Tennessee theatre at 9 p. m. Wednesday. It will symbolize Knoxville's observance of "June, the month of brides."

KNOXVILLE JOURNAL · MAY 31, 1936

the corner of Union Avenue and Walnut Street. Sure enough, when the movie started, several in the audience at the Tennessee reacted to the opening shot, the familiar KHS banner.

Hardly any mere movie or show-biz performer ever got as much attention as what happened at the Tennessee on June 3, 1936. On the stage was a man who was famous in some circles, even if he wasn't a performer in the usual sense. The Reverend W. Herschel Ford was in town that day to marry two brothers, Ben Howard Easterday and Claude Raymond Easterday, to their respective mates, Mary Alice Hall and Lula Myrtle Norman. The candlelit ceremony, bedecked with barrelsful of flowers, seemed to capture the imagination of a city in mid-Depression. Mrs. Fanny Daly was the organist and played Wagner's wedding march. Local tenor Jack Safford sang "I Love You Truly."

Rev. Ford, later based in El Paso, would be famous in Baptist circles for his nationally popular "Simple Sermons" series of inspirational books.

It's not known whether that was the first wedding ever conducted in the Tennessee. It certainly wasn't the last. As a later poll suggested, the Tennessee has a reputation as a matchmaker. In 2001, the Tennessee's management asked East Tennesseans at large for special memories of the theater. The most common response, by far, was that of married couples who had enjoyed their first dates at the Tennessee. Some reported that the proposal that changed their lives and started their families took place there at the theater, in the house itself or in the romantic lobby.

By the mid-'30s, the Tennessee was hosting occasional orchestral performances by groups like the UT Glee Club and Orchestra, which presented an annual concert at the theater, sometimes with a 70-voice chorus. Although the university on the Hill offered some events and audiences to the Tennessee, it was also presenting, for the first time in its history, a rival for the Knoxville performing-arts dollar. In 1934, UT's Alumni Hall opened. The versatile venue could work as an auditorium, a dance hall, or a gymnasium. Over the next quarter-century, most visiting classical performers, and several major popular musicians, would perform at Alumni Hall. For the general public, who for generations had been accustomed to seeing musical performances mainly on Gay Street, it was a change.

The holiday season of 1936 ushered in one hint of a distant destiny for the Tennessee. That December, the Knoxville Symphony Orchestra, founded one year earlier under the baton of Bertha Walburn Clark and composed of 40 volunteer musicians, performed at the Tennessee Theatre for the first time. It was a special holiday benefit for Knoxville's St. John's Orphanage. Although declared a success, the night did not suggest the symphony and the theater were a perfect match. The 500 who bought tickets occupied only one quarter of the house. The symphony soon settled more cozily into the smaller Bijou Theatre. Symphony concerts at the Tennessee would not be a regular attraction until almost half a century later.

The theater was by then managed by Atlanta-based Wilby-Kincey Theatre Service Corp., which seems to have been an offshoot of Valatenga, through the person of R.B. Wilby, who was known for his opposition to "salacious" or exploitative movies and advertising. Movies about adultery, drugs, and venereal disease, popular in some Knoxville theaters like the Roxy, had become almost a subgenre. They wouldn't be shown at the Tennessee.

In 1937 the Tennessee welcomed Mr. Billy Barnes. The elegant organist, who in his dapper suits and thinning, slicked-back hair resembled maybe a cross between Fred Astaire and Charles Boyer, was well known in New York, where he'd played at the Paramount on Times Square — a theater associated with one of the Tennessee's architects, Arthur Mayger. Barnes arrived in town first at the request of the new minister of First Presbyterian Church, behind the theater, but soon found himself playing five nights a week at the Tennessee. And frequently on Saturday mornings. A generation grew up thinking of Barnes as the genial host of the Popeye Club.

THEATRE TICKET FROM OCTOBER 21, 1936

Tickets from productions during the Tennessee's first decade are rare. This is for a 55-cent balcony seat for the midnight "Folies Caprice," one of several traveling shows in the mid-1930s that featured squadrons of dancing girls, "Hot from Hollywood," as the advertising had it, "A Revue of Revelations." Despite its late hour on a weeknight — it went on at 11:30 p.m. after a full day of showing the latest Shirley Temple film, "Dimples" — the Folies featured 35 girls wearing the latest fashions in 15 scenes.

"Those were the days for a little child who didn't get to do a lot of fun things." Imogene recalls when she was 9 or 10 going to the Popeye Club every Saturday with her brothers and sisters.

IMOGENE COILE TYREE

Mattie remembers when she was 11 or 12 taking the bus alone from Fountain City to the Tennessee to see the Popeye Club. "I won a little camera once; they called out a row number and a seat number and I was the winner."

MATTIE GALYON

BILLY BARNES AT THE WURLITZER · CA. 1940

The same year, half a block away, the S&W's grand new art-deco cafeteria opened. Considered modern, elegant, even futuristic at the time, cafeterias combined comfort and efficiency in a way that seemed to speak to the times. Though the S&W was closer to the Riviera, the grandness of the place linked it in many minds with the Tennessee. The vaguely Egyptian themes of the S&W reflected the vaguely Moorish themes of the Tennessee; it was all quite safely exotic. For four decades, the elemental Knoxville night on the town was dinner at the S&W and a movie at the Tennessee. They combined to create the illusion of a faraway adventure.

That year, on an evening stroll around downtown, Swiss writer Annemarie Schwarzenbach described downtown Knoxville in a travelogue written in German, for European consumption. She mentioned "the businesses and movie houses of the garishly lit main street" mainly to remark on the fact that much of Knoxville was not like that at all. In 1937, hundreds of residences just a few blocks east of Gay Street didn't even have electricity. The contrast was especially striking at night.

April 1938 witnessed an unusual personal event. Inventor Weston Fulton was one of Knoxville's most successful industrialists, owner of the Fulton Sylphon Co., which manufactured gadgets that made much 20th-century technology possible, from car air

THE S&W

For a couple of generations, the definitive night on the town in Knoxville meant dinner at the S&W and a movie at the Tennessee. Some might recall the Riviera in that mix. In fact, both of Knoxville's grandest movie theaters were just a few steps down the sidewalk from that big restaurant right between them. But in remembering the dinner-and-a-movie combination, people seem to mention the Tennessee more often.

Unlike any restaurant in any city today, the S&W was an elegant art-deco cafeteria, in an era when cafeterias were still brand-new, and modern, even futuristic. Knoxville's S&W was a sleek, shiny place sprawling across four floors of some radically remodeled old buildings on the 500 block of Gay, hardly half a block from the Tennessee. It defied the Depression to open in the early 1930s, within a few years blooming at a new, much-larger location in 1937. Technically a Charlotte-based chain—the initials stood for Sherrill and Weber—S&W maintained locations in several Southern cities from Atlanta to Washington, each location distinctly different in design from the others. It became a Knoxville institution, more beloved in its way than any locally owned establishment. A sweeping spiral staircase with polished brass led up to the mezzanine, to the sound of popular tunes played by Lois, the organist—everyone knew her, just as they knew Slim, the lanky, acrobatic waiter. She played often with a lightly exotic flair that sometimes seemed to presage what was playing at the Tennessee. Its revolving door seemed like something in an Astaire-Rogers film, and the S&W's extravagant but democratic interior was somehow a reflection of the Tennessee's. Both were places that made you want to stand up straight, like Cary Grant or Gary Cooper.

The dishes served in the cafeteria line were mostly inexpensive. Like the Tennessee, the restaurant was a little paradoxically able to maintain its elegance through volume.

S&W CAFETERIA, 516 S. GAY STREET · CA. 1937

"To my horror the 10-cent bottle of rubbing alcohol broke, and the fumes permeated the entire theatre!" Marie remembers a date at the Tennessee in 1936 with the man she later married. "We were sitting on the front row of the balcony, and during the showing of the movie, I accidentally knocked over [the railing] a package of articles I had purchased at S.H. Kress store."

MARIE DOYLE GIDEON

KNOXVILLE JOURNAL · APRIL 25, 1938

conditioners to depth charges. His daughter, Barbara Fulton, was a professional actress who'd been associated with a minor success on Broadway. With high hopes she moved to Hollywood and landed a starring role, albeit in a 12-minute short. A re-enactment of an ostensibly true story of a department store clerk who discovers a shoplifting ring, *Shopgirl's Evidence* co-starred well-known journalist Floyd Gibbons as the narrator and was shown between feature films in cinemas around the world for several months. It showed at the Tennessee for just two days, but during that time proud father Weston Fulton and his family attended to see the film.

And later that month, the Tennessee presented a remarkable movie called *Snow White and the Seven Dwarfs*. Walt Disney's first feature-length film had premiered in Los Angeles the previous December, in New York in January, and in February began a slow distribution across the nation, creating enormous anticipation for what was being declared, even by serious filmmakers, to be the greatest movie ever made. As of 1938 it was certainly the most popular movie ever made, a global phenomenon. In an extraordinary response, the Tennessee devoted an entire week to that one movie, and offered six shows daily. "Nothing Like It Ever Seen Before!" went the advertisements, accurately. It's possible that 70,000 people saw *Snow White* at the Tennessee that week in April 1938.

Described as a sensation similar to *Snow White* was another remarkable movie that opened at the Tennessee a year and a half later, on October 19, 1939. There had been buzz for months about *The Wizard of Oz*, "probably the most ornate and beautiful film ever produced," according to *Journal* critic Sam Adkin. He remarked that "the star is Tennessee's own little Judy Garland." That detail was a bit of a stretch, concerning the Minnesota-born, California-raised Garland. But before she was born, her parents had lived in Murfreesboro.

LITTLE MISS MARKER · 1934

TREASURE ISLAND · 1934

THE GAY DIVORCEE · 1934

THE THIN MAN · 1934

RAFTER ROMANCE · 1933

IT HAPPENED ONE NIGHT · 1934

IT'S A GIFT · 1934

TARZAN AND HIS MATE · 1934

By the accounts of some people who remembered those days, popular swing icon Glenn Miller played at the Tennessee twice, the first time in the late 1930s. The one we know about for sure was what may have been Miller's second appearance on that stage, a very short concert for radio broadcast on June 6, 1940. The trombonist-bandleader, one of the biggest pop stars of his era, came to town partly to be the entertainment at the Smoky Mountain Wildflower Festival's Coronation Ball at UT's Alumni Hall. While he was here with his two biggest singing stars, Marion Hutton and Ray Eberle, he agreed to give a 15-minute live broadcast from the stage of the Tennessee before the evening's movie — the Fred MacMurray, Jean Arthur, Melvyn Douglas comedy, *Too Many Husbands.*

Miller's show started at 8:00. We can only guess what he and his band played. Miller was then famous for "Tuxedo Junction" and his recent hit, recorded just a few months earlier, "In the Mood." Miller hadn't yet recorded one song, a favorite in this region, "Chattanooga Choo-Choo." Since he was featuring his singers, he probably chose other material to highlight their vocals. An advertisement for the event hails "Glenn Miller's Orchestra with Marion Hutton and Ray Eberle in the 'Moonlight Serenade,'" so it's likely they performed that slow-dance favorite of 1939.

Part of the Chesterfield Cigarette show, it was broadcast nationally on CBS, with local station WNOX, which broadcast live-audience shows almost daily from their own Gay Street studio, doing the honors. An ad advised, "See and hear the King of the Airlanes broadcasting the Chesterfield Cigarette Program on the Columbia Network." As is the case with most live broadcasts of that era, no recordings are known to exist.

IN PERSON-On Our Stage

ONE PERFORMANCE ONLY—TONIGHT AT 8:00 P. M.

America's No. 1 dance band broadcasting the CHESTERFIELD cigarette program over the Columbia coast-to-coast network . . . PAUL DOUGLAS, CBS announcer, at the microphone.

GLENN MILLER

AND HIS ORCHESTRA

FEATURING

MARION HUTTON — RAY EBERLE

Program thru courtesy CHESTERFIELD CIGARETTES. Broadcast originating by STATION WNOX.

— NOTICE —

"REGULAR" passes will not be accepted tonight.

NIGHT tickets go on sale at 5:00 P. M.

The most hilarious of them all . . .

. . . another uproarious comedy from the studios that gave you "Mr. Deeds" . . . "The Awful Truth" . . . "You Can't Take It With You" and "His Girl Friday"!

Even If You Haven't Any...

TWO'S TOO MANY!

She's KNEE-DEEP IN HUSBANDS . . . and head-over heels IN LOVE!

How happy she could be with either . . . if only the other would go away! One returned from the grave . . . BUT PROVED HE WAS NO GHOST! The other returned from the office . . . TO DISCOVER HE WAS NO HUSBAND! The most devastating deluge of hilarity to reach Knoxville in many moons.

FRED MACMURRAY · JEAN ARTHUR

MELVYN DOUGLAS in

"Too Many Husbands"

— Other Selected Units —

DONALD DUCK CARTOON "SEA SCOUTS"

METRO NOVELTY—LATEST WAR NEWS

TODAY — FRIDAY — SATURDAY

KNOXVILLE JOURNAL · JUNE 6, 1940

"If you worked at the Tennessee Theatre or had any connection with it, you were proud to be a part of its family." Paul worked at the Tennessee from 1938 – 40.

PAUL E. OTTINGER

GLENN MILLER

PROMOTING CHESTERFIELD CIGARETTES · 1940

THE SECRET ROOM

In April 1938 a maintenance worker discovered a peculiarity about the Tennessee that demonstrated both what a complicated building it is and how little even its management knew the place. The theater was not yet 10 years old, but its builders had long since departed, the original organizations were defunct, one of the architects was dead, and management had turned over so often that no one had more than a couple of years' experience with it. L.H. Smiley, a respected theater technician who has become something of a backstage legend, discovered, underneath the seats, a large "secret room," 25 by 70 feet, with a 15-foot ceiling. Its floor was unfinished, but it appeared to have had a door—which, for reasons unknown, had been carefully sealed shut.

It made for a couple of fun newspaper articles—manager Eugene Street said they'd probably use the space for storage—and it was then forgotten again.

Among Miller's instrumentalists at the time were several well-known musicians, including saxophonist Tex Beneke, who would later succeed Miller as leader of the famous orchestra.

It was over at 8:15. His band had to hustle to pack up their instruments to make a 9:00 dance at UT, almost a mile away, where more than 2,000 fans were waiting. It was a short show, at 15 minutes, but in those days a long pop concert by a single band playing before a seated audience was unusual. Audiences were still accustomed to the fast pace of vaudeville, and jazz bands were for dancing to. It was assumed that if the same band held the stage for too long in an auditorium, the seated audience would get restless. If the live radio show had been the motive for it, that might have accounted for the brevity as well; most live-music radio shows in those days were just 15 minutes long.

Short as it was, the broadcast marked the Tennessee's highest-profile moment, in terms of national exposure.

In Knoxville, it was a heck of a night. Two blocks down the street from the Tennessee, at the Lyric, Cab Calloway and his orchestra were playing to a mixed-race crowd. Forty years later he would perform at the Tennessee.

Miller's career wasn't nearly as long. Four years after his Tennessee show, Miller, who had become leader of the Army Air Force Band, had been entertaining troops with his music when his small plane disappeared over the English Channel. He became something of a legend, subject of a popular movie, a decade later, starring Jimmy Stewart.

Interesting vaudeville-ish attractions kept showing up at the Tennessee, sometimes not on stage. In September, a Professor H.L. Watling appeared several nights in a row at the Tennessee, but in the lobby. He was the "Famous English Graphologist," an analyzer of handwriting who would offer character analyses to all comers.

The movie that night was *Charlie's Aunt*, starring Jack Benny in a cross-dressing role. ("He's the Gayest Gal of the Year!" the ad line went.) To promote it, the *Journal* ran a "Most Embarrassing Experience" contest.

That fall, the nation's sports pages were following the fortunes of the Tennessee Vols. College football had never been more popular than it was in 1940, and it happened to be then that the Vols were the talk of the nation. That fact likely has a lot to do with the appearance of one of the theater's most surprising performers. *Too Many Girls* was a Rodgers and Hart musical based on a recent Broadway hit and aimed at the college crowd. Among its cast were Lucille Ball, Ann Miller, Eddie Bracken, and Van Johnson in his first movie role.

One of movie's several ad lines went, "Youth and Pep on Joyous Wing—Soaring to Collegiate Swing!" The movie was of greater than average interest to Knoxvillians. In this movie about an upstart college football team from the Southwest, the team to beat, nationally, was the Tennessee Vols.

That October 21, the Vols had just beaten Alabama, and Knoxvillians got to see film from that game in Birmingham for the first time just before this new football movie. There was also a Disney cartoon, *Donald's Vacation*. A special treat was that onstage was also a live performer from the movie itself.

PRESIDENT ROOSEVELT ON GAY STREET · SEPTEMBER 2, 1940

On Sept. 2, 1940, President Franklin Roosevelt's motorcade paraded through downtown Knoxville on its way to official dedication ceremonies for the Great Smoky Mountains National Park. The president is in the back seat of the front car, waving with his hat. The Tennessee was playing the new Bing Crosby musical comedy "Rhythm on the River," the week of its national release. During summer, the Tennessee advertised its air conditioning—"Cooled by Refrigeration"—during an era when few Knoxvillians experienced air conditioning elsewhere.

DESI ARNAZ

KNOXVILLE JOURNAL · OCTOBER 21, 1940

Desi Arnaz may have been the first actor to appear on the Tennessee's stage to promote a movie. The Cuban singer and musician was billed as a rhumba dancer. Almost exactly 11 years before his debut as early television's most famous husband, when he was in Knoxville, Arnaz was just 23, and single. The city swooned. "Arnaz is a handsome Latin fellow," reported the *News-Sentinel*, "who does the rhumba in such a manner as to cause girls to write him notes beginning, 'You're wonderful. I love you.'"

On the Monday afternoon and evening the film opened, the dapper Arnaz made three personal appearances on the Tennessee's stage, proving himself to be a "marvelous dancer ... his manner is modest and pleasing." He had a little back-and-forth with local sports-radio personality Tys Terway and gave a "nice little talk" about making the movie. The movie's football scenes were "honest-to-God stuff," Arnaz said, adding that he had to train on the gridiron for the role. Earlier in the day he had shared a family-style lunch with the Tennessee Vols, including heroes of the hour Bob Suffridge and Johnny Butler, who had just beaten Alabama in Birmingham. He declared he hoped Tennessee would make it to the Rose Bowl and beat UCLA, eliciting an approving "howl" from the Tennessee's heavily collegiate audience.

Then "Senor Arnaz sang, very beautifully, a Cuban slave song accompanying himself on the guitar" and rhumbaed with Milagros Velez, a Puerto Rican pharmacist who worked at St. Mary's Hospital.

About five weeks after his appearance at the Tennessee, Arnaz surprised his family and friends by eloping with his better-known co-star in *Too Many Girls*, the somewhat older Lucille Ball.

Despite these memorable exceptions, the expectation of finding live entertainment at the Tennessee diminished after 1935, to a degree that by the 1940s it was all but gone — with the exception of Mr. Billy Barnes at the Mighty Wurlitzer. War seemed to put an end to what little remained of the era of vaudeville and big shows.

PREMIERES AND THE POSTWAR ERA

CHAPTER 5

That first week of December 1941, the Tennessee had just concluded a popular run — so popular it was to be held over at the Riviera — of a movie of special regional appeal, the Gary Cooper classic about combat in World War I, *Sergeant York*. Its last showing at the Tennessee was just hours before the Japanese bombed Pearl Harbor.

The next day opened what had been expected to be a major film, *Honky Tonk*, with "Rough, lusty Clark Gable!" and "Luscious Lana Turner, the most exciting siren of your screen desires!" Though it was advertised almost as big as *Gone With the Wind*, it may have been a disappointing run. The crowds were distracted.

Knoxville saw images of that bombing, via newsreels at the Tennessee. Later they watched footage of the battles of Guadalcanal, Midway, Anzio, and the invasion of Normandy. The Tennessee showed Paramount's own respected newsreels, of course, but also the popular "March of Time" newsreels, a companion to the radio-news show of the same name. "March of Time" had specialized in exposing fascism in Europe even before the war. Knoxville heard news on the radio, but newsreels shown in movie theaters were the city's only access to what the battles looked like. Some were also directed at the home front, showing civilians how to help with the war effort and how to deal with realities like "How to Use Your Point-Rationing Book."

During the war, the Tennessee, still the largest auditorium in Knoxville, was the most logical place for war savings-bond drives, and served that purpose repeatedly. Some offered nylon stockings — a real rarity during wartime rationing — as a premium for those who bought the most bonds. Meanwhile, the Tennessee presented a regular diet of war-related movies. From 1942 to 1945, most of Hollywood's products were related to the war in one way or another, and Knoxvillians — the ones who weren't overseas — watched them all with interest.

In November 1942, the Tennessee advertised *Someday I'll Find You*, "Clark Gable's LAST PICTURE for the duration." They didn't have to explain the duration of what. And indeed it was just that. Gable was by then training to be an officer in the U.S. Army Air Force, and saw deadly combat aboard a bomber. He didn't make another movie until the war was over.

War was a trying time for everyone, and the Tennessee's management — at least two individuals, in the war's early days — enlisted. To take their place, Wilby-Kincey was lucky

TENNESSEE
KNOXVILLE'S OWN MOVIE STAR PATSY NEAL "THE FOUNTAINHEAD"
WITH GARY COOPER FROM THE BEST SELLER BY AYN RAND - NEWS
ALWAYS THE BEST SHOW IN TOWN!
IT'S AN EMOTIONAL EXPLOSION!
GARY COOPER · "THE FOUNTAINHEAD" · PATRICIA NEAL
GARY COOPER · PATRICIA NEAL "THE FOUNTAINHEAD"
AIR CONDITIONED
FOR KNOXVILLE'S
GARY COOPER PATRICIA NEAL
NOW PLAYING

SUMMER · 1949

to find Malcolm Miller. Son of a London actress, Miller had spent his early youth in England but, taking his mother's advice, went into the most practical of trades in America, the lumber business. That's what brought him to Knoxville, but he couldn't stay away from the stage. By 1922 he was the *Knoxville Journal*'s urbane music and theater critic, and soon he was teaching drama at UT and working with the effort to found a Knoxville Symphony Orchestra. He sometimes played the role of promoter, booking Knoxville shows by Paderewski, Rachmaninoff, Anna Pavlova, Jascha Heifetz, and many others.

By the time of World War II, Miller, in his late 50s, was no target for the draft, and took over the management of the Tennessee Theatre for three years, giving up his *Knoxville Journal* column during that period. Miller only occasionally wrote about movies, but when there was an issue of concern about whether movies were "moral" or not — an acute concern in those days — he always rose to the defense of artistic freedom.

During its first 15 years, the Tennessee showed hundreds of new movies without ever entertaining the prospect of a major regional "premiere," much less a national one. The outstanding publicity success of *Gone With the Wind*'s world premiere in Atlanta in 1939 may have suggested the idea that middle America, beyond Los Angeles and New York, might deserve an occasional gala "premiere."

Knoxville's day came on February 17, 1943. As part of an unusual studio strategy, the Tennessee hosted the "southeastern premiere" of MGM's newest historical film, *Tennessee Johnson*, starring Van Heflin in his first movie role, as well as Lionel

WAR BOND DRIVE · JUNE 1945

Barrymore and Ruth Hussey. During the war years, Hollywood took a hard turn toward the patriotic, with movies aimed at building the nation's confidence in itself and its own history. The movie's publicity attempted to link its story to the war effort. In early 1943, when Hitler controlled almost all of Europe, it was not going especially well. *Tennessee Johnson* was "a courageous man's stormy career ... an inspiration to an America facing the ordeal of today."

It was a natural that America's first heroic movie about Andrew Johnson should get a special early showing at a theater that shared part of the movie's title — and that was located on the same street where Johnson had once given wartime speeches, and that hosted, by then, East Tennessee's tallest building, a 17-story hotel named for the 17th president. There was reportedly a practical reason too. In early 1943, a time of tight gasoline rationing, the studio tried to target places where patrons wouldn't necessarily have to drive much to see the show. At the time, Knoxville still represented a density of population, and the city was still served by an efficient electric-streetcar system.

"During the summer I would ride the Fox bus from Concord, go to a movie at the theatre and then take the streetcar to my grandmother's house on Morgan Street. I remember the cool feeling of entering the grand lobby with its wonderful marble floors and brass handrails."

LIBBIE MCBEE HAYNES

"I would go early and pop the popcorn downstairs, bag it, and carry it up to the large booth in the middle of that grand lobby. Some evenings I would be completely surrounded by people — that huge lobby was filled to capacity!"

ANNA LEE COX
CONCESSION CLERK, 1943–44

Herb recalls one of his first dates at the Tennessee with his wife, Ruth, when during intermission, the organist passed a portable keyboard into the audience: "I was able to get it and proceeded to play an old ditty with only two fingers. In my haste to 'show off,' I had completely forgotten that my date was an accomplished classical pianist. She thought I was getting the keyboard for her… Even after all these years when my tendency to get attention manifests itself, Ruth will say, 'Remember the Tennessee.'"

HERB MAYS

KNOXVILLE JOURNAL · FEBRUARY 17, 1943

It was an unusual rollout for a movie. *Tennessee Johnson* had premiered at New York's Astor weeks earlier, but had been shown nowhere else until it opened at the Tennessee and in three other cities, Houston, Philadelphia, and Lincoln's hometown of Springfield, Illinois. A benefit for the Red Cross, an appropriate cause in wartime, Knoxville's "Southern Premiere" apparently didn't include any actors. It did draw some guests the other venues didn't, however, including the title character's granddaughter, Martha Johnson Patterson, and her own daughter Margaret.

At the theater, teacher and former state senator E.E. Patton gave a talk on the subject of President Johnson. It was perhaps persuasive; the following year, Patton was elected mayor.

The Andrew Johnson Hotel, Knoxville's finest hostelry, hosted a banquet beforehand and an Andrew Johnson Ball afterward, at 10 p.m. Johnson was never so thoroughly appreciated in Knoxville in his own lifetime.

Remarkably, the Tennessee's first "premiere" was the same evening as one of the most memorable live performances in Knoxville history. Sergei Rachmaninoff performed a concert a few blocks away, at UT's Alumni Hall. The Russian composer and pianist did not realize he was dying of advanced cancer; after he played here, he canceled the rest of his American tour and died weeks later, rendering the Knoxville concert his last. Rachmaninoff stayed in the Andrew Johnson that evening. When he returned exhausted after his final encore to encounter an Andrew Johnson Ball at the hotel, he must have wondered what the fuss was about.

It was just a few weeks later that the Tennessee debuted a classic movie with which future generations would closely associate the theater. Perhaps no other movie has been shown to more people in the Tennessee's post-1977 revival than *Casablanca*. The movie's sets seem to mirror the Tennessee's exotically Moorish interior. The movie had already been showing in the big cities for a few weeks when it opened for a four-day, 24-showing run at the Tennessee on Friday, March 12, 1943. *Casablanca* was not heralded as a timeless classic — the *Knoxville Journal* mentioned it as one of two "war pictures" the theater was showing that week, the other being the now-forgotten *Hitler's Children*, a heavy-handed anti-Nazi film.

KNOXVILLE'S LAST STREET CAR RUN · AUGUST 1, 1947

AUTOMOBILES ENCOURAGE SUBURBAN LIVING · 1952

POSTCARD · 1945

PIKE THEATRE, ON KINGSTON PIKE IN BEARDEN

PIKE THEATRE, INTERIOR

Still, *Casablanca* had a better-than-average rollout: four days. "As exciting as the landing itself," hailed the typically hyperbolic advertisement, referring to the successful Allied landing at Casablanca four months before. "They had a date with fate — in a city that rocked the world!"

It was shown with a Disney cartoon, *Donald Gets Drafted*. *Casablanca* apparently did well enough at the Tennessee, because it walked half a block over to the Riviera, where it was "Held Over" for two nights. "Here's the picture that has all Knoxville talking!" they declared.

One of the Tennessee's last bond drives made national trade news. In early June 1945, when the war in Europe was over but the war with Japan remained a question, *Motion Picture Daily* ran a photograph of hundreds of people crowding Gay Street outside the Tennessee Theatre, standing in the street and heedless of traffic, ostensibly to see a Carmen Miranda movie, *Something for the Boys*. The caption describes the impressive congregation as an "effective ... pep-up drive" aimed at retailers and their employees, for the seventh of eight national drives to sell war-related bonds.

Many Knoxvillians learned about the bomb that ended the war with Japan — and about what had really been going on over at Oak Ridge — via theater newsreels.

Postwar Knoxville was a different place in lots of ways, some of which didn't bode well for downtown theaters. In 1947, Knoxville's electric-streetcar system ended its 56-year run.

TOWER THEATRE, N. BROADWAY

With a new middle-class affluence and better roads every week, the city was getting more and more accustomed to automobiles, and to the strange new idea that stores, and restaurants, and even movie theaters might pop up and thrive almost anywhere. Small cinemas had been sprouting in the suburbs for several years. In 1946, the Pike, a theater with almost 900 seats, opened in Bearden. There were plans to build an even bigger new theater, bigger even than the Riviera, but not on Gay Street. The Tower Theatre emerged on North Broadway, a few miles from downtown. It was Knoxville's second-biggest theater, and most patrons got there by driving cars. It seemed incredible.

For the first time, Knoxvillians began looking for, and eventually expecting, free parking.

Knoxville had grown to be a city of more than 100,000. By the time the war was over, and thousands of young veterans were

"WE DANCED OUT IN THE FRONT LOBBY LOOKING IN ALL THE BIG MIRRORS AND UP AT THE BEAUTIFUL CHANDELIERS PRETENDING WE WERE BETTY GRABLE, JUNE HAVER, OR WHOEVER WE HAD SEEN IN THE MOVIE THAT DAY."

MARGARET F. BACON

flooding back into town, Wilby-Kincey was floating the idea that maybe it was time for another big theater on Gay Street. Their proposal, apparently uncontroversial at the time, was to tear down the 70-year-old Lyric Theater and replace it with a big modern million-dollar cinema with a capacity comparable to the Tennessee, perhaps 1,900 seats. It was to be called the Knox. Months of silence followed that first announcement.

It came up again in 1947, with Wilby-Kincey still talking about it as if it was a sure thing, but this time with downward-revised seating projections: about 1,200, closer in size to the Riviera. More months of silence followed, as perhaps theater developers were reconsidering whether the postwar version of downtown was an ideal investment.

The new Gay Street theater never happened. In fact, no new theater would be built downtown until another century.

Meanwhile, Knoxville and the state reconsidered a peculiar old custom. Blue laws, enforced statewide, had mandated that movies never be shown on Sundays. (The Tennessee had bent the law a little in May 1937, when it showed the Lily Pons musical romantic comedy *That Girl From Paris* on a Sunday. It earned a pass because it was a benefit for the Salvation Army.)

By the '40s, Knoxville was decidedly over state enforcement of the Ten Commandments, with their proscription of working on the Sabbath, but Governor Prentice Cooper pocket vetoed a 1943 effort to change the law.

In February 1947, repeal finally passed. A couple of small theaters held out for their right to remain closed on Sunday; one operator protested it was the only day he could go fishing. But the

"The year was 1946 and I was sitting in the balcony. This handsome young man who had just returned home from World War II sat down beside me and offered me a piece of Juicy Fruit Gum. We dated for eight months and saw a number of movies from the balcony. We were married in 1947, and he always joked that he got me at the Tennessee Theatre with a piece of Juicy Fruit gum."

JUNE NORMAN

"I never had much money, but sometimes I would get a snack, which was always a roll of Necco wafers. It was the largest candy and lasted the longest for only a nickel."

VIVIAN R. SLAUGHTER

A FASHION SHOW ON THE TENNESSEE STAGE · 1948

Tennessee Theatre celebrated the legislative change immediately, with a showing, on Sunday, February 16, 1947, of Errol Flynn's romantic comedy *Never Say Goodbye*.

Some damage was already done. In John Gunther's infamous assessment of Knoxville as "the ugliest city in America," in *Inside U.S.A.*, published that year, he mentioned the fact that the "extremely puritanical town" forbade Sunday movies — without mentioning that the city had been at the mercy of state law in that regard. By the time the book was a bestseller, the ban was no longer in effect.

In September 1948, the Tennessee showed *Tap Roots*, another historical drama starring Van Heflin — along with Susan Hayward, Boris Karloff, and Julie London. The theater took out much more advertising space than the typical new movie merited. *Tap Roots* was touted as another *Gone With the Wind*, and was of special local interest because it was "the first Technicolor-sound movie ever made in the Smokies." The fact that its shooting location, some of it near Gatlinburg, didn't necessarily match its setting — flat Mississippi — was an incongruity that didn't escape its critics. Whether it was a success at the Tennessee or not, it was a flop nationwide. It's almost forgotten today.

An era ended that year when beloved organist Billy Barnes departed for New York. He'd gotten an offer as a regular organist at Sheraton Hotels around the country. For the next 30 years, the once-famous organ got a workout when someone volunteered to play it. After Barnes, more than a dozen organists were generous with their time and talent. But the Mighty Wurlitzer was no longer an expected part of a night at the Tennessee Theatre.

By then, a night at the movies was just a night at the movies.

The fondest memories of the Tennessee belong to members of middle-class and affluent families, those who could attend regularly. Novelist David Madden, who grew up in a working-class household, had a different perspective. In 1946, when he worked as an usher at the Bijou, that older theater had become mainly a movie theater, with occasional dramatic productions. Madden's 1974 novel *Bijou*, which earned national attention, is centered on its title character, but the Tennessee appears, barely disguised, as the "Tivoli." Madden describes the culture among postwar Knoxville ushers, who were cliquish and loyal to the different personalities of the theaters that employed them, and at the time there was an extreme range of theater personalities in downtown Knoxville, from tiny, unkempt theaters on Market Square that showed third-run Westerns to the Roxy, which featured burlesque shows, to the Lyric, which by that time often offered wrestling and boxing. Ushers at the "Tivoli," Madden recalled, were snobbish and disdainful of the other usher fraternities.

Madden described the Tivoli/Tennessee from the point of view of his insecure working-class alter-ego, Lucius: "The marble floor of the main lobby sloped long as a football field as the sour-faced woman who took tickets, facing the bright sun and the street that flashed at her from streetcar windows passing. A miniature Taj Mahal, gold domed, wide, swooping marble stairs, oriental and Renaissance tapestries and suits of armor. But the Tivoli was too enormous, cold, forbidding. Among marble statues of goddesses, velvet drapes, and crystal chandeliers, he felt inferior."

Cormac McCarthy referenced the Tennessee, circa 1951, in his novel *Suttree*, but more subtly. His hard-bitten characters were not the sort who'd buy tickets to see Gene Kelly movies in a fancy air-conditioned theater, and McCarthy does not mention the Tennessee by name. But his characters spend a lot of time in Comer's walk-up pool hall, across the street from the Tennessee. Of his title character, the novelist writes, "He'd sit on the front bench at Comer's and watch through the window the commerce in the street below, the couples moving toward the box office of the theatre in the rainy evening, the lights of the marquee slurred and burning in the wet street."

Suburbanization, and the times, had their effects on downtown. The old Strand, on Gay at Wall, two blocks north of the Tennessee, closed in 1949 and was converted into a women's clothing store. Several small cinemas had closed, but the Strand was big and old enough — dating back to before World War I — that people noticed.

By 1950 there were a dozen newer, more modern cinemas than the Tennessee, most of them located in Knoxville's blooming new suburbs. They were convenient and offered free parking. But they were plain little things, not the sort of places you'd get dressed up to visit, not the sort of places you'd take visitors just to show them. None of them even tried to approach the Tennessee's scale and style.

The Tennessee, Riviera, and Bijou tried to keep up with the free-parking idea, a little awkwardly, offering a validated-ticket deal with the old Pryor Brown Parking Garage around the corner: three hours for 15 cents, with proof of purchase of a movie ticket.

Perhaps unexpectedly, the postwar years saw a glamorous second act for the already old theater. If not world premieres, the Tennessee was drawing occasional celebrity events.

ROXY THEATRE, UNION AVENUE

According to handed-down personal memories, postwar noir queen Lizabeth Scott (coincidentally, she's said to have derived her stage name from the successful *Mary of Scotland* and its leading character Elizabeth) appeared at the Tennessee, likely to promote a movie.

THE STRAND THEATRE INTERIOR, GAY STREET

JOHN PAYNE

DONALD O'CONNOR

In February 1950, John Payne, darkly handsome star of *Miracle on 34th Street* and several war movies, came to promote his new movie, *Captain China*. He appeared onstage at the Tennessee, alongside "guitar ace" Arnold Adler. (One written memory remembers Payne singing "Time on My Hands," which was a hit in the early '30s, when Payne was known mainly as a singer. He may have appeared on this stage back then.)

Four months later Donald O'Connor, the singer and dancer best known for his new comedy, *Francis*, about a talking mule, came to town to promote his newer comedy, *Curtain Call at Cactus Creek*. O'Connor's most famous role, in *Singin' in the Rain*, was still two years off.

To be sure the promotional trip got attention, the studio sent with him three other fledgling stars who weren't even in the movie: future Western hero John Russell, Lois Andrews (only 26, but already legendary comic George Jessel's ex-wife), and Peggie Castle, the sultry blonde who, perhaps coincidentally, had just played a bit role as a Knoxville waitress in the recently released noir film *Woman in Hiding*.

It represented a shift in America's response to show business. For a century, actors were expected to act, singers were expected to sing. After World War II, it was clear that patrons would turn out by the thousands just to catch a glimpse of a famous actor, maybe even hear them say a few words.

On July 29, 1953, when it was almost a quarter-century old, the Tennessee Theatre hosted the most glamorous, high-profile event of its career.

NEWSPAPER AD · FEBRUARY 2, 1950

GRACE MOORE

Grace Moore was East Tennessee's diva. She'd spent parts of her early childhood in rural Cocke County and on the industrial fringe of downtown Knoxville, but considered Jellico her hometown. Astonishingly beautiful, with a voice to match, the blonde soprano was first an opera diva, then one of Hollywood's first musical stars, the first actress ever nominated for an Academy Award for a musical role, for the 1934 movie *One Night of Love*. In 1947 she'd been traveling in Europe with a few others, including Prince Gustaf Adolph of Sweden, when their plane crashed. Her romantic life and sudden death seemed to demand a biopic. In 1953, Warner Brothers obliged with a light musical version of the story, *So This Is Love*, starring musical star of the moment Kathryn Grayson, the North Carolina-born singer and actress then at the height of her *Show Boat* stardom. Twice divorced at 31, she was reportedly dating reclusive aviator Howard Hughes at the time. Also in a leading role was a young, then little-known singer, musician and actor named Merv Griffin.

For a time, Knoxville, Jellico, and Chattanooga — home of some of Moore's surviving family — were all vying for the enviable distinction of hosting the movie's world premiere. Aubrey Couch, Knoxville manager for the Wilby-Kincey Theater chain, may have hit on just the right idea with a promise that funds raised would go to the Grace Moore Scholarship at UT. Ralph Frost, then manager of UT's University Concerts program, was instrumental in putting it together as a fundraiser for the Grace Moore Scholarship Fund, honoring the woman Frost declared to be "Tennessee's greatest contribution to the musical world."

Couch promised Warner Brothers "the second-biggest premiere in the nation's film history if the show comes to Knoxville." Wilby-Kincey eventually went farther, to declare the Knoxville premiere would be bigger than any in American history — including that of *Gone With the Wind*, 14 years earlier, still the world standard for world premieres.

Knoxville's first big "world premiere," if it can properly be called that — the movie had been released two weeks earlier, but hadn't yet been reviewed in *The New York Times* — was the biggest film gala ever held in Knoxville. Four recognizable film stars were in

KATHRYN GRAYSON

UNIVERSITY CONCERTS
INCORPORATED
UNIVERSITY OF TENNESSEE • KNOXVILLE

July 3, 1953

To University Concert Subscribers:

A very outstanding event in which I am sure you will be interested is taking place in Knoxville on the 29th of this Month. It is the World Premiere of "So This Is Love", depicting the life of Grace Moore - Tennessee's greatest contribution to the musical world. It is expected that many prominent Tennesseeans including the Governor and our Congressional representatives along with the Stars from Hollywood and members of Miss Moore's family will be present. The press and Radio will keep you informed as to who these personalities are.

Through the generosity of Warner Brothers Pictures and the Tennessee Theatre, all of the proceeds from the premiere will go to the Grace Moore Scholarship Fund here in the University. Tickets are not being sold, but invitations are being issued following contributions to the Scholarship fund. There will be three sections in the Theatre and invitations will be issued to these sections according to the amount contributed. You may contribute anything from a minimum of $2.50 up. These three sections are set aside on the basis of contributions of $2.50, $5.00 and $10.00. Larger contributions will gladly be received and are deductible from your income tax.

We understand this is Knoxville's first World Premiere, and we think it very appropriate that the life of Grace Moore be premiered in Knoxville. Make your checks payable to "The Grace Moore Scholarship Fund", box 8280 University of Tennessee, Knoxville, Tennessee and we will forward you an invitation. If more convenient you may come by the University Concerts office and make the transaction. I trust that you will be able to be present for this gala affair and help us honor the memory of this great singer.

Sincerely yours,

Ralph W. Frost
Ralph W. Frost
Manager

LETTER ANNOUNCING "SO THIS IS LOVE" WORLD PREMIERE

"On Oct. 5, 1951, in the beautiful lounge of the Tennessee, Jim proposed to me and gave me a lovely engagement ring." James and Hazel celebrated their 50th wedding anniversary on Dec. 28, 2001.

HAZEL WALKER

attendance, and for them it wasn't just a whistle stop, but a three-day pageant of formal dinners and country-club balls, an auction fundraiser, and dedications. Knoxville named its first highway cloverleaf for Grace Moore. UT commemorated her by giving her name to a set of steps to its Alumni Memorial Auditorium, where she'd once performed. Grayson, Griffin, and company had to be on hand for all that, shuttled from dedication to dedication.

The Tennessee Theatre show was the climax of it all.

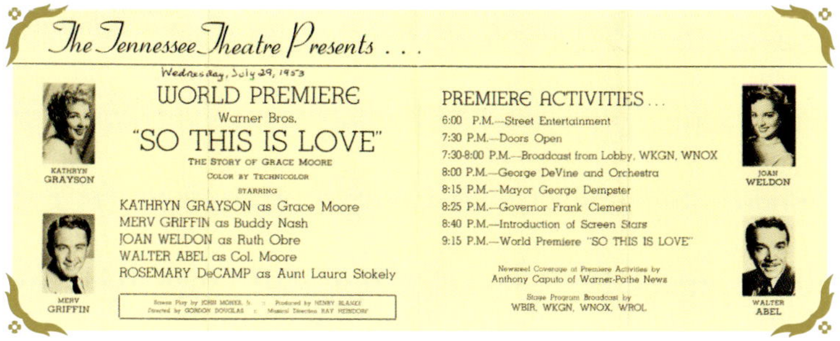

"SO THIS IS LOVE" PROGRAM

The big night might have seemed ill-starred in a couple of respects. Grayson came down with a bad virus, and there was a question about whether she could sing. The 28-year-old Griffin complained about the sweltering heat; he'd been put up in the hotel right across Clinch, the Farragut, which was not air-conditioned. And the huge crowds that gathered in the rain, blocking Gay Street in hopes of catching a glimpse of a star, were bitterly disappointed; citing time considerations, the celebrities had all been spirited in through a back entrance.

But for the 2,000-plus lucky enough to get in — the Tennessee was literally standing-room only — it was perhaps the most memorable night of the decade. Four stars attended, including Grayson, Griffin, familiar supporting actor Walter Abel (*Holiday Inn*, *Fury*), and 22-year-old Joan Weldon, who the following year would reach the height of her career as the female lead in the giant-ant epic, *Them!*

Those who arrived early were entertained by an organ recital by Pearl Francis, Jellico's favorite church organist, and a short concert by George Devine and his orchestra (culled from the KSO, especially for the occasion), followed by talks by Mayor George Dempster — by then famous as the inventor of the

CAPTAIN CHINA · 1950

HONKY TONK · 1941

TAP ROOTS · 1948

THE ROBE · 1953

CASABLANCA · 1942

I MARRIED A WITCH · 1942

THE FOUNTAINHEAD · 1949

NEVER SAY GOODBYE · 1946

Dumpster — and Tennessee governor Frank Clement. In the crowd were three men named Moore, brothers of the honoree.

Walter Abel was no singer, so the 55-year-old actor with the graying pencil-thin mustache served as a suave master of ceremonies. Accompanied by the orchestra, Weldon sang three tunes and awed the audience with a voice they hadn't heard about. To the surprise of the crowd, the young Merv Griffin proved himself a showman, playing piano, singing, and charming the crowd with his own rendition of "Tennessee Waltz," the song Patti Page had made a hit not three years earlier.

Despite her illness, Grayson sang "Sempre Libera," the famous aria from Verdi's *La Traviata*. When the enthusiastic crowd demanded an encore, she wept as she replied, "I won't sing anymore. You'll hear my songs in the movie. Just let me thank you for your kindness, and introduce you to the stars of tomorrow," whereupon she invited UT's first four Grace Moore scholars to the stage.

The movie itself was a fanciful retelling of the Grace Moore story whose positive reviews were mostly based on the music, which surprised a few critics by including some jazz. Ironically, the room was so full the four Grace Moore scholars, ostensibly the honored guests and the reason for the fundraiser, were not provided with seats and had to stand for the movie. Before it was over, one of them reportedly fainted, either from the excitement or the exhaustion of standing.

Word had gotten around about the disappointment in the streets, which had by then thinned out a little. Grayson, Griffin, Abel, and Weldon exited by the main front lobby at 11:15, pausing

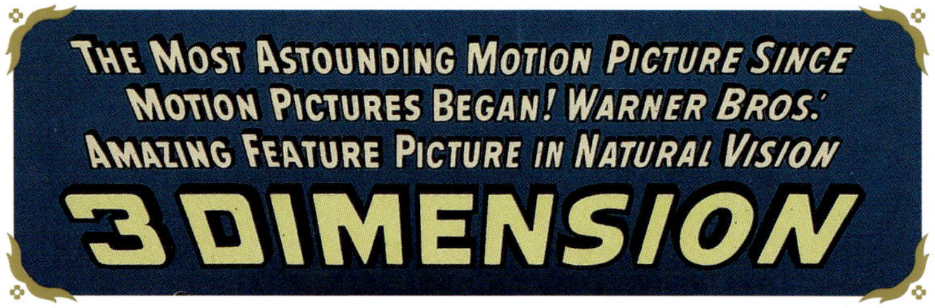

for publicity pictures of themselves walking into the theater, as if excitedly arriving. That's show business. Illusions were their specialty.

Of course, one of the stars attending Knoxville's first world premiere would play a major role in the development of television over the next 40 years. Through his numerous creations, especially game shows, Merv Griffin became one of the most powerful executives in television history. Knoxville didn't have television yet — but thanks to some engineers working long hours at a radio station on that same block just a couple of doors away from the Tennessee, that would soon change.

Television had been sweeping America since the end of the war, but efforts had stalled in Knoxville and several other mid-sized cities due to an FCC-mandated embargo aimed at letting technology and regulation catch up with the demand.

"The really good thing about being an usher at the Tennessee was that the girls seemed to be impressed."

PETE PIATT
USHER IN THE 1950S

Rhonda remembers as a child in the Tennessee Theatre in the 1950s, she would always look at the paintings in the lobbies and especially at the ceiling. "I believed I was in the Sistine Chapel or something like that. I thought the theatre was so grand and beautiful."

RHONDA BARLOW

"The Tennessee Theatre is the reason I'm here: it's where my parents met. I'm truly a child of the cinema." Bobbie recalls that while her father, Bill Davis, managed the Tennessee, he became "enamored" with a young woman who would attend the movies and would send her free passes.

BOBBIE DALTON
DAUGHTER OF THEATRE MANAGER IN 1950S

GUS KELLY, THE TENNESSEE'S FIRST STAGE MANAGER · 1958

AT THE STAGE LIGHTING SWITCHBOARD

Recognizing television's challenge for America's leisure hours, Hollywood hastened to give Americans experiences they couldn't get at home. One offensive was 3-D technology, which hit the Tennessee with a 1953 showing of *House of Wax*, Hollywood's first color 3-D feature. The movie starred Vincent Price as the villain and a few other familiar faces, and one that was not yet familiar in 1953, Charles Bronson, as Igor. Patrons peered at them through "Natural Vision" glasses issued at the door.

For decades, Americans had watched movies on a standard squarish screen. In October 1953, the Tennessee installed the latest in cinema technology, a CinemaScope system, including a wide screen for showing the latest sweeping color epics. CinemaScope offered the ability to film wide-screen movies on film of conventional width, converted to wide screen format by a special lens. Notably, it was a much broader image than could be presented on any television (a fact that would make broadcasting the same movies an awkward problem in years to come).

The broad stage gave the old movie palace an advantage over some theaters that had to adapt their proscenia to the wide-screen format. The Tennessee was a quarter-century old, but that fall it was the most modern theater in town.

The Tennessee's showing of Hollywood's first CinemaScope sensation, a religious epic starring Richard Burton and Victor Mature called *The Robe*, was modern in another respect, at least on one particular day. Knoxville's school system brought black school children to the Tennessee for a special occasion. This showing to students of both races was rare in the South, the year before the U.S. Supreme Court ruled that racial segregation was unconstitutional.

On November 1, 1953, one month after the Tennessee turned 25 years old, a dramatic event just a couple of doors down the sidewalk seemed ominous for the future of the Tennessee and all movie theaters. On the fifth floor of the old Mechanics Bank and Trust building, engineers successfully launched, into the air, East Tennessee's first-ever television broadcast. That first night, WROL-TV — it would later be known as WATE — showed a couple of old movies, including *I Married a Witch*, that had once drawn paying crowds at the Tennessee. People could now watch movies free at home.

Overnight, television changed the way East Tennesseans lived. For a generation, movies had become a weekly or even daily routine, a way to keep up with the news, hear the latest music, cheer sports. Within a few years, people had all that at home, on television.

The Tennessee played a small role in rock 'n' roll history, at least as a setting. In 1954, Phil and Don Everly were trying to make it as a duo. As part of a family act with their parents, they'd sung mostly country and gospel harmonies. By most accounts it was the brothers' interest in rock 'n' roll that caused their rift with Cas Walker, who'd sponsored their show on WROL. After an argument, the Everlys walked out of Walker's studio.

Don later recalled walking a couple doors down the sidewalk to the Tennessee, consoling himself with a new movie about young people falling in love in Rome: *Three Coins in the Fountain*.

Maybe the suggestion of travel helped. They moved to Nashville to reconnect with another former Knoxvillian, Chet Atkins, who was considerably more impressed with their work than Walker

THE EVERLY BROTHERS

was. The Everly Brothers would become one of the great, defining early voices of rock 'n' roll, and a major influence on future groups like the Beatles. Many years later they'd perform for large, appreciative houses at the Tennessee.

The Tennessee rarely made room for live performers in the '50s, but made an exception for Vaughn Monroe and his orchestra. By 1955 they were known mostly for smooth '40s memories but occasionally still hit the charts with a new song like "Ghost Riders in the Sky." According to one fan, they performed "Racing With the Moon."

Most performances, though, were at the Wurlitzer. Breck Camp was just 19 when he became a volunteer organist. He was one of the first to remark on the instrument's rarity, claiming even in 1957 that there was only one other in Tennessee, in Nashville. (Camp later became a manager at the Tennessee, and, much later, a member of its foundation's board.)

The Everly Brothers, shown here during the height of their rock 'n' roll idol fame — Phil is at left, Don at right — were West High School kids when they visited the Tennessee in 1954, seeking solace watching the European travel romance "Three Coins in a Fountain" after losing their radio show on local WROL due to creative differences with sponsor-host Cas Walker. It was a dramatic day that left the Everlys more determined than ever to succeed, and the brothers would tell the story onstage the first time they performed at the Tennessee — almost 40 years later.

Many Knoxvillians had televisions by 1956, but national programming offered only glimpses of the new rock 'n' roll stars. Elvis Presley's first movie, "Love Me Tender," appeared at the old Tennessee in November, the month of its national release, but a few weeks after its title song became a radio hit. It was technically a Civil War melodrama, but its draw was the 21-year-old rock 'n' roll phenomenon from Memphis, who performed a few light rock tunes in the film and even demonstrated some of his distinctive dance style banned on national television. The cartoon that week was a 10-year-old Disney cartoon, "The Purloined Pup," starring Pluto.

NOVEMBER 1956

Suburbanization and television took their toll. Staub's Opera House, more recently known as the Lyric, was torn down in 1956. Then the 42-year-old Crystal Theater, a storefront third-run cinema on Market Square, closed. Two years later, the Roxy, on Union, closed too. Built two years after the Tennessee, the Roxy claimed to be the South's last vaudeville theater—though their live show generally consisted of the same performers every week, scantily clad dancing girls and a bizarre clown. In the six years after local television arrived in Knoxville, eight local movie theaters closed.

Downtown, only the Tennessee, the Riviera, and the Bijou were left, and the old Bijou was not doing well. Somehow the Tennessee and the Riviera maintained their dignified rivalry, half a block away from each other. But the Tennessee took down its towering 1920s vertical sign, and replaced the old marquee with a more conventional one.

TRANSITION AT THE TENNESSEE

CHAPTER 6

For over 30 years the Tennessee had been not only the grandest but the largest auditorium in Knoxville. That changed, suddenly, with a new decade that would be dramatic in other ways.

After decades of discussing the prospect, the city completed, in 1961, a Civic Coliseum and Auditorium on the edge of downtown. Built almost suburban-style, with a lawn and dedicated parking, it allowed visitors to attend shows without having much to do with the rest of downtown. The Coliseum was a multipurpose arena, bigger than any covered venue ever built downtown. Even the smaller Civic Auditorium was about 20 percent bigger than the Tennessee, and much more modern, in ways respected in 1961. Maybe it didn't pose any direct challenge to the Tennessee, in spite of the fact that both theaters occasionally showed Sunday afternoon travelogues. Live performances had almost vanished from the Tennessee's schedule anyway. But the new municipal auditorium across the way seemed to suggest that that time was utterly over. If a modern equivalent of Fanny Brice or Glenn Miller came to Knoxville in the brave new 1960s, they'd perform over there at the Civic, or perhaps at UT's Stokely Athletics Center, but almost certainly not in this old 1920s movie palace.

Any narrative history of the Tennessee Theatre has to acknowledge an unbecoming reality: that for its first 35 years, the Tennessee was with very few exceptions a whites-only theater — as were, to be fair, almost all theaters in the South, and whether by law or habit or local demographics, most theaters in the nation. Except for extremely unusual exceptions like *The Robe*, which permitted some black schoolchildren to attend, the only black people who ever got to see the Tennessee's famous interior were those who worked there.

Poet Nikki Giovanni spent much of her childhood on Mulvaney Street, a short walk from the Tennessee. Giovanni tells a story about her family in the 1940s, when her older sister, Gary Ann, was just learning to read. "One day we were walking down Gay Street, when it was really *Gay Street*, and my sister stopped to read the poster for *Snow White and the Seven Dwarfs*," a favorite that made the rounds for a few years after its 1938 release. "She asked my father if we could go in. My father didn't know whether to say we can't go in there because we don't have enough money, or we can't go in there because we're black."

PRESTON SPAULDING AT THE MIGHTY WURLITZER · EARLY 1970S

KNOXVILLE COLLEGE STUDENTS PROTESTING SEGREGATION · 1963

STUDENT PROTESTOR · 1963

NIKKI GIOVANNI

AT THE TENNESSEE
MARCH 2007

Giovanni leaves the story there. According to Giovanni's friend and biographer, Virginia Fowler, however, Jones Giovanni tried to get his family into the theater, but was refused. For him, a college graduate unable to find any but menial work here, it was Knoxville's last straw. He determined to move his family north, to Cincinnati.

Despite Knoxville's segregation, young Nikki often preferred to stay here, at her grandmother's house on Mulvaney, attending the all-black Gem Theatre on Vine Street.

In 1963 the Tennessee was the focus of a demonstration, organized partly through students at historically black Knoxville College.

All of Knoxville's theaters were segregated. The Tennessee wasn't worse in that regard than any other downtown or suburban cinema, but it was the most famous of them all, and the logical focus of multiple demonstrations. Several of downtown's lunch counters had already desegregated as the white theaters, represented by the Tennessee and the Riviera, still banned black patrons. A demonstration in October 1961, during a showing of the British war comedy *Invasion Quartet*, led to a few arrests.

A much larger demonstration, largely fueled by Knoxville College students, came in March 1963. (They didn't wait for a movie of any symbolic gravity; it was a Connie Francis musical comedy, *Follow the Boys*.) Among those who demonstrated were Bob Booker and Avon Rollins, both of whom would remain leaders in Knoxville's black community for many years to come — Booker would serve a term as a state legislator, and both men would become directors of the Beck Cultural Exchange Center. Another of the demonstrators in front of the Tennessee was controversial future Washington, D.C., mayor Marion Barry, who was then enrolled in a doctoral program at UT.

RIVIERA ON RE-OPENING NIGHT · JANUARY 1964

POSTCARD · 1961

Nonviolent demonstrations persisted through the spring, when a film arguably more relevant showed — *To Kill a Mockingbird* — and management finally relented.

Nikki Giovanni was by then a student at historically black Fisk University in Nashville, on her way to national prominence as a black activist. She never saw the inside of the Tennessee Theatre until the 1980s, some 40 years after her family was refused admittance, when she was invited by Governor Lamar Alexander to attend a Tennessee Homecoming event. In later years, she has returned as the featured speaker.

Weeks after desegregating, the Riviera caught fire. It was the biggest theater fire in Knoxville history, and though no one was hurt, it was such a big fire that at first the Riviera appeared to be done for. But it reopened months later as a smaller, plainer, more modern theater. Once Knoxville's biggest theater, the post-fire Riviera had just 800 seats, making it less than half the size of the Tennessee.

"ALL THE WAY HOME" REGISTERS SMASH OPENING IN KNOXVILLE WORLD PREMIERE!

Filmed and set in Knoxville, Paramount's "All The Way Home" was the main topic of conversation weeks before its opening. The premiere of this poignant David Susskind production shoved other news off the front pages of the Knoxville News-Sentinal and the Knoxville Journal.

In a front page story accompanied by three photographs, the News-Sentinal's Dwayne Summar wrote that "Knoxville has never been more glamorous. There were movie stars, film officials, wads of out-of-town press, exciting parties, a motorcade with brassy bands, bright lights and thousands of movie fans. Together they made a perfect premiere."

In an unprecedented move, the News-Sentinal also ran its review of "All The Way Home" on the front page, noting **"it is a beautiful, sensitive story and has been artistically told. Knoxville, be proud you had a part in 'All The Way Home.'"**

2

A TRADE JOURNAL PROMOTION

Theatergoers might have assumed there'd never be an event to compare to *So This Is Love*. But 10 years later, *All the Way Home* at least came close, and it may have been the boost that the officially desegregated Tennessee needed after the unwelcome spotlight of the spring.

It was a smaller movie, a black-and-white film in a color era, and not a movie that received as much national hype. And it was less of a "world premiere," in the literal sense, than the previous event had offered. *All the Way Home* had been reviewed in the New York press weeks earlier.

But the opening night gala brought a major star, Robert Preston, at the height of his fame in *The Music Man*. The new movie, based on screenwriter James Agee's Pulitzer-winning autobiographical

ROBERT PRESTON AT "ALL THE WAY HOME" WORLD PREMIERE

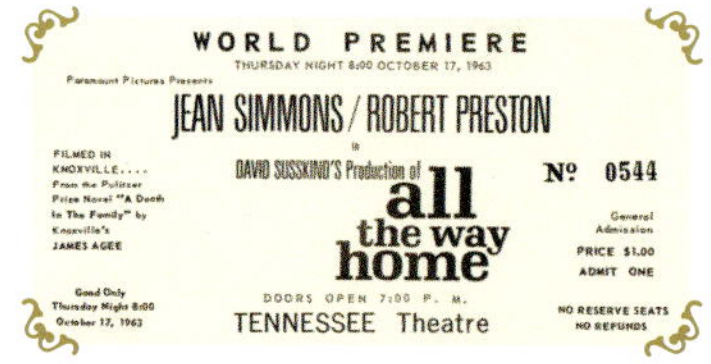

OPENING NIGHT SOUVENIR TICKET

Peggy remembers being in the huge crowd in front of the Tennessee in 1963 for the "All The Way Home" world premiere. "I remember seeing Robert Preston for just a moment. He turned all the way around to wave at the crowd."

PEGGY F. RAILEY

OPENING NIGHT SOUVENIR PROGRAM

novel, *A Death in the Family*, was already especially well known here because it had been shot in Knoxville, a few months before, mainly in the Fort Sanders neighborhood.

Appearing at the Tennessee for the gala premiere on October 17, 1963, were Preston himself, who arrived at the theater with his longtime wife, Catherine—a familiar Hollywood actress herself—in a small fleet of 1915 flivvers, along with 8-year-old Michael Kearney, who before this movie had appeared in only a few episodes of the soap opera *The Secret Storm*. David Susskind, well-known television personality, produced the film and spoke at its premiere showing. Young Kearney was introduced on the stage but was so overcome that he wept at the microphone.

Just months after the civil rights actions out front, the audience couldn't have missed dialogue that included some subtle civil rights messages: the father, played by Preston, gently admonishes his son not to use a certain word in referring to people of another race.

Movies were changing, and culture was changing. The Tennessee never seemed more old-fashioned than it did in the '60s, when all new theaters were plain and modern, lacking big organs, chandeliers, and plaster ornamentation. Still, it kept introducing East Tennessee to the latest in movies and movie technology. The unprecedented wide-screen (and almost three-hour) epic *How the West Was Won*, a challenge to all television formats ever since its 1962 release, played at the Tennessee.

In September 1964, a limited four-showing engagement of Richard Burton in a stage performance of *Hamlet* introduced "the Miracle of Electronovision," a technologically interesting early experiment in high-resolution videotape production.

The Tennessee played family movies like *Kisses for My President*, starring Fred MacMurray as "the First Male First Lady"—oddly, the Tennessee's initial advertising didn't mention his co-star, well-known former Knoxvillian Polly Bergen, who played the president — but also some serious, controversial dramas, like Tennessee Williams' *Night of the Iguana*.

Cleopatra, the three-and-a-half-hour 1963 sensation — billed at the Tennessee as "the No. 1 Attraction of All Time" — played there for three solid weeks. Long runs became more common in the '60s, a very different model from the early days of three-night stands. And major motion pictures, which had once arrived at the theater almost simultaneously with their national release, didn't make it to the Tennessee until they were weeks or months old. *Cleopatra*'s three-week stand came almost a year after its national release.

Tony Perkins, famous for recent movies *Psycho* and *Fear Strikes Out*, came to town to make a new movie with avant-garde Mexican director Servando Gonzales — another horror film called *The Fool Killer*. Its gala "world premiere," in April 1965, the Tennessee's third in 12 years, drew Perkins himself, who smiled and shook hands and sat amongst the mostly puzzled audience.

The movie may have been too unconventional to evoke a strong response from either audiences or critics. Perhaps ironically, this otherwise daring movie was one of the last new black-and-white movies ever shown at the Tennessee.

The theater still showed some extras, like cartoons and occasional holdout newsreels. (Paramount had quit the newsreel business in 1957, acknowledging television's obvious advantages, while Universal and Hearst Metrotone kept producing newsreels until 1967.) But management no longer advertised these extras as if they might be a draw in themselves. The feature film was considered the main draw, maybe the only one.

OPENING NIGHT SOUVENIR TICKET

In general, as some theaters experimented with new horror movies, science fiction, and an occasional adults-only film, the Tennessee tried to play it safe, with Westerns and war movies featuring well-known stars like John Wayne, and light comedies, especially big colorful family movies. It showed nearly everything issued by Disney, whether cartoon or live action, movies starring Fred MacMurray and Hayley Mills and Dean Jones.

By the mid-'60s, though, the Tennessee wasn't always the place for local premieres of blockbuster movies. Management often funneled major-event movies to the Park Theater in East Knoxville, where they could camp out for weeks of expected crowds, while the Tennessee kept refreshing weekly with moderate hits. Hence *The Sound of Music* opened at the Park as the Tennessee was showing the John Wayne / Dean Martin Western, *The Sons of Katie Elder*. John Wayne movies were among the Tennessee's few constants over the decades.

Television didn't seem to bode well for cinema in general. In the era of color TV sets, *NBC Saturday Night at the Movies* (it debuted in 1961), and Jiffy-Pop Popcorn, who would keep paying

ANTHONY PERKINS

THE PARK THEATRE AT MAGNOLIA AND OLIVE STREETS

APRIL 28, 1965

FIRST CROWD AFTER THE 1966 REMODEL

1966 RE-OPENING FEATURING ORGANIST HUGH LIVINGSTON

to go see new movies in a theater with strangers? Some theaters adapted by showing movies that would never be shown on TV.

The venerable Gem Theatre, the large cinema at Vine and Central that had served the black community for most of the century, closed, partly a victim of urban renewal and also the fact that its traditional clientele suddenly had access to mainstream theaters. In 1965 the creaky old Bijou restyled itself the Bijou Art Theatre and began its nine-year run showing adults-only pornography.

By then the Tennessee's longtime parent company, Wilby-Kincey, had withdrawn from the scene. The Tennessee Theatre was run by ABC Southeastern, an efficient national corporation.

The Tennessee's opulence, designed for 1928 audiences, kept TV-age customers interested, at least for a while. But it was obviously a new era, and seemed time for a makeover. The Tennessee's biggest renovation during its cinema era came in 1966, with new carpet, a new concession stand, big mirrors, and a paint job that—a little unusual for remodelings in the 1960s—respected the original 1928 stencil patterns. They replaced seats, rendering the theater more comfortable but reducing the Tennessee's total capacity by almost a quarter, to 1,545. One unfortunate result of the renovation was that it left the balcony with a flatter slant that made the stage hard to see from some seats. That fact seemed of little importance in 1966, because by then the old stage was rarely used.

And the lobby was freshly decorated with framed pictures of Vol stars, a new "UT Wall of Fame" similar to a football homage at the theater's closest relative, Birmingham's Alabama Theatre. (It had been an 8-3 winning season, but in 1966 the Vols had lost to the Crimson Tide by one point.) Interest in college football was more general in the '60s than it had been in previous generations,

THE BIJOU FEATURED ADULT FILM 1965–1975

LITTLE HOLLYWOOD

In the early 1960s, on-location shooting in the area's richly diverse setting, for movies like "All the Way Home" and "The Fool Killer," both of which had their star-attended "world premieres" at the Tennessee, gave Knoxville the impression it was becoming a little Hollywood. Near West High School, the city even sponsored the construction of a sound stage (known for a time as James Agee Studio), though it may never have been used for that purpose.

when it had been chiefly an interest of students and alumni. The Tennessee Theatre had played a role in fanning that interest, since the days of 1930 when the theater first showed a game film. It reopened to a showing of Fred MacMurray's newest, *Follow Me, Boys*, the scouting comedy whose peculiar cast included both child star Kurt Russell and 73-year-old silent legend Lillian Gish. (A supporting role was that of "Melody Murphy," played by Ken Murray, who had appeared live at the Tennessee 32 years before as the headliner of "Earl Carroll's Vanities.")

Rarely known for hyping horror movies, in 1967 the Tennessee made an exception for an A-list suspense film starring Audrey Hepburn called *Wait Until Dark*, which became famous for one especially startling scene. In ads, theater management prudently warned patrons to stay away from the edge of the balcony — just because it would be a hazardous place to be when they jumped out of their seats.

For many years the Tennessee offered occasional special features, like travelogues. An almost-forgotten outgrowth of the newsreel era, travelogues were long-form documentaries about exotic faraway places, traveling one-time shows often introduced onstage by the film's intrepid hero. Typically sponsored by a local service organization, travelogues were usually shown on Sunday afternoons, often to crowds still dressed for church.

The October 3, 1968, showing of a now-obscure film called *Bill Wallace of China* was hailed with "sweeping searchlights." A film about a Baptist missionary, a UT alumnus who had died in a Communist Chinese prison, it was hailed as a "world premiere," though some sources indicate it was first released the previous year. Whatever it was, it did draw an in-person appearance of the movie's star. Gregory Walcott was familiar to fans of B movies, notably *Plan 9 From Outer Space*. Along with him was local actress Jo Helton, who had recently had a minor role in the Sidney Poitier movie *The Slender Thread*.

It may have seemed a sign of the times, though, two years later when the locally filmed movie *A Walk in the Spring Rain*, starring Ingrid Bergman and Anthony Quinn, debuted at the suburban Capri 70 in Bearden, where parking was free — and where they were soon boasting of Knoxville's own patch of Hollywood Boulevard, a concrete sidewalk with handprints and signatures. Bergman herself, who had once glowed on the Tennessee's screen in *Casablanca*, arrived in a limousine to inaugurate it with her own hands.

That tradition began at Hollywood's Grauman's Chinese Theatre, an exotic 1920s movie palace like the Tennessee. Those who thought of Gay Street as Knoxville's Hollywood Boulevard could hardly ignore a reality. In 1970, fewer people were coming downtown on a regular basis, especially at night. Ticket sales at the Tennessee were declining.

In that turbulent era, when UT students were demonstrating against the war, the Tennessee began a tradition that may not have seemed quite as revolutionary at the time as it turned out to be. The theater was still mainly devoted to big new releases, but on one Tuesday night, in a three-hour program called "Sounds of the Silents," the Tennessee showed some very old films. On March 25, 1969, the theater featured organist Lee Erwin, who played the score behind several silent comedies, followed by the Rudolph Valentino movie *The Eagle*.

Erwin was one of America's best-known organists of the day, from his network TV work, but in years to come he would be credited, partly through his original compositions, with re-awakening a national interest in silent film. Years after his first Tennessee Theatre gigs, Woody Allen would pay tribute to him by giving Erwin a cameo in the nostalgically autobiographical movie *Radio Days*.

Erwin's performance that night is sometimes recalled with some irony: it was possibly the first time the 41-year-old Mighty Wurlitzer was ever used for its ostensible purpose — that is, playing accompaniment to a silent film. Though the theater had been built for silents, the first silents actually shown in the theater came with a Vitaphone soundtrack and did not call for organ accompaniment.

It's likely the organ might have been used for some silent shorts, or on the rare early occasions when the theater showed older pre-soundtrack features. In any case it's safe to say that most of the Wurlitzer's use in accompanying silent feature films has come in the years since 1969.

That particular silent film was an interesting choice. *The Eagle* was one of Clarence Brown's earliest directorial triumphs, but that fact wasn't advertised in promotions. In 1969 few Knoxvillians would have recognized the name. There was yet no theater bearing his name at UT. The long-retired MGM director, who lived in California, was then working with his alma mater about a major bequest.

It was the beginning of a significant era. Even when the Tennessee was only 40 years old — not old enough to be officially considered "historic" and still serving its original purpose as a first-run movie theater — the rare old movie palace was generating interest among prominent people who wanted to preserve it. It faced no immediate threat, but some in the cinema industry believed its days were numbered.

WESTOWN ULTRA-VISION THEATRE

West Town Mall's movie theater opened in 1972, an unusual, round-shaped, freestanding 800-seat cinema. An ABC executive was overheard to remark that the mall theater would eventually replace the Tennessee, which he assumed would eventually be demolished, for parking. As the Tennessee's advocates like to point out, it was West Town's suburban theater that was eventually razed for parking.

Perhaps for the first time there was coalescing interest in "saving" the Tennessee. Chief among the Tennessee's champions was Wallace Baumann, a businessman who'd grown up with the

Built as a freestanding round theater in the mall's big parking lot in 1972, the modernistic WesTown Theater, at what was later spelled as West Town Mall, was emblematic of the suburbanization of the movie market, which had been underway for decades. The large theater seemed poised to replace the Tennessee in the Knoxville market; one local industry insider even suggested the 800-seat theater, one of the two largest suburban theaters at the time, would result in the Tennessee's demolition. At a time when the Tennessee was struggling, the WesTown was showing the 1980 musical "The Jazz Singer," a remake of the groundbreaking 1927 talkie. It was WesTown that was eventually demolished — replaced by a multiplex-style theater inside the mall itself — as Knoxville rediscovered the Tennessee.

theater and emerged as the theater's unofficial historian and advocate, a role he held for 40 years.

WALLACE W. BAUMANN

1925 - 2009

WALLACE BAUMANN'S GRANDFATHER, ARCHITECT A.B. BAUMANN, SR. IN "MEN OF AFFAIRS" 1921

Descended from a local family of well-known retailers and architects, Baumann (1925 – 2009) grew up with a natural fascination for this lavish phenomenon. He claimed to have vivid memories of it from its earliest years, of celebrating his sixth birthday there in 1931. A few years later he learned of the Nazi's formidable Siegfried Line by way of the Tennessee's newsreels, never guessing that when war came he'd be one of the soldiers to help break through it. Baumann returned to his hometown eventually to run his family's old furniture store, Woodruff's, a block and a half away from the theater. A middle-aged bachelor without the distractions of family, Baumann loved the Tennessee as few have.

In 1972, Baumann wrote a glowing feature article about the Tennessee and its Wurlitzer for *The Console*, a small and short-lived but national magazine about organs and organists.

"Fortunately, the Tennessee's box office is still as busy as ever, and top first-run films still grace its giant silver screen," Baumann wrote, "assuring Knoxvillians of many more years of fine theater entertainment in the grand manner." The optimistic Baumann put the theater's best face forward for this select national audience. Others, looking at the same theater, might not have been so cheerful. Crowds were smaller and smaller, and many of the movies playing there were not of the same caliber as those of previous eras.

Despite some memorable events, on a nightly basis, the Tennessee had become just another movie theater, and not necessarily one of Knoxville's more appealing ones, often showing movies that were playing at other theaters simultaneously. Sometimes

JUNE 8, 1973

it showed the modern equivalent of B movies, like horror and martial arts films, and sometimes even second-run movies, even in tandem with drive-ins. In advertisements, the Tennessee no longer appeared in big letters. At some point, management installed pinball machines in the grand lobby.

The Wurlitzer hadn't been a regular feature in about 20 years, but young organist Preston Spaulding volunteered to play it three nights a week, even for brand-new movies. He'd keep the organ in workable shape with parts ordered from a supplier in Iowa.

A Junior League fundraiser for the Knoxville Symphony Orchestra highlighted the theater, and a newspaper feature about it brought Mr. T.C. Bigler, projectionist, out of his "lofty snuggery" to reminisce. He had been the Tennessee's projectionist since 1955.

Showing old movies was a rarity at the Tennessee in its first-run era, but the practice, which seemed odd at first, gained momentum. In September 1973, the theater showed the old Buster Keaton comedy *The General*. The rare old organ began getting more exercise, with frequent guest organists, some of national stature.

In 1975 the new preservationist group then known as Knoxville Heritage, in the midst of efforts to salvage the Bijou Theatre, naturally turned its attention to the Tennessee. On November 13, 1975, the organization, led by modernist architect Glenn Bullock, hosted "An Evening at the Tennessee Theatre," featuring a 1925 silent comedy, Buster Keaton's *Seven Chances*. Organist Lee Erwin returned to the Tennessee to do the honors. The famous organist played at the Tennessee at least four times. A younger organist of similar caliber, Lyn Larsen of Los Angeles, performed at another Knoxville Heritage special event in 1976: "Silent Night at the Movies," featuring Harry Langdon's 1926 comedy, *Saturday Afternoon*.

The Tennessee Theatre
...presents...
Tom's
Fresh!
Knoxville, Tenn.
1973
CHIP-MUNK CLUB
EVERY WEDNESDAY MORNING 10:00
(Except 5th Show on TUESDAY, JULY 3rd)
FREE ADMISSION

DATE	ADMISSION	ON THE SCREEN
Wednesday June 6	39c Worth of Tom's Bags or Wrappers	Mark Twain's "THE PRINCE AND THE PAUPER" A Childhood Production ....and Reels-of-FUN
Wednesday June 13	39c Worth of Tom's Bags or Wrappers	"THE BRAVE LITTLE TAILOR" A Childhood Production ....and Reels-of-FUN
Wednesday June 20	39c Worth of Tom's Bags or Wrappers	"ALLADIN AND HIS MAGIC LAMP" A Childhood Production ....and Reels-of-FUN
Wednesday June 27	39c Worth of Tom's Bags or Wrappers	"THE CLOWN AND THE KIDS" starring Emmett Kelly A Childhood Production ....and Reels-of-FUN
Tuesday July 3	39c Worth of Tom's Bags or Wrappers	"THE TENDERBOX" (HANS CHRISTIAN ANDERSEN) A Childhood Production ....and Reels-of-FUN
Wednesday July 11	39c Worth of Tom's Bags or Wrappers	"SLEEPING BEAUTY" A Childhood Production ....and Reels-of-FUN
Wednesday July 18	39c Worth of Tom's Bags or Wrappers	"TOM THUMB" A Childhood Production ....and Reels-of-FUN
Wednesday July 25	39c Worth of Tom's Bags or Wrappers	"BROTHER OF THE WIND" ....and Reels-of-FUN
Wednesday Aug. 1	39c Worth of Tom's Bags or Wrappers	"THE 7 DWARFS TO THE RESCUE" A Childhood Production ....and Reels-of-FUN
Wednesday Aug. 8	39c Worth of Tom's Bags or Wrappers	"PUSS 'N BOOTS" A Childhood Production ....and Reels-of-FUN
Wednesday Aug. 15	39c Worth of Tom's Bags or Wrappers	"LONG JOHN SILVER RETURNS TO TREASURE ISLAND" A Childhood Production ....and Reels-of-FUN
Wednesday Aug. 22	39c Worth of Tom's Bags or Wrappers	"LITTLE RED RIDINGHOOD" ....and Reels-of-FUN
Wednesday Aug. 29	39c Worth of Tom's Bags or Wrappers	"GOLDEN GOOSE" ....and Reels-of-FUN

(Any Combination of Tom's Empty Bags or Wrappers Accepted As Admission)
Admission limited to Children 12 years of age & under unless accompanying smaller children.
DOORS OPEN AT 9:30 A. M.
On Stage!
BoBo the Town Clown
(Bill Croxdale)
with BILLIE ANN, MELODY & GUEST
FREE PRIZES
TO LUCKY BOYS AND GIRLS ATTENDING
Tom's Products can be purchased in Theatre Lobby

THE CHIPMUNK CLUB

The Chipmunk Club was the third and last of the children's shows that started with the Popeye Club in the 1930s. This 1973 program mentions BoBo the Town Clown, portrayed by Bill Croxdale, who was clowning in Knoxville by the 1940s. The Chipmunk Club met on Wednesday mornings, not Saturdays. Mothers might have been grateful for the free babysitting either day. While early children's clubs like the Popeye Club and the Donald Duck Club showed current comedies and adventures made for general audiences, the latter-day club's offerings seem to be off-brand and mostly older films made for children — and perhaps less tap dancing.

KNOXVILLE HERITAGE'S ANNUAL MEETING · 1975

"Suddenly, he was awakened by smoke...! The popcorn machine was on fire! What did Gary do? Why he ran out of that room as fast as he could right up aisle 1, screaming FIRE!!! FIRE!!! FIRE!!! to the top of his lungs!" Donna recalls a day at the Tennessee when a napping co-worker forgot his training never to scare the audience!

DONNA HENSLEY

Downtown had been losing affluent residents since before the Tennessee opened. The old neighborhood was now losing retail too, especially as West Town Mall opened in 1972, with its own movie theater. Downtown declined, and to make things worse, many were predicting the end of motion pictures altogether. As improvements in network television programming were followed by the debut of cable TV, with new movies on HBO, box office receipts dwindled nationally. Hollywood seemed unsure of how to respond, whether with more and more extreme movies, with nudity and violence, or dumber and dumber ones. Some philosophers were predicting the final days of cinema.

In downtown Knoxville, it was easy to believe. With the Bijou on the way to a renovation with a new emphasis on live shows, downtown's only remaining cinemas were the Riviera and the Tennessee, showing new major releases to smaller and smaller audiences.

THEATER OR THEATRE?

When Noah Webster put out his American dictionary in the early 1800s, he delineated how American spellings were distinguishing themselves from British spellings. In general, Webster's recommendations were no-nonsense and more phonetic than old British spellings, which still had vestiges of ancient origins. One change he was noted for establishing was the –er ending, as opposed to the British –re endings, which were usually a remnant of the original Norman French.

When the Tennessee Theatre opened in 1928, it was spelled in the British or French style, with the –re ending. It was typical, even in the vaudeville era of the 19th century, to evoke British spellings, just as thespians sometimes affected British accents. In theater at least, the land of Shakespeare was the ideal.

For reasons unannounced, around 1950, the Tennessee began using the –er ending. Maybe the Cold War prompted a new swell of patriotism that gave the theater management a reason to fall back on the more purely American. Or maybe it was just an oversight by a manager who didn't make it a priority to spell it consistently with its past.

In any case, for the first time, it was Tennessee Theater. That red-blooded American spelling remained unchanged for the rest of the theater's era as a first-run cinema. As the cinema market shriveled in the 1970s, however, and the Tennessee began hosting more live performances, the original –re spelling mysteriously re-emerged.

FOLLOW THE BOYS · 1963

SEVEN CHANCES · 1925 · SHOWN 1975

HAMLET · 1964

CLEOPATRA · 1963

TO KILL A MOCKINGBIRD · 1963

WAIT UNTIL DARK · 1967

KING KONG · 1933 · SHOWN 1973

THE EAGLE · 1925 · SHOWN 1969

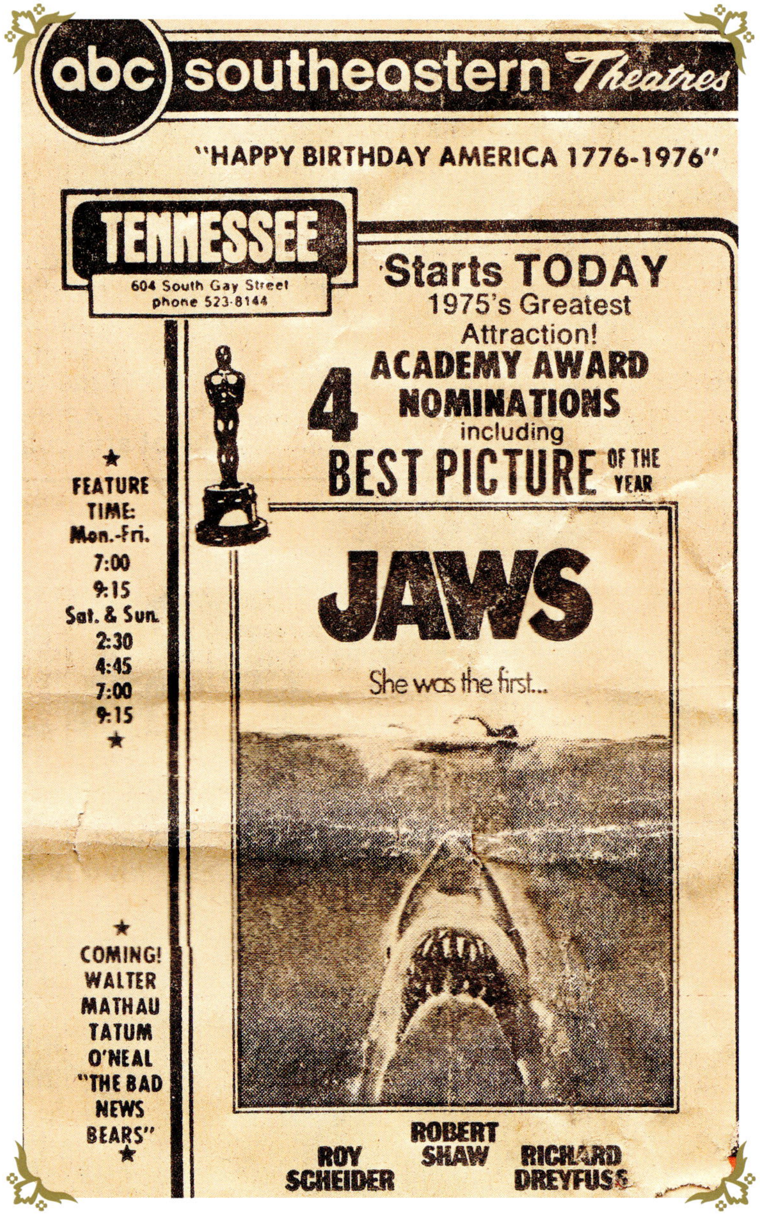

NEWSPAPER AD · 1976

As the Bijou Theatre's new mission as a historically valued live-performance space got traction, fans of the Tennessee wondered if a comparable effort might be appropriate for the bigger theater, that maybe the old movie palace was no longer just a moneymaking business but a cultural landmark deserving of non-profit support. Future Tennessee technician Tim Burns was then working at the Bijou and recalls the Tennessee's last movie theater manager, Glenda White, asking why the Bijou was then generating more passion for preservation than was the Tennessee. Burns replied, "Because the Tennessee is still open, and the bulldozer was knocking at the door of the Bijou," he responded. "I think we both knew then that one day in the near future the Tennessee would need saving." In fact, when approached for contributions to the Bijou effort, Wallace Baumann and other philanthropists replied they were saving for a potentially bigger job, the Tennessee.

The nation's bicentennial year brought nothing for downtown cinema to celebrate. In January 1976, after more than half a century, even bouncing back after an almost-ruinous fire, the Riviera closed. The press enjoyed joshing about the fact that the last new movie ever shown there was called *Adios Amigo*, with little interest in the movie itself, which apparently few saw. It was a black-cast Western comedy starring the not-yet-legendary comedian Richard Pryor. Unkindly reviewed in the national press, it marked the unceremonious end to a 56-year run of a theater that had ushered in the era of sound.

The Tennessee was hardly doing better. A 1976 showing of the suspense classic *Dog Day Afternoon* was described in ABC ads as showing "at Both Theaters"—the Tennessee and the Knoxville Drive-In, in Bearden. It was a step up from the B fare the Tennessee had been presenting of late, but when it played at the Tennessee, the movie was a year old.

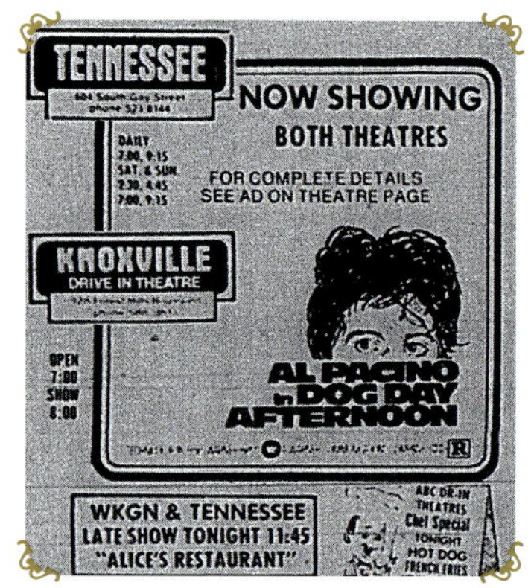

KNOXVILLE JOURNAL
OCTOBER 1, 1976

Downtown's deterioration was one problem. Another originated in Hollywood and made things tough for single-screen theaters everywhere. The studios were demanding more and more of the cut for their releases' opening weeks, leaving theater managers to try to make a profit in subsequent weeks. That plan was workable for small rooms, especially in combination with others, as in the new business model of the Cineplex. But the practice was ruinously terrible for big theaters, who couldn't expect commensurately big crowds to keep coming week after week to see the same show. It was especially hard on old-fashioned theaters that required a lot of maintenance.

The largest movie theater ever built in Knoxville became downtown's only movie theater. The year 1977 might have offered some reason to hope, as the modernist new Plaza Tower, the tallest building ever built in East Tennessee, rose just two blocks to the south — on the site of the old Lyric.

NOVEMBER 1977

NOVEMBER 1977

It made an ironic coincidence. When the Tennessee Theatre opened in 1928, the tallest building in East Tennessee history, the Andrew Johnson Hotel, was under construction. It had been almost half a century, but Plaza Tower was to be the Knoxville area's first building taller than the Andrew Johnson.

NOVEMBER 4, 1977

On October 22, 1977, Tate & McCallie Realtors, agents for C.B. Atkin Realty Co., made an announcement about the Tennessee Theatre. Though ABC Southeastern had another two years on its lease, the 49-year-old theater would be closing in two weeks. The development caught the owners by surprise. ABC's John L. Huff said it was "a business decision based on economic conditions and changing times."

The last new movie ever shown at the Tennessee was an action-comedy called *A Piece of the Action*, starring Sidney Poitier, Bill Cosby, and James Earl Jones. It's hard not to note another irony: that the final movies ever shown at both the Riviera and the Tennessee, which had admitted only whites for most of their history, were movies with black casts.

That showing was not specially promoted as the end of an era, or something not to be missed. It was mentioned in just a small ad listing the Tennessee and an interstate-exit theater, the Cedar Bluff, as one of two places where the movie was playing. Then, on November 4, the Tennessee's famous cursive logo disappeared from the movie-ad page forever.

As it turned out, it was only the anticlimactic end of Chapter One. In several respects, the Tennessee's biggest years were ahead of it. But for a while, it would be dark and quiet.

And as unlikely as it might seem, one of the stars of that last new film shown at the Tennessee would become, in person, the theater's most popular celebrity-fundraiser attraction.

NOVEMBER 3, 1977

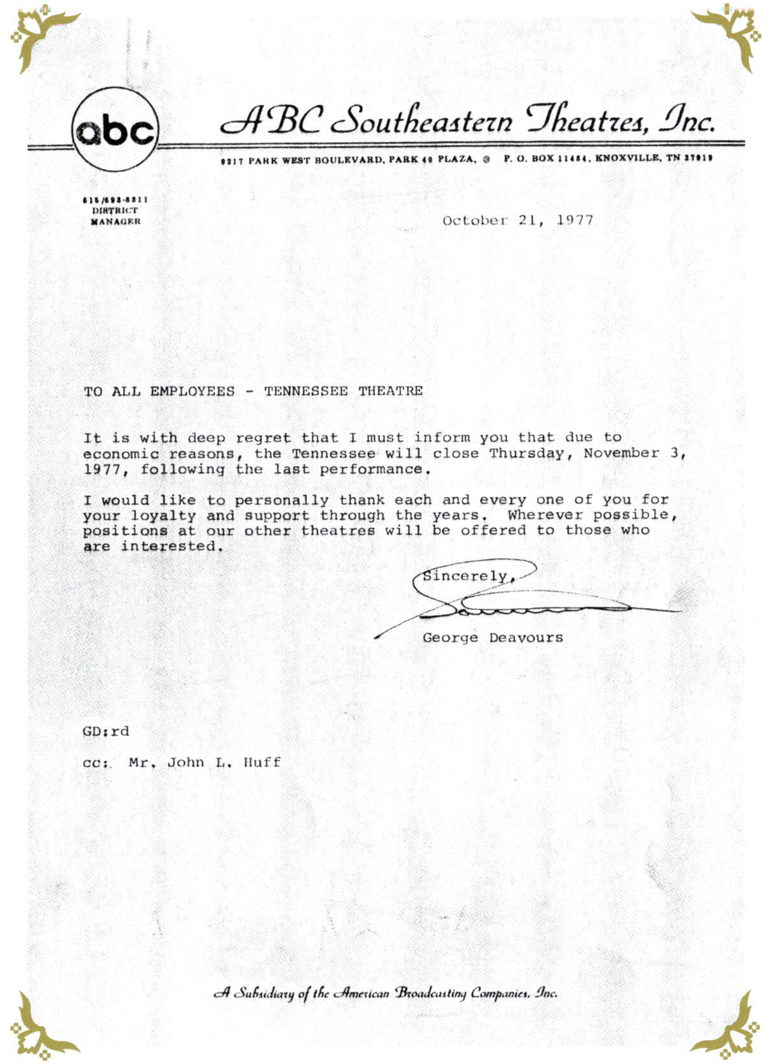

ABC Southeastern Theatres, Inc.

9217 PARK WEST BOULEVARD, PARK 40 PLAZA, P. O. BOX 11484, KNOXVILLE, TN 37919

615/693-8811
DISTRICT
MANAGER

October 21, 1977

TO ALL EMPLOYEES - TENNESSEE THEATRE

It is with deep regret that I must inform you that due to economic reasons, the Tennessee will close Thursday, November 3, 1977, following the last performance.

I would like to personally thank each and every one of you for your loyalty and support through the years. Wherever possible, positions at our other theatres will be offered to those who are interested.

Sincerely,

George Deavours

GD:rd

cc: Mr. John L. Huff

A Subsidiary of the American Broadcasting Companies, Inc.

NOTICE OF CLOSURE

A NOSTALGIC ERA

CHAPTER 7

In late 1977, no one knew what would become of the place. Across the nation many of the Tennessee's movie palace peers were deteriorating beyond repair, being knocked down or radically remodeled, stripped of their old-fashioned ornamentation and subdivided into smaller theaters to meet the modern economic model for movie distribution.

It may be fortunate that despite the new towering office building, downtown had cooled as an entertainment center. The more radical solutions, like dividing the theater into smaller parts, didn't seem promising economically, because few were coming downtown at night.

Since its closing almost two years earlier, the Riviera had remained empty. It would remain empty for years. Developers did make proposals for the Riviera, to render it a dinner theater or an "ultramodern office building." Nothing ever worked out.

For the Tennessee, one group proposed making it a "bluegrass emporium."

One 1970s trend seemed a path to salvation. After a decade of turbulence and change, the 1970s was unexpectedly an era of nostalgia, and college campuses were showing old Humphrey Bogart, Marx Brothers, Fred Astaire, and W.C. Fields movies. Young people were fascinated with them, and old people enjoyed the memories. The surprise re-release of the Marx Brothers' infectious 1930 comedy *Animal Crackers* in modern theaters across the country in 1974 — in Knoxville, it played at the Capri Cinema on Kingston Pike, to big crowds — suggested an untapped market for old movies, many of which could be shown cheaply.

Naturally, an old theater could show old movies. At a time when few people had access to old movies at home — both cable TV and home video were in their early development — it made sense.

There was more than one old theater downtown, of course. By the mid-1970s a giant mural on the old Riviera, an image of Charlie Chaplin in sharply defined black and white, was clearly visible from new James White Parkway.

But the Tennessee looked much older than the redesigned Riviera, and the idea of showing old movies there, in the theater that had debuted *Animal Crackers* back in 1930, appealed to an eccentric UT economics professor named Tony Spiva. He was interested in the idea of showing inexpensive old black-and-white movies to modern crowds in an interesting place for little

A RAY OF HOPE

Woodruff's

WOODRUFF'S, INC. • 424-426 GAY STREET, S.W. • KNOXVILLE, TENNESSEE 37902

October 21, 1977

Editor, Knoxville News Sentinel
208 Church Ave., S.W.
Knoxville, Tennessee 37902

Attention: Letters To The Editor Dept.

Gentlemen:

The closing of the Tennessee Theatre November 3rd by ABC Theatres marks the end of an era in Knoxville entertainment. This great movie palace, which opened October 1, 1928, at a cost of $1,000,000.00 couldn't be duplicated today for twenty times that amount - if craftsmen could be found to execute the workmanship involved.

This Knoxville landmark must be saved! Here is a theatre in excellent condition of modern concrete and steel construction with a fully equipped stage, dressing rooms and, of course, a "Mighty Wurlitzer" pipe organ in fine playing condition. This theatre is one of the last great showplaces left in the south - or the country.

Hopefully, Knoxville Heritage, the city or some other group can find a way to save this theatre from demolition. Interested citizens need to think of ways this theatre can serve the community so that future generations can enjoy the beauty and splendor of this important part of our heritage.

Sincerely yours,

Wallace W. Baumann
3612 T[illegible] Ave.
Knoxville, Tennessee 37919

WWB:MW

OVER A CENTURY OF SERVICE

WALLACE BAUMANN'S PLEA

money. Spiva was central to a new organization called Tennessee Theatre Classics, Inc. (TTC), which included young attorney John Duncan, Jr., who only later assumed his father's seat in U.S. Congress, and later still would play a key role in the future of the Tennessee.

Dreams for the theater were modest in 1978. "We're not trying to get rich," Spiva said. "We're trying to keep the theater from falling apart."

Wasting no time, they started on Wednesday, March 15, 1978, hardly four months after that final new movie. At a gala re-opening, Mayor Randy Tyree cut the ribbon to show the 1932 all-star classic *Grand Hotel*, accompanied by Preston Spaulding on the Wurlitzer. With that, the group launched a grueling schedule of old movies, usually shown as double features, and changing every three days or so — about 20 feature films a month, a pace that almost imitated the theater's 1930s schedule.

STATE STREET, SHOWING REAR OF RIVIERA

Tennessee Theatre Classics

presents

HUMPHREY BOGART

Double Feature

The Maltese Falcon

Tonight at 6:15/10:00

and

They Drive By Night

Tonight at 8:20

BILL DEXTER at the Mighty Wurlitzer

Ph. 524-1426

NEWSPAPER AD · MAY 26, 1978

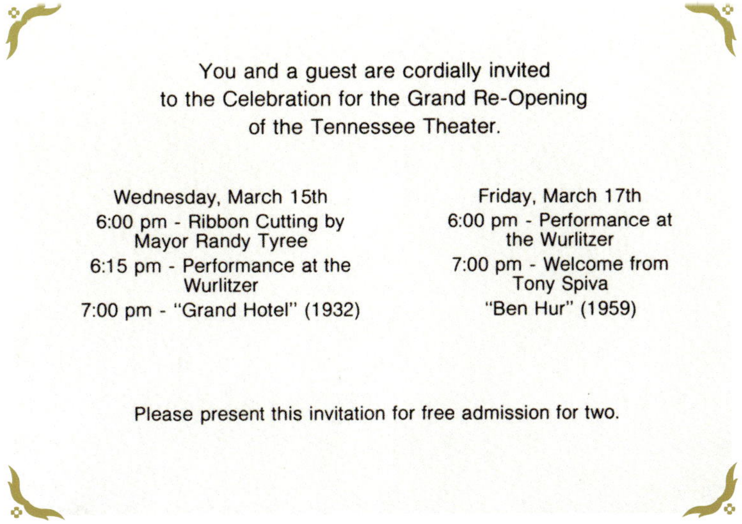

You and a guest are cordially invited to the Celebration for the Grand Re-Opening of the Tennessee Theater.

Wednesday, March 15th	Friday, March 17th
6:00 pm - Ribbon Cutting by Mayor Randy Tyree	6:00 pm - Performance at the Wurlitzer
6:15 pm - Performance at the Wurlitzer	7:00 pm - Welcome from Tony Spiva
7:00 pm - "Grand Hotel" (1932)	"Ben Hur" (1959)

Please present this invitation for free admission for two.

1978 GRAND RE-OPENING INVITATION

That June saw the return of a local legend. After an absence of almost 30 years, Billy Barnes took his customary place at the Wurlitzer. After decades playing in Sheraton Hotels, he had settled in North Carolina, but it wouldn't be his last return. Scenes at the Tennessee in the late '70s and early '80s must have had patrons checking their calendars. Barnes, the favorite of the 1930s, proved he was keeping up. He played themes from *Star Wars* and *Rocky*, plus a tribute called "Hello, Knoxville" to the tune of "Hello, Dolly." The show included live mimes, an appropriate accompaniment to a couple of Valentino silents, *Son of the Sheik* and *Blood and Sand*.

The August 1978 showing of the 1944 film *Shine On Harvest Moon* might have seemed another typical oldie except for the fact that the male star, 69-year-old Dennis Morgan, was in attendance. Morgan's career had peaked in the '40s; he'd done mostly TV work since then. By the '70s, he was practically retired from show business. When he made his personal appearance at the Tennessee, he had only one more acting gig left in him, a *Love Boat* guest spot.

SCREENED AT 1978 GRAND RE-OPENING

DENNIS MORGAN VISITED THE TENNESSEE IN 1978

But he had his fans. The event was played up as if it were a premiere. The Tennessee's marquee proclaimed, "DENNIS MORGAN COMING TO TOWN."

Spiva's group, which underwent some leadership turmoil in its short tenure, showed more than 100 movies at the Tennessee, and raised its profile, bringing it to the attention of a city that had come to think of it as just another movie screen.

They drew crowds, bigger than might be expected — even a few sellouts, albeit not many. The typical old movie drew about 450, some just a couple hundred. It wasn't dependably popular enough to justify the rent and utilities on a 1,500-seat theater. When it was all over, Professor Spiva, the master of supply-and-demand curves, had to admit that he turned a profit only with the Bogart films. Somehow Humphrey Bogart, who had been dead for more than 20 years, was especially hot in the late '70s.

On October 6, 1978, not quite a whole year after the first-run theater chain gave up on it, the *News Sentinel* ran a discouraging headline about the Tennessee: "Tennessee Theatre Closes Again." Tate & McCallie told reporters, frankly, the TTC organization wasn't paying the rent.

Its second closing came just as the Tennessee and its seeming revival were getting a bit of national attention. Wallace Baumann got another illustrated feature story about the Tennessee's Wurlitzer into another national trade publication, the October-November issue of *Theatre Organ* magazine.

At the end of 1978 came confirmed reports that an "out of state party" was interested in taking over the theater. It never materialized.

PATRICIA NEAL

FESTIVAL PROGRAM

MS. NEAL IN THE GRAND LOBBY · 1978

Even without TTC, the Tennessee hosted a previously planned event, a showing of the 1949 war drama *The Hasty Heart*, starring Ronald Reagan — by then better known as a presidential contender — and a local hero, Patricia Neal, who had grown up in East Knoxville and gotten her start in acting when she attended Knoxville High. It was billed as the Patricia Neal Homecoming Film Festival, co-hosted by former Knoxville comedian Archie Campbell, who by then was nationally recognizable as a regular on the long-running comedy show *Hee Haw*. Patricia Neal herself, then only 52 but already sidelined by a stroke, was in attendance. The title may have been partly a play on Neal's return to the screen, not quite seven years earlier, in a television movie called *The Homecoming*, which would be remembered as the pilot for a new series called *The Waltons*. She gave a brief talk on the Tennessee's stage. It was also the year's second homecoming for Billy Barnes, who did the honors at the keyboards.

Robert (Bob) Frost had grown up in local show business. His father, Ralph Frost, was the Indiana-born businessman who'd been one of Knoxville's most successful promoters, beginning with his work as head of University Concerts back in the 1930s; the elder Frost had been instrumental in putting together the *So*

This Is Love premiere back in 1953, and was still involved in local show business. Both Frosts had been promoting shows at the Civic Auditorium/Coliseum since it first opened. Son Robert Frost leased the Tennessee in September 1979 with intentions to carry forward the previous management's plan of classic-film programming. Frost had been involved in a successful classic-movie project at Chattanooga's Tivoli, and despite the early departure of Spiva and company, found their basic idea sufficiently encouraging. It had been just popular enough to show promise but not popular enough to turn a regular profit.

Frost pledged to fix the place up, especially with better lighting. He made one major improvement by hiring Tim Burns to help maintain the place. Raised in a cinema-operator's family, Burns had previously worked at the Bijou. For him, the Tennessee became a career. A trip to Atlanta's famous Fox Theatre in 1975, the last night it showed new movies, commenced a lifelong fascination with movie palace architecture, of which Burns became a student — and eventually the expert on the nooks and crannies of Knoxville's particular example of that style.

ACTOR JOHN CULLUM WITH ROBERT (BOB) FROST · 1981

TIM BURNS AT THE 1928 LIGHT BOARD · 1977

November 1977: The original 1928 stage switchboard. The left side of the panel controlled white, red and blue lights in the auditorium. The right side controlled all the stage lighting. Tim Burns, shown here, was working at the Bijou at the time. Wallace Baumann asked him to come to the Tennessee to turn on as many lights as possible, for what he feared would be its final opportunity to be professionally photographed.

Burns remained with the Tennessee as technical director well into the 21st century and became the theater's chief host and historian, the longest-tenured professional ever associated with the theater as a full-time job.

The longest-tenured organist in the Tennessee's history began his career on the bench in an unlikely manner, on October 18, 1979. It was the first night of the Frost era, and they were showing the 1936 Clark Gable/Jeanette McDonald classic, *San Francisco*.

BILL BURNS

TENNESSEE PROJECTIONIST
1984 - 2001

BILL SNYDER · 1980

1979 RE-OPENING MOVIE

With that event approaching, a middle-aged fellow approached a young employee of the theater and asked if anybody was going to play the old Wurlitzer; she responded, "We'd like to, but we don't have any money."

"I don't need any money," the man responded. Bill Snyder, department head of UT's School of Engineering — he would later be chancellor of the entire university — had learned to play the organ 30 years earlier, when he took lessons from organist Bess Shugart at old Second Presbyterian Church when it was downtown. It was for him the beginning of a lifelong fascination with an unusual instrument.

The second problem was that the old organ was locked. The building's maintenance man, Jim Hensley, didn't have a key, but he thought one of the theater's enthusiasts, Wallace Baumann, then manager of Woodruff's Furniture on Gay, might have one. Snyder walked down the sidewalk and introduced himself to Baumann, who took a break to show Snyder the organ pit. Finding the key, he unlocked the 50-year-old Wurlitzer and then said, "Now, Bill, that's all I know about this organ."

Snyder learned several *San Francisco* tunes and played a medley of them before the movie. And that first night the professor added a flourish that became a tradition: he played "The Tennessee Waltz."

After the showing of this love story centered on the San Francisco earthquake of 1906, an older woman came up to Snyder in tears. Her late husband had proposed to her in a balcony watching *San Francisco* in 1936, and the movie and the music he played moved her to remember that moment. Professor Snyder rarely got that sort of a response in engineering class. Unbeknownst to Snyder, it was the beginning of several decades

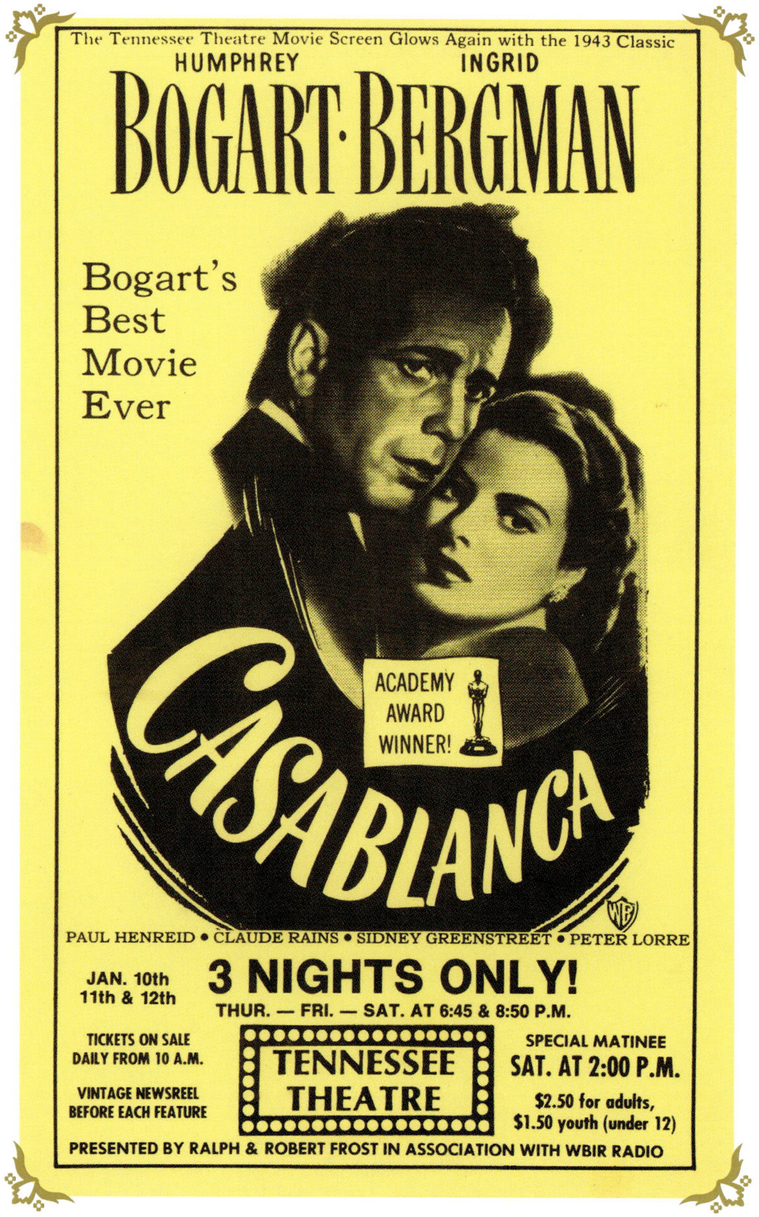

CASABLANCA SOLD OUT FIVE SCREENINGS IN 1980

THE TENNESSEE WALTZ

There's no question that organist and former UT chancellor Bill Snyder has played "The Tennessee Waltz" almost every time he has sat at the bench of the Mighty Wurlitzer since 1979. His performances have made the popular tune part of the lore of the theater.

The familiar and much-beloved tune so much associated with the Tennessee Theatre is not as old as the theater. Written in 1946 by Redd Stewart and Pee Wee King, the Milwaukee-born Western Swing star who had once been based in Knoxville, the now-familiar tune was first recorded by Cowboy Copas, who was at the time a Knoxville radio performer, in late 1947. Copas is not known to have performed the song on the Tennessee's stage, at a time when live musical performances were rarer than they had been in earlier eras. It's just possible that the Tennessee's signature organist, Billy Barnes, heard the song before leaving Knoxville in 1948, but assuming he ever arranged a version of it for the big pipes might be a stretch. "The Tennessee Waltz" did not become a familiar tune even in Tennessee until Patti Page had a major national hit with it in 1950. By then the Tennessee Theatre was showing mainly movies, without live performances; the Wurlitzer was played only occasionally.

It's unknown who first performed the song on the Tennessee's stage. As strange as it may seem, it may have been California-born future television producer Merv Griffin, who sang "The Tennessee Waltz," accompanying himself on piano, during the premiere of "So This Is Love" in 1953.

FIRST TOURING SHOW OF THE MODERN ERA · 1980

as the Tennessee Theatre's chief organist, and a relationship with the theater that would go even deeper.

Frost showed old films that fall and into the winter. Six January 1980 evening presentations of the classic *Casablanca* — maybe the perfect movie for a Moorish-revival theater — were packed, and five showings were sold out.

Frost's multiple showings, combined with sentimental touches like rehiring the movie theater's popcorn lady, Easter Russell, proved popular, and for the first time in years the Tennessee regularly generated a line down the sidewalk. Old-line restaurants like the Brass Rail, across the street, reported unusual business on the Tennessee's old-movie nights.

Late 1979 saw a live show on the stage, a presentation by several local alumni of *The Lawrence Welk Show*. But Frost was interested in bringing full live concerts back to the Tennessee's stage. Already a concert promoter for the world's most famous Dixieland band, Frost brought New Orleans' Preservation Hall Jazz Band to the Tennessee in February 1980, probably the first full show by a touring performer since World War II. For the legendary group, which still included several of its original members, it was the first of several visits to the Tennessee.

But in September Frost "had to give it up," according to a newspaper story that didn't elaborate more fully. By later accounts, the owners, interested in selling the building, did not wish to renew Frost's lease. Frost would only say, "reopening the Tennessee and having the success we had is one of my proudest achievements."

GRAND HOTEL · 1932 · SHOWN 1978

THE SON OF THE SHEIK · 1926 · SHOWN 1978

BLOOD AND SAND · 1922 · SHOWN 1978

THE MALTESE FALCON · 1946 · SHOWN 1980

SHINE ON HARVEST MOON · 1944 · SHOWN 1978

YOU CAN'T TAKE IT WITH YOU · 1938 · SHOWN 1980

THEY DRIVE BY NIGHT · 1940 · SHOWN 1978

SAN FRANCISCO · 1936 · SHOWN 1979

DIRECTOR FRANK CAPRA'S PERSONAL APPEARANCE · 1980

This time a member of the owner family took charge. Bill Akers, Jr., a great-grandson of C.B. Atkin, became the third party to try showing old movies at the theater. Rather than shifting to a completely different business plan, he raised the stakes. On the weekend of December 4–6, 1980, the Tennessee offered Knoxville seven screenings of Frank Capra's 1938 classic, *You Can't Take It With You*, starring Jimmy Stewart, Jean Arthur, and Lionel Barrymore. Before two of the showings, on subsequent nights, Frank Capra himself was on the Tennessee's stage, speaking and fielding questions from the audience.

Capra wasn't on a speaking tour. "It was just a wild hair," recalled Akers, who flew Capra to Knoxville for the Tennessee event, and he stayed at the old Atkin estate on the south side of town. The 83-year-old director talked about the importance of speed and pace in his comedies, about modern special effects of the *Star Wars* era (they impressed him), and about dealing with Jimmy Stewart's disillusionment with Hollywood, a crisis of faith that almost ended his career until Barrymore convinced him of the importance of entertainment. Capra may have been the highest-profile Hollywood director who spoke to the public in Knoxville, but the visit drew only polite attention from local newspapers. Still, the theater was packed for one of his talks, and another drew several hundred.

Though he hadn't made a movie in decades, Capra's fame swelled later in the 1980s, as his movies became available on tape and on cable, and one in particular half-forgotten film was just becoming a holiday classic on television. Somehow, in years to come, it would become one of the first movies ever released on DVD. But when Capra referred to *It's a Wonderful Life* in 1980, it's likely that most in the audience, especially those under 50, weren't familiar with it.

FRANK CAPRA

Linda Whitmire, center, speaks with the Tennessee/Burwell maintenance man Jim Hensley and an unidentified woman in the Orchestra Foyer in late 1980. Note the carpet and draperies, dating from the 1966 remodel. The carpet was soon replaced in the 1982 renovation, but the curtains hung until 2003.

ORCHESTRA FOYER IN 1980

At the time, the Tennessee was quietly for sale. After the theater chain's lease was up, the building reverted in ownership to the grandchildren and great-grandchildren of C.B. Atkin, the real estate developer who had died almost 50 years earlier. They favored saving the old dame somehow, but they weren't entertainment-industry professionals. And if Knoxville, circa 1980, had much practical need for the Tennessee Theatre, it was hard to prove.

In an era of small-house multiplexes, the large single-screen movie theater was just over. The numbers didn't work anymore.

For live performances, the larger, cleaner, more modern Civic Auditorium was only 20 years old, and had much handier parking. The university's Clarence Brown Theatre was even newer than that; since 1970 it had drawn most of Knoxville's market for live drama, while also showing some special-interest vintage and foreign movies. The Bijou, two blocks down the street, which had declined for most of the Tennessee's glory years, was a renovated acoustic marvel, and seemed to be the answer to any city's need for an historic theater. What American city Knoxville's size could support two historic theaters?

At least one prospective buyer, given a tour of the Tennessee, was overheard to marvel at the old movie palace's "wasted space." Some prospective buyers were reportedly interested in gutting the building for offices.

Space was at a premium. Downtown's decline was obvious, and some believed the suburban wisdom that lack of free parking was the main problem. Although the Tennessee was never publicly slated for demolition, more than one witness to that era remembers hearing proposals that the Tennessee be torn down to make way for a city parking garage.

The four years since the Tennessee had stopped showing first-run movies had seen mixed results at best, and in 1981, downtown's future was hardly assured. The venerable S&W, the elegant cafeteria paired with the Tennessee in the minds of a few generations as a Night on the Town, closed for good, suggesting no obvious future for that large old hulk near the Tennessee. The S&W would remain empty for more than a quarter-century to come.

And after five years, the Riviera remained quiet. The Tennessee would be an exception, largely thanks to an unlikely savior.

NEW DIRECTIONS

CHAPTER 8

The Tennessee was hardly an ideal investment in 1981. Still, some were interested in buying it from the Atkin family, who'd been involved in the property since the 1920s. Among them was Robert Frost, who was still interested in proving he could do something with the place.

But in June of that year, radio magnate James Dick, via his company, Dick Broadcasting, Inc., made a better offer. For $1.5 million, Dick bought the landmark. Associates said he was partly motivated by the upcoming world's fair, and the idea that an interesting old theater might play a role in it.

A native of Paris, Tennessee, Dick (1919 – 2011) had moved to Knoxville in 1947 to take a job in radio. Later, he nurtured a new station called WIVK in its early years, broadcasting little-known talents from the Everly Brothers to Dolly Parton. He built WIVK into what was reputedly the nation's most popular country music station.

Dick was a pianist himself — he kept a small keyboard in his office — and an aficionado of several musical genres, including classical. He was on the board of the Knoxville Symphony Orchestra, and upon his purchase he suggested the KSO might occasionally do concerts at the Tennessee.

Dick's manager, Bobby Denton, immediately announced sweeping changes to the Tennessee, including a new air-conditioning system, re-upholstered seats, new carpets, and new stage curtains. He also embarked on a renovation to the Mighty Wurlitzer, enlisting several professionals in that effort.

The original five chandeliers in the Grand Lobby were still there, but not altogether intact. Giving them individual names — Angie, Molly, Suzy, Windy, and Gretchen — Tim Burns, Janet Acker, and Bill Cheverton painstakingly restored them, one by one. With new crystal prisms imported from Czechoslovakia, replicas of the long-lost originals, they refurbished the chandeliers with more than 37,000 individual crystal beads.

Dick spent about $800,000 in renovations alone.

When Dick bought the theater, it had rarely hosted classical music in almost half a century, since that one KSO benefit in 1936. The KSO had performed in various locations around town, but its home had been the Civic Auditorium since its completion in 1961. Dick's connection to the KSO reintroduced the symphony to the Tennessee, but gradually.

FLAGS REPRESENTING WORLD'S FAIR PARTICIPANTS · 1982

The first year of Dick's ownership, the KSO's smaller chamber orchestra, under the baton of Maestro Zoltan Rozsnyai, settled in at the Tennessee for a season, favoring its acoustics to that of their previous home, the Civic Auditorium. It had certain advantages, including even that old Wurlitzer. An April 1982 chamber concert included a Poulenc organ concerto, to be played by local church organist William Brice.

For a while, watching serious symphonic music in the old movie palace might have seemed a temporary novelty, and in fact the chamber group eventually settled at the cozier Bijou. But hundreds more classical concerts would follow. It was the beginning of a marriage of Jim Dick's two favorite causes.

"Jim was just a wonderful human being," Snyder recalled later. "A very gentle but determined person. He was strongly committed to his ideas"—and chief among them was making the Tennessee Theatre "the premier arts and entertainment venue in East Tennessee."

Some of Dick's 1981 ideas never came to pass. He also proposed opening a restaurant on the ground floor of the Burwell, one with an entrance directly into the Tennessee's lobby. Although a New York-themed restaurant-bar called the Exchange opened in the corner space, the planned entrance into the lobby was never constructed.

Projecting Broadway-style shows in the Tennessee's future, but recognizing the problem with the shallow stage, Dick first suggested that the stage be extended into the audience section, covering the old orchestra pit. That problem would be addressed 20 years later, with a much more ambitious solution.

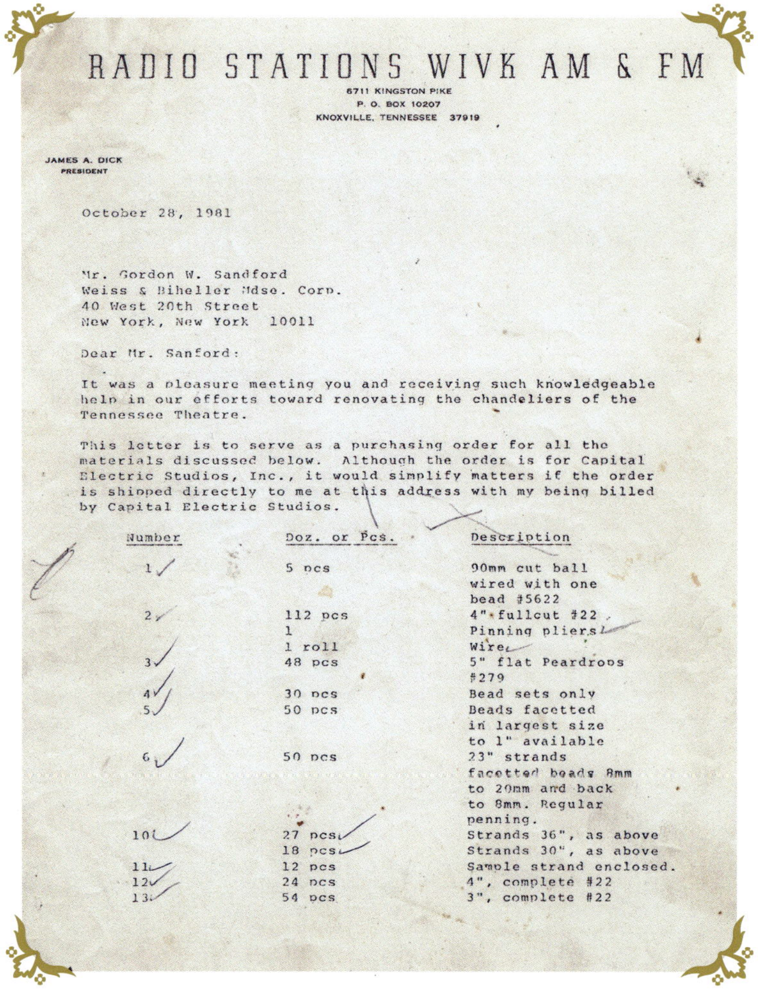

RADIO STATIONS WIVK AM & FM
6711 KINGSTON PIKE
P. O. BOX 10207
KNOXVILLE, TENNESSEE 37919

JAMES A. DICK
PRESIDENT

October 28, 1981

Mr. Gordon W. Sandford
Weiss & Biheller Mdse. Corp.
40 West 20th Street
New York, New York 10011

Dear Mr. Sanford:

It was a pleasure meeting you and receiving such knowledgeable help in our efforts toward renovating the chandeliers of the Tennessee Theatre.

This letter is to serve as a purchasing order for all the materials discussed below. Although the order is for Capital Electric Studios, Inc., it would simplify matters if the order is shipped directly to me at this address with my being billed by Capital Electric Studios.

Number	Doz. or Pcs.	Description
1	5 pcs	90mm cut ball wired with one bead #5622
2	112 pcs	4" fullcut #22
	1	Pinning pliers
	1 roll	Wire
3	48 pcs	5" flat Peardrops #279
4	30 pcs	Bead sets only
5	50 pcs	Beads facetted in largest size to 1" available
6	50 pcs	23" strands facetted beads 8mm to 20mm and back to 8mm. Regular penning.
10	27 pcs	Strands 36", as above
	18 pcs	Strands 30", as above
11	12 pcs	Sample strand enclosed.
12	24 pcs	4", complete #22
13	54 pcs	3", complete #22

ORDER FOR CHANDELIER CRYSTALS

JAMES A. DICK

1919 - 2011

Still, it was clear that Dick was thinking outside the box, almost literally, and that his era would be altogether different from anything before it. So many things had happened in the theater over the decades that there were few things left that had never

WORLD OF WONDERS BROCHURE

happened there, but one was a French film festival, sponsored at the Tennessee in February 1982. Over the next several years, the Tennessee's offerings would be remarkably eclectic, keeping the popular classic-film model but adding an extraordinary variety of live entertainment, from classical music to gospel to rock to experiments with Broadway-style shows.

On April 1, 1982, thanks to Dick's initiative, the Tennessee Theatre earned a listing in the National Register of Historic Places, just three and a half years after its age made it eligible. It had been a long time since the Tennessee was the center of that kind of attention. The theater may have gotten a fast-track approval thanks to an upcoming event; the listing came just four weeks before the opening of Knoxville's World's Fair.

That April 9, Reba McEntire performed at the Tennessee. Barely 28, she had just recently scored a few hits on the country charts, but was not yet an arena superstar.

Though the theater was four blocks from the nearest gate to the big six-month exposition, it played a role in that unprecedented party almost daily, serving as a sort of theatrical pavilion. The theater hosted a regular film about world's fairs, *World of Wonders*, narrated by Knoxville's most successful Broadway star, double-Tony-winner John Cullum.

The same tall, deep-voiced fellow on the film would be on stage, in person, as part of the biggest World's Fair-related event on Gay Street. That extraordinary summer was the debut of a new musical drama called *The Conversion of Buster Drumwright*—eventually billed, simply, as *Drumwright*. Based on a Jesse Hill Ford script, a reworking of a story that had been nationally televised 20 years before, the makeover included new songs written by a Nashville songwriting team. Cullum would direct the production and play a leading role, alongside local singer-actor Jim Turner, a sometime Broadway performer who was better known by 1982 as a regular on *The Lawrence Welk Show*. Also in the cast was Cullum's teenage son, J.D. Cullum.

For the female lead, producers had eyed Nashville singer Lynn Anderson, whose "Rose Garden" had been a major crossover hit a decade before. Her presence would have guaranteed crowds from the fair, and negotiations were reportedly underway just weeks before the play was to open. But when *Drumwright* opened in late June, the role was filled by Bobbi Jo Lathan, a Texas actress on the brink of a TV career, but unknown in 1982.

To make things worse, the Broadway professionals found the Tennessee lacking in several respects, perhaps as Helen Hayes had, 46 years earlier. Its stage and backstage were too shallow, its lighting was very limited, and the floor didn't offer the facility to move large sets around.

Though *Drumwright* drew positive local reviews, audiences were sparse, some shows playing to fewer than 100 people. It turned out to be hard to compete with a World's Fair. The play closed in mid-August, earlier than hoped, but its final show drew 1,163. Producers cheerfully spoke of another production lined up in Nashville later that year, and allowed rumors of a Kennedy

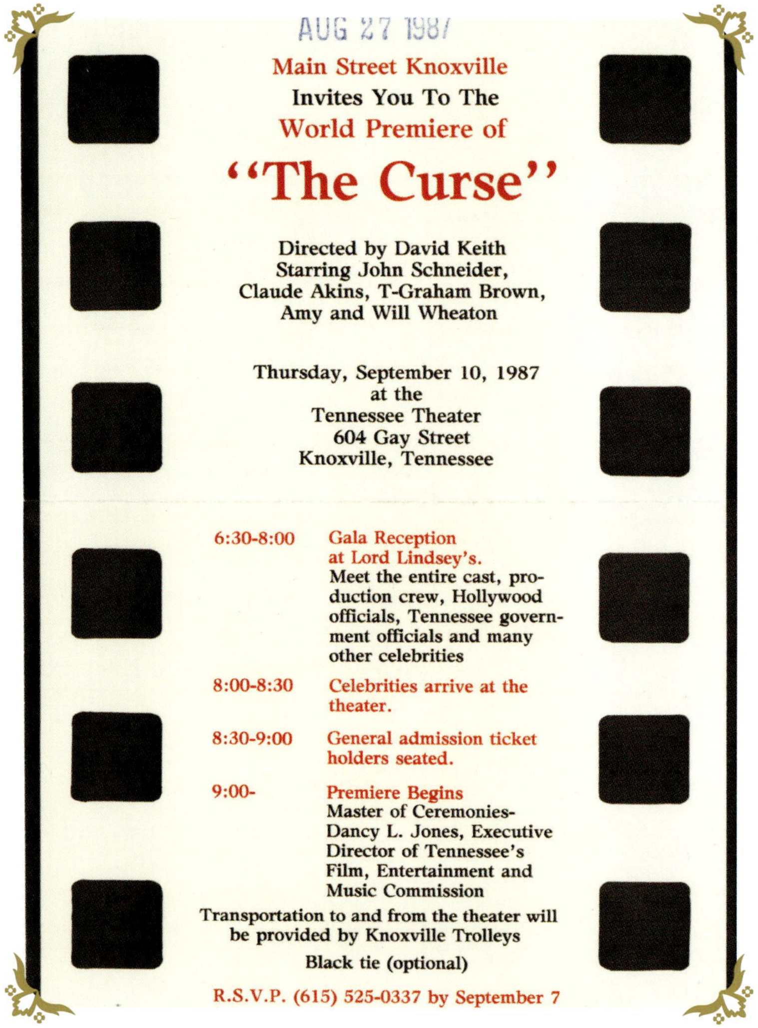

AUG 27 1987

Main Street Knoxville
Invites You To The
World Premiere of

"The Curse"

Directed by David Keith
Starring John Schneider,
Claude Akins, T-Graham Brown,
Amy and Will Wheaton

Thursday, September 10, 1987
at the
Tennessee Theater
604 Gay Street
Knoxville, Tennessee

6:30-8:00	Gala Reception at Lord Lindsey's. Meet the entire cast, production crew, Hollywood officials, Tennessee government officials and many other celebrities
8:00-8:30	Celebrities arrive at the theater.
8:30-9:00	General admission ticket holders seated.
9:00-	Premiere Begins Master of Ceremonies- Dancy L. Jones, Executive Director of Tennessee's Film, Entertainment and Music Commission

Transportation to and from the theater will be provided by Knoxville Trolleys

Black tie (optional)

R.S.V.P. (615) 525-0337 by September 7

INVITATION TO "THE CURSE" PREMIERE

Center performance. Drumwright never made it to Broadway. But its 58-show run made it Knoxville's longest-ever production of a dramatic play. In spite of the disappointments, an estimated 25,000 people saw *Drumwright* in the Tennessee Theatre.

Some might have assumed the Tennessee's era of "world premieres" ended back in the mid-'60s, the last days of the theater's regional primacy as a first-run movie venue. But in July, during *Drumright*'s World's Fair run, the theater hosted the premiere of a family comedy called *Six Pack*, starring Kenny Rogers, Diane Lane, and Erin Grey. It was popular singer and TV star Rogers' first theatrical release. A younger generation might remember *Six Pack* as the film debut of Anthony Michael Hall, the teenage actor soon to be associated with the Hollywood Brat Pack. It's not clear he attended the event, but Rogers and his wife, Marianne Gordon, a semi-familiar actress herself, did attend, and thousands jammed Gay Street to greet him. Among others who attended were the movie's producer, Michael Trikilis, who happened to be Gordon's ex-husband — he later made a career producing *Playboy* videos — and director Daniel Petrie, who'd made the groundbreaking *A Raisin in the Sun*, 20 years earlier, and who had recently been in charge of some major movies starring the likes of Laurence Olivier and Paul Newman.

Five years later, actor and recent Golden Globe nominee David Keith, a Knoxville native, chose the Tennessee to unveil his own rare directorial effort, a horror movie called *The Curse*, based on an H.P. Lovecraft story. The movie's actors, including well-known television actors Claude Akins, John Schneider, and Wil Wheaton, attended, after a gala reception at the Lord Lindsey.

SHOW POSTER · 1982

On September 30, 1982, while the World's Fair was still on, the one and only Cab Calloway stepped onto the Tennessee's stage to present a show called "Cotton Club Revisited." At age 74, the 1930s swing showman still had it, and was popular with a new generation, thanks to his recent appearance in a movie called *The Blues Brothers*. He performed what was described as a "Razzmatazz Musical Journey Down Memory Lane," with renditions of "Get Happy" and "Goodtime Charlie's Got the Blues."

The following month, the World's Fair's last, the Tennessee hosted an "animation festival" in the room where East Tennesseans saw *Snow White* for the first time.

As the big fair closed, Dick hired an old friend of the Tennessee, Robert Frost, to be its general manager.

Drumwright might have disappointed some of its producers and promoters, but it brought the prospect of the Tennessee as a performing arts venue out in the open.

A lively new era opened for the Tennessee one evening in February 1984, when a brash young jazz fan, still in his 20s, organized a concert by two of the nation's most popular jazz-fusion stars,

vibraphonist Gary Burton and keyboardist Chick Corea. It was a success, and the very first of hundreds of Tennessee Theatre shows promoted by Ashley Capps. Then best known as a public-radio announcer, Capps was in the early years of a remarkable career that would lead him to help create one of the world's most popular rock festivals.

The Corea-Burton show at the Tennessee must have been a surprise in the days when most shows that big went to UT or the Civic Auditorium. Few Knoxvillians came to Gay Street at night, except when there was something happening at the Bijou, and downtown often seemed abandoned. To Capps, who'd grown up watching new movies at the Tennessee, the old theater seemed a natural. He'd seen successful shows in historic theaters in New York and elsewhere. The famous Fillmore East, known by the late '60s as the "Church of Rock 'n' Roll," was an elaborately exotic old 1920s movie palace not unlike the Tennessee.

The Tennessee's unusual shape presented some acoustical challenges, Capps noted, but compensated, in part, by bringing more audience closer to the stage than is possible in most theaters. "Using the Bijou and the Tennessee for shows seemed a logical thing to do," Capps thought. "Why would you not do that?"

Encouraged, a few local performing arts organizations, like the Tennessee Valley Players and the Appalachian Ballet Company, began mounting live productions at the old movie theater.

The most ambitious of them was the nine-year-old Knoxville Opera Company, then under the direction of its new conductor from Texas, Robert Lyall. When they began performing there, it brought up decades-old complaints about both the depth of the stage and the size of the orchestra pit, which limited their prospective repertoire. Still, they accomplished some impressive feats, sometimes featuring performers so famous even non-opera fans knew their names. The great Roberta Peters performed there in the title role of *Lucia di Lammermoor* in November 1984. A year later, Jerome Hines appeared as Mephistopheles in Gounod's *Faust.* And in April 1986, opera fans enjoyed a treat extremely rare in most opera repertoire: a visit from a composer who conducted the performance. Carlisle Floyd appeared to conduct his best-known opera, the Tennessee-based *Susannah.* The performance was filmed and broadcast regionally on public television.

During the early part of Dick's ownership of the theater, the Knoxville Symphony Orchestra was still committed to the Civic Auditorium. According to Tim Burns, the day of reckoning came after the opera had already been using the Tennessee. "What really pushed the KSO to move from the Auditorium was a concert that they had there in November or December of 1984. There was also a rock show going on at the same time in the Coliseum, and the sound bled over into the Auditorium." They shared a wall, and amplified rock is hard to control. After 22 years in the Civic Auditorium, the KSO felt compelled to look for other venues, and Mr. Dick was happy to oblige.

In early 1985, the Tennessee got a more thorough checkup than it had ever had before. Robert C. Coffeen, an engineer and nationally recognized acoustical consultant, came to the Tennessee to appraise its sound. Some were skeptical about whether an old plaster-adorned movie palace could be any better, acoustically, than the modern Civic Auditorium, which was designed for big live performances.

"I think you have a great place here," Coffeen said. "And there is so much you can do with it." The theater wasn't acoustically

ROBERTA PETERS

KSO UNDERNEATH THE ACOUSTIC CLOUDS · 1985

perfect, he said, but much better than average, and could be much improved with the addition of some basic acoustical aids, like an orchestra shell.

The verdict surprised some, but confirmed a quiet rumor among musicians that the Tennessee sounded better than the Civic Auditorium. Guest conductor Paul Polivnick, filling in after the departure of Rozsnyai, came out and said so.

The following season of 1985–86, the Knoxville Symphony Orchestra began using the Tennessee on a regular basis, under the baton of English-born conductor Kirk Trevor, who oversaw the introduction of an orchestra shell on the Tennessee's stage, as well as 15 hanging acoustic disks known as "clouds" above the stage. Although they helped solve some sound problems, they became controversial, as years passed, because they hid some of the proscenium's elaborate detail.

The KSO launched its Tennessee Theatre era with some internationally prominent guest soloists. In October 1985, at Trevor's debut as conductor, an absent-minded young Hungarian-born pianist named Andras Schiff played a Beethoven concerto with the KSO on the Tennessee's stage; Schiff was then 31, early in his career, but coming years would bring him multiple international awards (including a Grammy for best instrumental soloist) and acclaim as one of the world's greatest interpreters of Beethoven and Bach. One year later, 19-year-old Joshua Bell, before his fame as one of the world's greatest violinists, played a Mendelssohn concerto with the KSO there. (He would return, years later, as a solo artist.) And the following September, the Japanese violinist Midori performed a Paganini concerto for a packed house at the Tennessee when she was just 15.

Meanwhile, the KSO's Pops series brought famous performers like Judy Collins and Ray Charles to the same stage. In 1985, vibraphone legend Lionel Hampton performed at the theater. It's hard to tell the story of the Tennessee without sounding like a name-dropper. In fact, no individual in history could claim to have known all the great performers who have stepped on stage at the Tennessee.

Mr. Billy Barnes came back to Knoxville to play his favorite Wurlitzer one last time to accompany the showing of *Yankee Doodle Dandy* in September 1985. His experience with the organ had spanned almost half a century.

For fans of Western movies, the Tennessee is one of the region's holiest places, ever since it introduced East Tennessee to John Wayne back in 1930, and then hosted icon Tom Mix and his

AUTOGRAPHED MOVIE POSTER · 1987

horse, Tony, in person. But rivaling those dates was April 5, 1986, when colorful Western aficionado "Marshal Andy" Smalls put together a summit conference of surviving cowboy heroes he called "Saturday Morning at the Movies." Attending were 1940s cowboy hero Sunset Carson, universally recognizable sidekick Dub Taylor, and perhaps the most dashing of all the B-Western stars, Lash Larue, the cowboy named for his bullwhip. They all appeared on the Tennessee's stage for a double feature that included Larue's classic, *The Black Lash*.

BILLY BARNES RETURNS · 1985

Actor Butterfly McQueen, whose portrayal of slaves and servants in film informed her later career as a political activist, appeared at each of three August 1987 showings of *Gone With the Wind*. She had once been ambivalent about the implied stereotypes in her memorable portrayal of Prissy, but at 76, she posed with the local winner of a Scarlett O'Hara look-alike contest. Two years later, she would participate in golden-anniversary celebrations of the famous movie.

A series of shows packed the theater with audiences expecting to see familiar television celebrities. In 1988, when WBIR, a longtime CBS affiliate, switched to NBC, it hosted a party to celebrate the move, bringing *Golden Girls* stars Betty White and Estelle Getty, plus *Night Court*'s Harry Anderson, who performed card tricks on stage.

BUTTERFLY MCQUEEN

AUTOGRAPHED SHOW POSTER · 1987

Another event that might have offered more nostalgic than dramatic appeal was a presentation of *The Odd Couple*, featuring TV comedy stars Tim Conway and Pat Harrington, in 1987. Stagehands like Tim Burns enjoyed Conway's lively humor even backstage.

Crowds would return a few years later to see old TV stars John Schneider in *Brigadoon* or Barbara Eden and Don Knotts in *Last of the Red Hot Lovers*. Eden, then 61, commented on the multi-level backstage: "At least I don't have to use my Stair-Stepper this week!"

When *MASH* star Jamie Farr was performing in a production of *Oklahoma* in summer 1990, along with John Davidson and Kim Crosby, he caused a stir among autograph-seeking tellers during a visit to a local bank.

Many of those who attended may have come just to see those TV celebrities on stage right here in Knoxville. But that trend demonstrated that some dramatic shows with modest demands could work there.

At least it could sometimes. The Fats Waller revue *Ain't Misbehavin'* worked all right. A 1989 production of the extravagant musical *Evita*, featuring Saundra Santiago, a star of the trendy detective show *Miami Vice*, was a near disaster. One technician recalled it as "embarrassing." Because of the shallow stage, two-thirds of the set had to be left on the trucks.

AUTOGRAPHED SHOW POSTER · 1990

Despite multiple efforts to save the Riviera, and premature announcements that it was indeed saved, to become a restaurant, or "ultramodern offices," or a dinner theater, the old theater, still displaying its black-and-white Charlie Chaplin mural in back, was demolished in 1988. Except for a poignant effort by the group Main Street Knoxville to save its façade, which would have called for $15,000 that apparently nobody had, there was little public complaint or press commentary. People kept saying they wanted more convenient parking downtown. Here was a new patch of it. To some old fans who hadn't been paying close attention to the old landmark, the Riviera just vanished. For years to come, old acquaintances expressed surprise upon learning it wasn't there anymore.

By then, the Tennessee's owners wanted to keep their own old movie palace around, even when community support, or a workable business plan, seemed elusive.

Ashley Capps, who by then had started his own regular music promotion company, AC Entertainment, had been presenting a few live shows a year at the Tennessee. In the early days, the crew was learning from mistakes. A show by electric-guitar icon Johnny Winter drew crowds to their feet, and to the front of the auditorium, unaware they were standing on a slim covering for the orchestra pit, which eventually collapsed. "We're very, very lucky no one was hurt," Capps recalled later.

Most AC shows were by former stars like Leon Russell — major performers but perhaps no longer at the arena-filling peaks of their popularity — or Lyle Lovett, a cult figure whose star was just rising.

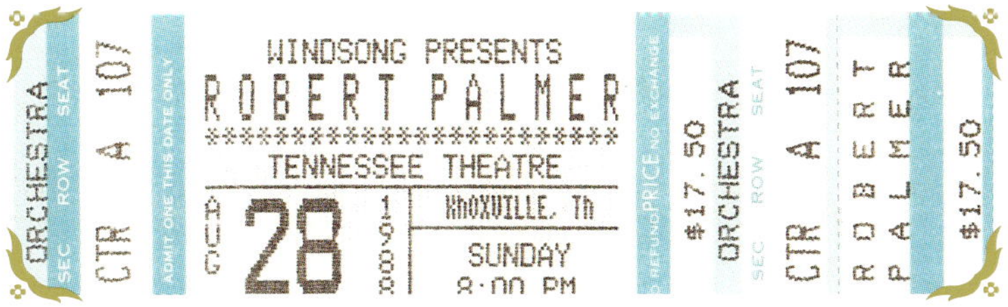

On August 28, 1988, Capps got a surprise call that turned out to be a serendipitous moment in the Tennessee's history, a new sort of landmark. British superstar Robert Palmer, whose MTV-fueled popularity was at its height — "Simply Irresistible" was peaking on the U.S. charts that month — needed to fill an unexpected gap in his American tour. Capps put him at the Tennessee. "It was one of my first experiences with an instantaneous sellout," he said.

In August 1992, the Everly Brothers returned to the Tennessee for the first time since 1954, when they were customers slipping into the theater licking their wounds after being fired from Cas Walker's live country show just a few doors down the sidewalk. Performing with virtuoso guitarist Albert Lee and a band, the Everlys drew 1,150, not a sellout, but probably the largest crowd who'd ever seen them in the city where they spent their formative years before breakout success as rock legends. They played all their old hits like "Bye Bye Love" and the Knoxville-inspired "Cathy's Clown" and told the story of the last time they were in that room. "We were out there," said Don Everly, pointing to where they sat. "Now we're up here."

Meanwhile, the KSO and Knoxville Opera kept putting on memorable shows. Some especially remember two successive revues, in 1993 and 1994, featuring Broadway star Laurie Beechman (one of Broadway's early Grizzabellas, from *Cats*, among other roles), who appeared alongside versatile television performer Ron Raines and Tony winner Michael McGuire, from the original Broadway cast of *Les Miserables*. The show, organized in cooperation with Knoxville Opera, was billed as "Music of the Night." Although Beechman was an energetic performer in her early 40s when she appeared at the Tennessee, she was near the end of her life; she died of cancer at age 44.

But perhaps the most famous opera star in modern history sang at the Tennessee without an audience. In October 1990, Luciano Pavarotti, the black-bearded Italian tenor at the height of his global renown, came to Knoxville to perform an arena show at Thompson-Boling Arena, but the night before, came to the Tennessee to rehearse in an empty theater.

The Tennessee was more versatile than its planners and promoters projected. During its first 60-odd years, it rarely

TENOR LUCIANO PAVAROTTI · 1990

if ever served as a lecture hall. It showed movies, and live performances of singing, dancing, or acting, and any talking was done in conjunction with those noisier attractions. A new wrinkle appeared on October 15, 1991, when Pat Conroy, the 45-year-old Southerner who authored *The Prince of Tides*, spoke on the Tennessee's stage. Notably given the venue, three of his semi-autobiographical novels had become major motion pictures, two of them Oscar contenders.

The sellout, extraordinary for an author in a venue of that size, was a fundraiser for the Friends of the Library, and the non-profit was sufficiently encouraged to try it again a year later when novelist William Kennedy, the Pulitzer-winning author of *Ironweed*, which had also been a major motion picture, spoke there. A third author appeared in January 1994 and was such a legend that the fact he spoke at the Tennessee might, to some readers, be the theater's single greatest moment. John Updike had recently won his second Pulitzer, and so many other prizes that he was already counted among the greatest American novelists of the 20th century, but he wasn't the movie star, or the Southerner, that Conroy was. Maybe those facts, combined with bad weather, accounted for the fact that that turnout was disappointing. The non-profit moved its annual author events to the smaller Bijou.

Dick worked with several WIVK staffers on tending to the theater, including radio personality Mickey Dearstone, "the Voice of the Lady Vols," who proved himself adept at working with the theater. In 1994, Bob Frost stepped down after 12 years as manager, and Dearstone took his place.

At 77, Dick, widely acclaimed as the savior of the Tennessee, and known to have invested about $3 million in the theater, was reconsidering his role. After 15 years, it was still losing money. Not much, relatively, but too much to justify it as a functional private business. After almost half a century in the entertainment business, Jim Dick wanted to find a responsible way to take a big step back from the daily struggle of keeping the lights on.

He first offered to donate the Tennessee Theatre to the City of Knoxville, with the proviso that the government assume responsibility for taking care of it. Victor Ashe's administration considered Dick's offer, but asked for a private endowment of $2.5 million to cover maintenance of the complicated old place. Unwilling to mount a fundraising campaign for that purpose, Dick told a reporter that he was frankly "demoralized."

He offered the same deal to UT, which had begun its life on that plot of ground. Even with former Chancellor Snyder's encouragement, they declined too.

The Tennessee's future was anything but assured. At a time when much of Gay Street, as well as Market Square, was still vacant and downtown often seemed deserted on evenings and weekends — especially when there wasn't a big show — it was hard to blame the skeptical.

Ashley Capps worried. "I was surprised when they said no," Capps said. "But when they did, my first response was, 'Oh, no, what's going to happen?' By then we were scheduling eight to ten shows a year there, and we didn't want to lose it."

He called Dick to set up a meeting at Dick Broadcasting headquarters, and proposed that AC Entertainment assume

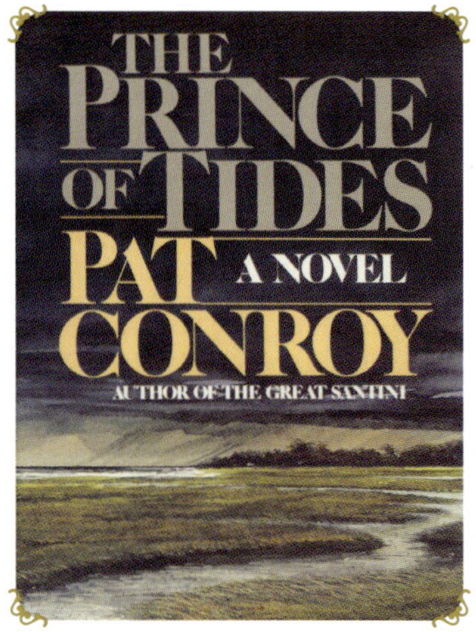

THE PRINCE OF TIDES

IRONWEED

management of the historic Tennessee Theatre. At the time, Capps had never managed anything but a small basement nightclub that, while impressive in its live-music lineups, didn't survive more than a couple of years. He and Dick were more than 30 years apart in age, and, despite Capps' occasional success with booking shows at the Tennessee, they didn't know each other well.

"As far as he knew, in his eyes I was just a punk kid promoting rock concerts. I had never managed a theater. But by then I had experience promoting shows in historic theaters across the South," Capps recalled. "Most of those were poorly managed, poorly run. I knew what not to do."

BRUCE HARTMANN

HTTF PRESIDENT
1996 - 2010

Perhaps lacking other options, Dick responded positively to Capps' offer, and called Bill Snyder for a meeting. He wanted to set up a non-profit to take care of the theater indefinitely, and he wanted Snyder to serve on its board of directors. As the organist and former chancellor took a leadership role in the future of the theater, Dick worked out details with attorney Bill Davis, Sr., and in May 1996, Dick announced the formation of the Historic Tennessee Theatre Foundation (HTTF).

To lead it, Pilot magnate Jim Haslam, whom Dick had recruited as a board member, nominated Bruce Hartmann, well-connected publisher of the *News Sentinel*, to be its first president. Originally from New Jersey, Hartmann had moved to Knoxville in the '80s, long after the Tennessee's movie era, when Dick was struggling with various strategies to keep it open.

"He was just a very charismatic personality," Hartmann says, "very dedicated to Knoxville, and he had a love for the Tennessee Theatre. He put his own money into it for a long time."

"I don't know a whole lot about running a theater," Hartmann admitted.

"You'll figure it out," Haslam responded.

AC was the management company that would keep it booked.

Within six months, the theater was profitable for the first time since the first-run cinema era. "We proved it had a purpose in the 21st century," said Capps.

"He ended up being so supportive and appreciative," recalled Capps of the perhaps-skeptical Dick. "He loved that theater, and appreciated having someone else come in who loved it too."

The well-connected music enthusiast, who'd already brought many heavy-hitters to the theater over the previous 15 years, conjured a steady stream of major rock, jazz, and country acts, including several legendary figures, at the Tennessee. The first act AC booked in its tenure as the Tennessee's official managing company was the alt-rock band Cowboy Junkies. And one early booking posed a dilemma.

For years during Dick's tenure, one of the Tennessee's most regular customers was octogenarian gospel impresario Reverend J. Bazzell Mull and his semi-regular gospel jamboree Mull's Singing Convention.

Singer-songwriter Shawn Colvin could only come on one of Mull's nights. AC budged Mull out of his expected spot, but the legendary preacher didn't balk at keeping his business at the Tennessee until management started charging a 50-cent-per-ticket preservation fee. Mull moved his show to Sevierville.

AC ENTERTAINMENT STAFF · 1996

The team at AC Entertainment in 1996 handled booking, marketing, production, and management of the Tennessee Theatre.

Front, left to right: Ashley Payne, Ashley Capps, and Monica Galloway. Rear, left to right: Tom Bugg, Troy Sellers, and Matthew Range.

MARY COSTA

CLIPPING FROM THE KNOXVILLE NEWS SENTINEL SEPTEMBER 13, 1997

To help manage the Tennessee, Capps hired a man he'd first known as a bartender at Capps' short-lived Old City nightclub, Ella Guru's. Tom Bugg had helped with shows at the Bijou, and figured out a system to keep up with audiences' beer demand. He had an unexpected challenge with some early acts. When Ani Difranco played at the Tennessee, the cult-following singer-songwriter had reportedly gotten death threats over a personal issue, and her people demanded guards at every entrance throughout the show.

When Ray Charles returned for a visit, his people boosted the previous asking price by $6,000. AC had already been promoting the show, and knew the change would put it out of any possibility of breaking even. They presented it anyway, partly for the publicity value.

Occasionally, a local band would play there. One of Knoxville's most popular rock bands of the 1990s, the V-Roys, earned some national attention through Billboard and late-night television, especially through the support of their producer, Steve Earle. The title of their 1996 debut album, *Just Add Ice*, was an inside joke, considering that attorneys had advised the band to abandon their original name, the Viceroys, due to a copyright-infringement issue. The V-Roys made a practice of big shows at the Tennessee, especially on New Year's Eve, and their album cover showed its marquee, with the album title proclaimed there.

The theater hosted a short film festival when the National Film Registry, on a coast-to-coast tour, made their only Tennessee state stop at the Tennessee Theatre in March 1997, and over a period of three days showed about a dozen films deemed important by the authoritative organization, from the Marx Brothers' *Duck Soup* to *Dr. Strangelove*.

SEPTEMBER 12, 1997

One of many offbeat events that proved the diversity of the Tennessee's legacy was in September 1997, when the theater hosted the world's only "premiere" of the DVD of Disney's 1957 film, *Sleeping Beauty*. On hand was an audience regular at the Tennessee, Knoxville native Mary Costa, who supplied the singing voice for the title character. After a parade on Gay Street, attended by costumed characters from the animated film, the sold-out event raised money for ChildHelp USA, one of Costa's favorite charities.

Among the greatest singer-songwriters in the history of country music, Johnny Cash played at the Tennessee on October 23, 1997. Ashley Capps met Cash backstage for the first time. "Hi,

ENNESSE THEATRE?

In 1998, when actor Jake Gyllenhaal walked down Gay Street, he didn't turn heads. Just 17 years old, he was not yet famous, but playing the lead role in a movie about the youth of rocket scientist Homer Hickam. The movie, to be called October Sky, was set in the late 1950s, mostly in coal-mining country, the reason director Joe Johnston, between his films Jumanji and Jurassic Park III, chose to do the shooting on location in East Tennessee. But for a scene ostensibly set in downtown Indianapolis, Johnston liked Gay Street. The picturesque urban setting was perfect for a couple of shots set in downtown Indianapolis, and he liked having a movie theater marquee in the picture. But there was one problem. Indianapolis was unlikely to have a theater called the Tennessee. They solved it, sort of, by temporarily removing the first and last letters of the problematic state's name, yielding the "Ennesse Theatre," briefly visible in the final cut of the movie.

MODIFIED MARQUEE FOR OCTOBER SKY · 1998

PAT SUMMITT WITH LILY TOMLIN · FEBRUARY 2010

I'm Johnny Cash," he introduced himself in his trademark rumble, before giving a show that included all his classic hits like "Ring of Fire" and "I Walk the Line."

No one expected it, least of all Cash, but it turned out to be one of his final full-length shows. His assistants never knew how ill the 65-year-old legend was until he played the Tennessee. He stumbled down the stairs backstage. Cash played one more show that year, in Michigan, but canceled the rest of his tour due to a health crisis, an obscure neurological disorder that troubled his final years. He recovered enough to play a couple of short shows in New York in 1999, and later did several small-audience shows at the Carter Family Fold outside of Bristol, Virginia, before his death in 2003. His legend has only grown since then.

Most of the Tennessee's "world premiere" experience had been with fiction-oriented motion pictures. March 9, 1998, saw an unusual event that drew lots of dignitaries, many in black tie, including Governor Don Sunquist and Congressman Jimmy Duncan. HBO doesn't always host world premieres for its documentaries before they're actually broadcast, but this one seemed to call for it. *A Cinderella Season: The Lady Vols Fight Back* was the story of UT's women's basketball team's astonishing come-from-behind national championship the year before. On hand for the premiere was former player Abby Conklin, assistant coach Holly Warlick, and already famous head coach Pat Head Summitt, who would mention the gala evening in her upcoming book, *Raise the Roof*. The makers of the 75-minute film, Jon Alpert and Maryann DeLeo, were there too, not as famous as they would be in years to come, which would bring them both Academy Award nominations. DeLeo would win the 2004 Oscar for her documentary, *Chernobyl Heart*.

Summitt, Warlick, and other legends of women's basketball would return to the Tennessee in years to come, when it hosted the annual Women's Basketball Hall of Fame induction ceremonies. Honorees who walked across the Tennessee's stage include championship coaches Van Chancellor, Gene Auriemma, Sue Gunter, and Lin Dunn.

The Tennessee hosted several performers associated with Knoxville's own musical history, in connection with the East Tennessee Historical Society's "Cradle of Country Music" tour in 1998. The Everlys returned for a second show. Charlie Louvin, the surviving half of the Louvin Brothers, played one of their signature songs, the ancient murder ballad "Knoxville Girl" — but only after the audience demanded it, in an encore, and after he shyly apologized for the content of the grisly lyrics.

One of the most influential figures in popular music performed at the Tennessee, probably for the first time. At 74, Chet Atkins had all but retired from touring, but was persuaded to make an emotional return to Gay Street, where he had begun his radio career in the 1940s. On the afternoon of June 12, 1998, he walked around town some, reminiscing and attending the dedication of a plaque in his honor. And that night he played his famous guitar with a band before an adoring crowd at the Tennessee. Although Atkins lived another three years, and played a bit here and there, it's been claimed by some national sources that the Tennessee Theatre show was Atkins' last full concert.

Neither Cash nor Atkins' shows seemed fateful. But it's worth noting that both legends of American popular music, who might have retired from the stage a bit earlier than they did, made time for one more full-tilt show at the Tennessee.

On its 70th birthday in October 1998, the Tennessee threw a party. By then, the HTTF was considering a major renovation that went far beyond previous renovations. They weren't sure what shape it would take, and hired the New York firm of Hardy Holzman Pfeiffer as consultants to look at the Tennessee and see what could be done with it. Architect Malcolm Holzman arrived and was surprised at what he found. He'd seen a lot of old movie palaces that had been picked apart over the years. The Tennessee was almost intact. "The community is so remarkably fortunate that 90 percent is still there."

It wouldn't be easy, though. The firm offered several options for improving the Tennessee, each one in the millions of dollars, ranging from a thorough spruce-up to a comprehensive reinvention of the theater as an unusual performing arts center.

BILL COSBY WITH ASSISTANT MANAGER HEATHER SEIBER · 2009

A publicity rush helped, a little at least. *Southern Living*'s Tennessee edition included a feature about the Tennessee and its prospects.

Bill Cosby came to the Tennessee, the first of several visits, to help raise funds. Things had changed. Cosby would not have been allowed in the door, even as a paying customer, 40 years earlier, but in 1998 he was here helping raise funds for its preservation, and was so popular his appearance sold out within 36 hours of the announcement.

KENNY CHESNEY FILMS A MUSIC VIDEO AT THE TENNESSEE · JUNE 30, 1994

EVELYN GLENNIE WITH KSO · OCTOBER 1998

JOHNNY CASH · OCTOBER 23, 1997

JOSHUA BELL · 1986

KIRK TREVOR AND THE KSO · 1985

V-ROYS · 1999

JOHN UPDIKE · 1994

WILLIE NELSON · FEBRUARY 1999

CHET ATKINS · 1998

Ebet Roberts

CLINCH AVENUE STAIRWELL

RUN-DOWN DRESSING ROOM

AUDITORIUM WITH 1960S SEATING

BACKSTAGE DETERIORATION

FAILING PLASTER IN CLINCH AVENUE STAIRWELL

Cosby wanted to help, but like many artists, made one very specific request: in his case, it was for a salad with specified sorts of lettuce, radicchio, and other certain ingredients. Bugg called several well-reputed restaurants, and none could comply. So Bugg just drove to the grocery, went home, and made Bill Cosby a salad. After delivering it, he got a call. "Mr. Cosby wants to see you." The legendary comedian wanted to tell Bugg that he loved the salad. He was surprised to learn that Bugg made it himself.

In 1999 the Tennessee State Legislature in Nashville gave the Tennessee the singular designation State Theater of Tennessee — perhaps especially remarkable considering the state's capital city had become famous for live entertainment. Nashville had the Ryman, but didn't have a historic movie theater.

The Tennessee had rarely been involved in anything but entertainment, but in 1999 some private developers promoting a massive plan called Renaissance Knoxville presented it to an almost-packed house of the interested public. It may have been the largest group in Knoxville history ever assembled to consider a municipal-improvement issue. The controversial plan flopped, but may have catalyzed interest in downtown's revival.

A year later, the large-scale "visioning process" known as *Nine Counties. One Vision.* held some of its largest public meetings at the Tennessee, laying out a generally progressive series of suggestions for the city and its surrounding region.

To any audience, the Tennessee remained a point of pride. "So this is what the inside of the genie's bottle looks like," famously offbeat comedian Stephen Wright once observed from the stage, but to some professionals it was becoming clear the Tennessee needed a genie-sized miracle.

The Tennessee was deteriorating in ways more obvious to performers and those obliged to look at the theater closely. In 1999, Knoxville Opera featured a guest conductor, New York City Opera veteran Brian Salesky, to conduct *Don Giovanni*. Salesky loved the look of the theater. "It's great to put on theater in a place that's theatrical in itself, an architectural wonder," he said. He was much less impressed with the parts the audience doesn't see. "Backstage, it was totally run down, just a mess."

By that time, plans were afoot to make something even more remarkable of the old movie palace, bringing it closer to Jim Dick's ideal of a performing arts center. The turn of the century seemed a particularly propitious time to strike. After years of failed attempts to revive downtown, major investments seemed to be transforming the neighborhood, and Gay Street in particular, where bold and expensive renovations of large buildings like the Miller's Building and the Sterchi Building were bringing both business and, more surprisingly, hundreds of residents back to the old main street. And there was talk of a major city-sponsored redo of nearby Market Square.

Architect Doug McCarty, of the firm McCarty Holsaple McCarty, began consulting on the project early in the process. He'd grown up with the Tennessee. As a kid aspiring to be a race-car driver, he went to the Tennessee in 1966 to watch the James Garner movie *Grand Prix* — three times. "When you go in that space, it's just a magical experience," he said. "A fantasy, really."

Among performing arts organizations, opera had been one of the early settlers in the post-cinema Tennessee. In the dark, at least, the old movie palace resembled a European opera house more than the clean, plain Civic Auditorium, and many liked the acoustics better as well. But there were multiple problems with mounting operas at the old movie house, and the main problem may have been the toughest to fix. The shallow stage was not designed for anything more elaborate than 1920s vaudeville. Both full-production Broadway shows and grand opera seemed unlikely to figure in the Tennessee's future unless the backstage area could be significantly deepened.

One perfect-world proposal called for extending the theater all the way across State Street, supported by pillars beside Knoxville's oldest cemetery, maintained by the two-century-old First Presbyterian Church. The church objected, and so did the city until an unusual idea emerged, apparently in several minds at once, of cantilevering the theater over State Street.

"Necessity is the mother of invention," according to Capps. "The theater needed a stage twice as deep. And the stage is 22 feet above State Street, which is right behind the theater." After the city declined a proposal to hold up the extension with pillars, the cantilever option began to seem the only option.

Doug McCarty discussed the prospect at length with Nashville engineer Edwin McDougle, a Knoxville-raised member of the Nashville firm of Ross Bryan. McDougle studied it. Sure, it could work, he said.

McCarty had been consulting about the theater for some months, but working in his own office on other projects, putting off the site visit. He had an unusual opportunity. On the morning of September 11, 2001, his staff was crowded around the firm's television set, watching the horrible news. "I'm a little too hyper for that," McCarty says. He knew he couldn't work, and had to get his mind distracted. "I'll just call Tim Burns and do the tour," he thought. He spent the next three hours with Burns, above the Tennessee's dome, the eeriest part of the theater, inspecting architecture unlike anything else in the region.

1928 STAGE LOADING DOOR

Near the corner of State Street and Clinch Avenue, the 1928 loading door opened 2 stories above street level and was a constant reminder of the arduous load-in of the early days. Its position necessitated loading in from Gay Street during the modern era (1980–2003).

The mezzanine foyer just before closing in 2003. The 1982 carpet was worn and stained, and the faded draperies were leftover from 1966. The ceiling shows plaster damage which was prevalent throughout the public areas.

"I could not even concentrate on the movie. I was so upset that the Tennessee Theatre could look so sad. Where had all the glimmer and glitz gone that I remembered as a young girl?" Glenda, who lived in Knoxville until she was 15, recalls visiting family here in the 1990s and attending a movie showing at the Tennessee. "My best wishes to the restoration effort, I truly believe and support it."

GLENDA ROBINSON

MEZZANINE FOYER · 2003

REBIRTH IN A NEW CENTURY

CHAPTER 9

A huge coordinated private-led effort set out to raise an unprecedented amount of money for a performing arts facility in Knoxville. Old Tennessee stalwarts like Wallace Baumann, Jim Dick, Bruce Hartmann, and Bill Snyder were on the front lines.

The Wurlitzer required significant refurbishing, and in 2000 it was removed from the theater for the first time since its installation in 1928 and shipped to nationally known theater-organ expert Ken Crome in Reno, Nevada, for a complete overhaul. The work was expensive, reportedly $300,000. Only later was it revealed that Baumann paid the bill himself. It was re-installed a year later. On October 1, 2001, the 73rd anniversary of the theater's opening, guest organist Lyn Larsen, a recording artist from California who had worked on improving the tone of the organ, played a concert on the fresh-sounding Mighty Wurlitzer. The same evening, the Historic Tennessee Theatre Foundation publicly announced an ambitious $20 million fundraising campaign.

The campaign came with a terrible coincidence. Journalism professor and recently retired UT administrator Sammie Lynn Puett was one of the early leaders of the effort. She was killed in a car accident in Texas, just 10 days after helping launch the campaign.

Capps, looking for a theater manager, remembered a young woman, a UT music major, he'd known when he was a radio announcer at WUOT. By then Becky Hancock had been living in New York for several years, working for ASCAP and for a classical musicians' public relations firm. She'd always loved the Tennessee, though, even back to the days when she used her clarinet to bluff her way into the State Street stage door to hear KSO concerts. When Capps offered her a job managing the theater, she jumped at the opportunity to come back home and work at a landmark in the midst of a radical transformation.

Before closing for the massive renovation, in 2002 and 2003, the Tennessee had been the centerpiece of Knoxville Opera's first two Rossini Festivals. The theater presented sellout opera performances as a huge party thronged the streets outside. The attendance well into the thousands surprised even its promoters. The unusual festival captured Knoxville's imagination in ways that couldn't have been predicted. Within a few years, other downtown festivals were hitting higher marks than ever before. Anchored by the Tennessee, Rossini seemed to presage a much livelier new era of festivals and of downtown events in general.

THE KNOXVILLE SYMPHONY ORCHESTRA

BIG EARS FESTIVAL · MARCH 2014

BECKY HANCOCK

IN 2005

LYN LARSEN AT THE ORGAN REDEDICATION · OCTOBER 2001

Early in the fundraising planning, the old, unrehabilitated Tennessee earned a star turn. At the height of his fame, country star Travis Tritt shot a video there for his hit "It's a Great Day to Be Alive" in 2000.

Popular neo-folk singer-songwriter Nanci Griffith did him one better a couple of years later. She did a show at the Tennessee in March 2002, liked it, and was encouraged to use the theater as a setting for a live concert DVD called *Winter Marquee*. She wanted to come back and do another show in Knoxville for the camera, leaving AC with a dilemma: would Knoxville come out and see her do the same show again? They charged just $10 a ticket, a price just low enough to almost pack the house with a sufficiently appreciative audience. Those funds went directly to the restoration campaign.

So despite its name, *Winter Marquee* was filmed on a warm evening in late May. Though much of the associated CD was recorded elsewhere, the only marquee depicted on its case was the Tennessee's old 1950s marquee, with the words "Knoxville's Grand Entertainment Palace."

There was a bit of serendipity associated with the recording. As she introduced the song "Good Night New York," Griffith remarked casually, "speaking of my wonderful friend and sister in arms, Emmylou Harris, it just so happens she's passing through town"—and the singer, at least as famous as Griffith, stepped out on stage, to ecstatic applause, and harmonized with Griffith on the song. That moment is captured on both the CD and the DVD. Harris had performed at the Tennessee a few times before, as the headliner.

DVD ARTWORK FEATURING THE TENNESSEE MARQUEE

Once fully underway, the fundraising effort awed even the organizers. "The thing that amazed me most was the grassroots connections," says Hartmann. "The personal connections so many people had to it. The community wanted to make it succeed, and willed it that way."

The final cost of the Tennessee's transformation was close to $30 million—even adjusted for inflation, the renovation and reconstruction was arguably more costly than the actual construction of the theater. It was some 50 percent more than the original estimates, and paid for by a diverse array of sources, with federal, state, city, and county funds, each in the millions. The City of Knoxville, under Mayor Victor Ashe, who had previously declined to accept ownership of the theater, chipped in a substantial $4 million.

THE DORMANT MARQUEE

Knox County government contributed $6 million, more than might be expected. Hartmann credits County Mayor Mike Ragsdale's leadership. "He said, 'We have such a hard time doing things right in Knoxville. We want to do this right.'"

Historic tax credits accounted for about $6 million. With public funding totaling about $12 million, some 3,300 private donors, large and small, made up the rest. Perhaps the most generous corporate sponsor was Regal Entertainment Group. Regal had made substantial contributions to the Tennessee since the 1980s, and had recently donated two 35-millimeter projectors to the theater, as well as welcome advice. It's something more than a footnote in Knoxville's movie theater history that, by then, the Knoxville-based Regal operated more cinemas than any company in the world.

The restoration drive hit Knoxville on all fronts, from exclusive black-tie soirées to an unusual telethon, a June 2003 simulcast of the 1951 musical *Show Boat*, being projected to a live audience in the theater as it was being broadcast around the region on WATE-TV, the station that had begun life a couple doors down from the Tennessee in 1953.

McCarty Holsaple McCarty got the contract to guide the reconstruction from an architectural point of view; Denark got the construction contract. Both were local companies but relied heavily on national experts, most of whom were familiar with 1920s movie palaces, some of whom were specifically interested in the work of Graven and Mayger. By then, the Tennessee was one of only two substantially intact examples of their work in the nation.

LAST PERFORMANCE BEFORE CLOSING · JUNE 2003

Before the original stagehouse was demolished in late 2003, support bracing was erected in the auditorium. This stabilized the proscenium wall, which would soon become an exterior wall for most of the construction period. The proscenium opening was sealed tight to protect the interior from the elements.

SUPPORT BEAMS IN THE AUDITORIUM

What happened at the Tennessee Theatre over a period of more than a year, from mid 2003 to early 2005, was a transformation more than a restoration. It was the most painstaking renovation of any building in Knoxville history. Darlene Smolik, a tax-benefits expert who had previously been chief operating officer of the Public Building Authority, was project coordinator.

Architect Doug McCarty led the project and enlisted an international team of vintage-theater experts. The consulting architect was Paul Westlake, partner in the Cleveland, Ohio, firm of Van Dijk Westlake Reed Leskosky, along with Luis Peris, a Venezuelan-born old-theater expert. In charge of reviving the Tennessee's long-muted original colors was Jeff Greene, of New York's Evergreene Architectural Arts.

These were national experts, with extraordinarily high standards, by any accounts, but they were always as high as the standards of Wallace Baumann. By then nearing age 80, Baumann inspected each improvement, and sometimes demanded that it be thrown out and that these experts start over again.

For almost half a century the Tennessee Theatre had been content with a conventionally flamboyant '50s-style marquee, which to a couple of generations was sufficiently nostalgic. However, it was also important to Baumann that the theater

COMPLEX SCAFFOLDING IN THE AUDITORIUM

During the last renovation (2003 – 2005), the entire Grand Lobby and Auditorium, shown here, were covered in a complex scaffolding system which cost over $100,000. Painters and plaster workers were able to reach every inch of the walls and ceilings to bring them back to their 1928 grandeur.

restore an approximation of the original five-story-high vertical sign of his youth. By 2003 few remembered it, but Baumann did, and found a way to bring it back, in combination with a modern computerized marquee that informed sidewalk viewers of upcoming shows.

Naturally, considering the theater's Windy City heritage, a Chicago firm was involved too: Kirkegaard Associates considered the Tennessee's perhaps unique acoustic challenges. They were able to solve them without the widely loathed acoustic "clouds" in front of the proscenium.

Some of these national experts were already familiar with the short story of Graven & Mayger, and eager to work on one of the duo's only two intact theaters. Several connoisseurs remarked at how remarkably unspoiled the Tennessee was, compared with typical theaters of its era.

With painstaking techniques, sometimes using computer imaging, the team refashioned the interior of the theater closer to its 1928 appearance than it had been since about 1929. Along with it came significant acoustical improvements.

The most ambitious phase of the work was expanding the backstage area over State Street encroaching on the tree canopy over First Presbyterian Church's cemetery. It was much less invasive than the first idea, to extend it all the way across. The halfway cantilever option still didn't sit well with some church members, and might have been more of a problem if not for the fact that Wallace Baumann was an influential elder in that church.

It was an enormous, and enormously complex, project: more transformation than makeover. It added 19 feet to the backstage, deepening it to 45 feet. The backstage increased not just in depth, but in height, 15 more feet to accommodate modern theatrical sets, and serviced by a large new freight elevator.

Local contractor Denark Construction did the heavy lifting. When it was all over, the Tennessee became perhaps the nation's only theater with a cantilevered backstage.

The re-creation of the Tennessee added the much-better dressing rooms, partly with the help of acquiring retail space along Clinch Avenue. When it was done, the Tennessee's dressing room space had quintupled to 10,000 square feet.

There were dilemmas, some especially awkward, and one concerning unloading for show trucks, many of them large tractor-trailer rigs. One plan for ensuring access to the new backstage called for a new loading dock, and that would have called for demolishing the Glencoe, the century-old apartment building on State Street. It had been derelict for years. However, it began to seem workable for trucks to unload on one lane of State into a large new freight elevator—just as new interest in upscale residences downtown inspired a renovation of the Glencoe into an upscale residential building.

VERTICAL BLADE SIGN INSTALLATION · DECEMBER 2004

GRAND LOBBY CHANDELIERS REMOVED FOR REPAIR

RE-PAINTING THE FOYER

WORKERS LOOK INTO THE AUDITORIUM

RE-GILDING OF AUDITORIUM CEILING

AN EMPTY GRAND LOBBY

PLASTER RESTORATION IN AUDITORIUM

REFINISHING THE TERRAZZO FLOOR IN THE GRAND LOBBY

RE-PAINTING OF AUDITORIUM CEILING

THE BALCONY EMPTIED OF ITS SEATING

ORIGINAL STAGEHOUSE DEMOLITION

DEMOLITION DEBRIS

THE 1928 LOADING DOOR IS DEMOLISHED

STAGE EXTENSION OVER STATE STREET

NEW CANTILEVERED STAGEHOUSE CONSTRUCTION

THE 1956 MARQUEE IS DISMANTLED IN LATE 2004

NEW SEATING INSTALLED

WURLITZER CONSOLE ON ITS WAY TO MILLER'S BUILDING

At one point there was talk of actually adding real box seats where the faux box seats are, on either side of the balcony. It would have offered acoustical advantages for the whole theater, but might have added a few million more to the rising bill.

More doable dreams included the new elevators and other amenities for the disabled, a second bar and snack counter, upstairs restrooms, an expanded orchestra pit, a total of 13 dressing rooms, a small increase in the seating to to as many as 1,645 (depending on use of the orchestra pit), and a reverse of the 1966 balcony renovation to improve visibility of the stage.

During construction, the Mighty Wurlitzer's console — the part the audience sees — was removed for display and safe-keeping in the lobby of the Miller's Building, a little more than a block away. It was rolled there by hand, with police escort.

"It was so intense, we just didn't stop," Becky Hancock recalled later. "I lost 15 pounds. It was all worth it in the end. It was great, but it was scary." The memory of it is "one of those things I wouldn't take away for the world — but I'm not sure I'd ever want to do it again."

NEW CANTILEVERED STAGEHOUSE

LOUNGE

TENNESSEE CHILDREN'S DANCE ENSEMBLE REHEARSES ON NEW STAGE

R. B. MORRIS

ON OPENING NIGHT

BILL SNYDER

CELEBRATING AT THE MIGHTY WURLITZER

BETHEL AME CHURCH CHOIR ON OPENING NIGHT

The Tennessee reopened on January 14, 2005, with a gala almost reminiscent of the variety-show extravaganzas of the '30s, a black-tie occasion attended by philanthropists and politicians, including Governor Phil Bredesen and Mayor Bill Haslam, as well as all the people who'd been involved in its rebirth, from the theater's longtime champion Wallace Baumann to Cleveland architect Paul Westlake, who's supervised much of the renaissance. They experienced a diverse stage show titled "The Tennessee: A Waltz Through Time," written and produced by Tom Jester. Somehow that one night suggested the variety of shows to come, including the Knoxville Symphony Orchestra, Knoxville Opera, actress Carol Mayo Jenkins (Knoxville native and star in the 1980s TV drama "Fame") as Norma Desmond, local rock heroes R.B. Morris and Hector Qirko, Robinella and the C.C. String Band (featuring Cruz Contreras, who would soon front his own band, the multiple Grand Ole Opry attraction the Black Lillies), numbers by the Austin-East High School Jazz Band and the Bethel AME church choir, and the Tennessee Children's Dance Ensemble.

The next evening, the reimagined theater opened to the public at large with the same show.

The opening year coincided with the Knoxville Opera's recruitment of a new executive director, Brian Salesky, the same New York conductor who had been horrified at the theater's backstage facilities six years earlier. "What a spectacular transformation had occurred," he later recalled of his return. The hall itself was not just up to speed, but superior. Salesky called the Tennessee "certainly one of the finest acoustical theaters I've ever been in in my life. You don't need any amplification at all. Voice just shoots out to the back wall. It's an amazing place to be a performer."

AUSTIN EAST HIGH SCHOOL JAZZ BAND ON OPENING NIGHT

The new Tennessee opened onto a downtown changing so rapidly it was not exactly the same neighborhood that had bid the Tennessee farewell in 2003. The East Tennessee History Center, a huge expansion of the old Customs House, with its new entrance directly across the street from the Tennessee, had opened during the Tennessee's renovation. Hundreds more people, mostly affluent, were living downtown, dozens in the Holston Building; the 1913 office building diagonally across the street from the Tennessee became home of reportedly the most expensive condominiums in Knoxville. A few months after the Tennessee's opening, even the Burwell, previously an office building, opened to residents, and was almost instantly occupied. And, of course, the city's project to redo Market Square was completed in 2005 too, drawing more residents and new businesses. Many of these almost-simultaneous events were technically independent of the Tennessee's renovation, involving different investors, different developers — but it turned out seeming symbiotic. Many of Knoxville's affluent new residents cited the conveniences of the Tennessee's cultural offerings as one motive for their move; it seems likely the theater was helped by the presence of new residents and attractions too.

That celebratory first year after the reopening may have outmatched any other in the theater's history for sheer star power. Wynton Marsalis, Dave Brubeck, Elvis Costello, Emmylou Harris, Earl Scruggs, Lyle Lovett, B.B. King, Al Green, Doc Watson, Alison Krauss, Buddy Guy, Steve Earle, Nickel Creek, Pat Matheny, John Hiatt, Laurie Anderson and dozens of others all appeared at the Tennessee in 2005. Speakers that year included comedian Paula Poundstone, humor author David Sedaris, actor Hal Holbrook as Mark Twain, and, that September, poet Maya Angelou speaking (and singing, a little) an inspiring presentation aimed at university students.

That year, the music business greeted the theater with an unprecedented symbolic ranking. Industry organization *Pollstar* ranked the Tennessee Theatre number 47 — in the world — in ticket sales for a theater. For the Tennessee, it was the first of several appearances on *Pollstar*'s annual list of the planet Earth's 100 most popular theater venues.

The following year was hardly less impressive, spanning icons Tony Bennett and Dionne Warwick; violinist Joshua Bell; jazz saxophone legend Sonny Rollins; alternative-pop star Fiona Apple, singer-songwriters Bob Dylan, Merle Haggard, and Kris Kristofferson; and alternative groups My Morning Jacket, Old Crow Medicine Show, and Wilco. But promoters didn't forget the theater's permanent instrument. Jelani Eddington, one of the organ world's new stars, performed the first of several shows at the Tennessee that August.

WYNTON MARSALIS & ASHLEY CAPPS · MARCH 12, 2005

"The Tennessee Theatre in Knoxville ... [is among] some of the best theaters in the country."

ELVIS COSTELLO

"I'd be alright playing in places like this for the rest of my life."

JASON ISBELL

2014: BILL SNYDER AND TIM BURNS HOLD THE POSTER FROM 1979, THE FIRST SHOW THEY WORKED TOGETHER

As unlikely as it might have seemed, the Tennessee's successful revival presaged the return, after an absence of over 30 years, of first-run movies to downtown.

After first expressing skepticism of downtown movie theaters in the modern era, with encouragement (and investment) from Mayor Bill Haslam, as well as other partners in a complex, multi-part redevelopment that included the swank old S&W building, Knoxville-based Regal Cinemas built the Regal Riviera, downtown's first-ever multiplex cinema, half a block from the Tennessee, in the vacant space left years before by the demolition of the original Riviera Theatre. Opening in 2007, the eight-screen cinema was an immediate success, almost as its namesake had been, 87 years earlier. Its arrival presented a surprising new version of the old Tennessee-Riviera dynamic that had ruled Gay Street at night half a century before.

The rebirth of the Tennessee happened to coincide with its manager's development of a major new music festival. Bonnaroo, the wildly popular not-just-rock festival held every June in Coffee

County, was more than 100 miles from the Tennessee Theatre, but it put AC in touch with some major acts. Ashley Capps, in charge of booking much of Bonnaroo's talent, remained the man in charge of programming music at the Tennessee Theatre, and sometimes the festival and the theater seemed to exchange talent. Thanks to that association, and to Capps' own wide-ranging tastes and connections, the Tennessee hosted shows by some of the groundbreaking performers of their eras, including Lou Reed, Loretta Lynn, David Byrne, Joan Baez, Jackson Browne, John Legend, Burt Bacharach, Béla Fleck, Morrissey. The Tennessee Theatre's lineup in the decade after reopening could almost be used to make a documentary of influential and popular music of the previous 50 years.

Earl Scruggs, probably the world's most influential banjoist — he'd been based in Knoxville early in his career and, later on, played the Tennessee more than once — remarked to a reporter, "It's the most beautiful theater I was ever in in the United States."

Blues guitarist B.B. King performed there several times, as did Bonnie Raitt and Australian guitar virtuoso Tommy Emmanuel — who was an old friend and admirer of Chet Atkins. Crosby, Stills & Nash played there, as did Chicago and many other revived bands of the '60s and '70s.

The Broadway shows that had been problematic — and rare — since the mid-1930s returned in a big way with the "Broadway at the Tennessee" series, bringing multiple touring productions of major New York musicals to the Tennessee's newly enabled stage every year. With shows from *Les Miserables* to *American Idiot* to *Mary Poppins* to *Spamalot*, some of them with extravagant stage effects that would have been impossible at the Tennessee before 2005, the series became one of the theater's most reliable draws. Despite the legendary razzle-dazzle shows of the mid-1930s, the Tennessee has hosted more Broadway shows in the 21st century than it did in its first 75 years.

Of course the Tennessee continued to attract current performers. The modern cult phenomenon, Widespread Panic, has played two- and even three-night stands at the Tennessee, selling out each show. Alternative old-time band Old Crow Medicine Show recorded part of a concert DVD here in 2009. Just as they were gaining national attention, local favorites The Dirty Guv'nahs recorded a live album there in 2012.

When Elvis Costello, the British songwriting icon of the punk era, performed at the Tennessee in 2008, he sang a cappella and without notes the ancient (and long) murder ballad, "Knoxville Girl." He repeated the stunt on a return visit.

The theater drew a trickle of popular comedians, and seemed to suggest broadcasts and recordings to several. Kathy Griffin shot a Bravo cable special on the Tennessee's stage, and comedians Ralphie May and local favorite Henry Cho both recorded comedy DVDs in the same room.

And somehow that same room sometimes accommodated ethereally classical performers like pianist Emmanuel Ax and violinist Itzhak Perlman.

During a 2009 show of the offbeat West Coast crypto-swing band Pink Martini, lead singer China Forbes remarked, "You don't see rooms like this all the time. It's like being inside a Fabergé egg." Since then the vivid analogy has been ascribed to other performers as well as journalists.

LYLE LOVETT

AUGUST 26, 2014

"The Tennessee Theatre is one of the best places to play in the country... I can't tell you what a privilege it is to play in a place like this."

LYLE LOVETT

Rapidly rising soprano Rachele Gilmore happened to be the talk of the opera world, thanks to a triumphant unscheduled debut at the Met, when she appeared with Knoxville Opera on the Tennessee's stage in 2010, taking the title role of *Lucia di Lammermoor.* A balcony video of her performance of the famous "mad scene" went viral.

Knoxville opera has mounted dozens of full-scale operas at the Tennessee, inviting both well-known singers from the Met and local talent, but in 2013 the opera did something that had never been done before on the Tennessee's stage — or at least not in the last 80 years. It's still not proven how Tom Mix got a horse on stage in November 1933. But for Puccini's American-based opera, *Girl of the Golden West*, two live, healthy full-grown horses joined the singers on stage, loaned by local farmer John Niceley and brought to the stage from State Street via the heavy-duty set elevator.

The Tennessee's stage has drawn some of the most interesting speakers of the era too, including insurgent chef Anthony Bourdain, and confessionary author Elizabeth Gilbert, who finished her famous autobiographical book *Eat, Pray, Love* (which, of course, became a major motion picture, starring Julia Roberts) when she was living about two blocks away from the Tennessee, at the St. Oliver Hotel.

In 2011, Garrison Keillor, novelist and iconic host of *A Prairie Home Companion*, made an appearance at the Tennessee. Keillor's a well-known connoisseur of historically classic old theaters, but when he'd brought his nationally broadcast show to Knoxville 12 years earlier, he presented it at the larger and then-less-problematic Civic Auditorium, disappointing some longtime fans. His inevitable arrival at the Tennessee, for a non-broadcast show, helped make up for it.

WIDESPREAD PANIC · SEPTEMBER 25, 2011

ALLISON KRAUSS · JANUARY 20, 2005

MERLE HAGGARD & KRIS KRISTOFFERSON · MARCH 8, 2011

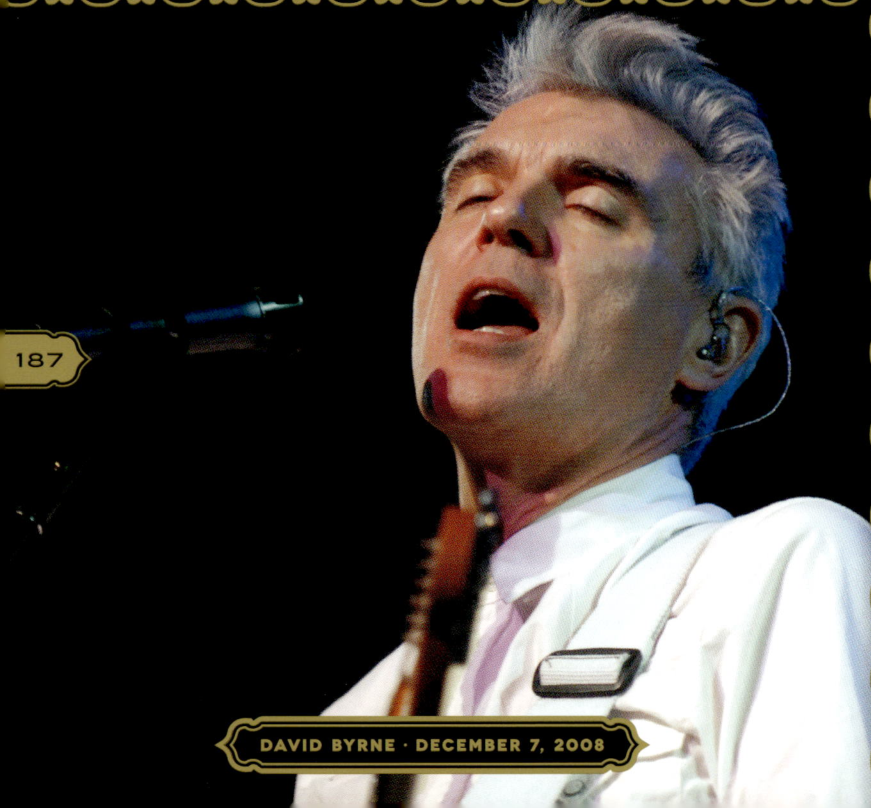

DAVID BYRNE · DECEMBER 7, 2008

EMMYLOU HARRIS · SEPTEMBER 11, 2005

JOHN LEGEND · APRIL 19, 2014

LORETTA LYNN · APRIL 21, 2006

KNOXVILLE OPERA'S "GIRL OF THE GOLDEN WEST" · FEBRUARY 2013

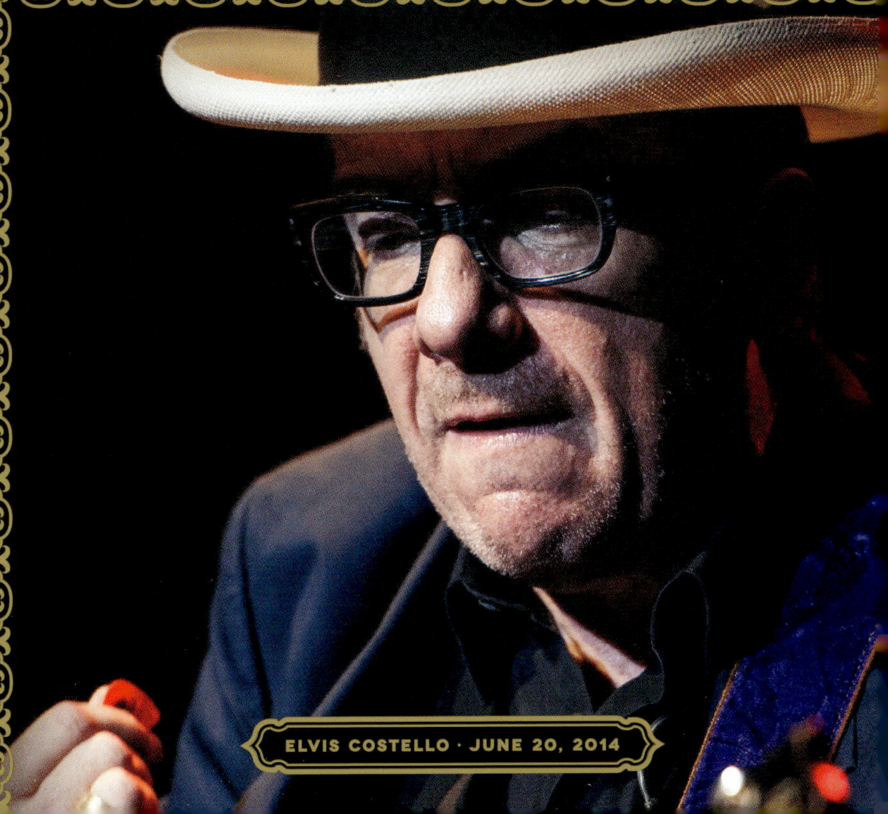

ELVIS COSTELLO · JUNE 20, 2014

SONNY ROLLINS · MARCH 25, 2006

NEEDTOBREATHE · APRIL 3, 2013

DIANA ROSS · JUNE 2, 2010

MOMIX · FEBRUARY 7, 2005

JACKSON BROWNE · MAY 9, 2011

BB KING · JANUARY 8, 2010

GRIZZLY BEAR · SEPTEMBER 16, 2012

TERRY RILEY AT BIG EARS FESTIVAL · MARCH 30, 2010

TONY BENNETT · MAY 3, 2006

KRONOS QUARTET · MARCH 31, 2006

GEORGE JONES · FEBRUARY 31, 2008

DOC SEVERINSEN WITH THE KNOXVILLE JAZZ ORCHESTRA · DECEMBER 20, 2011

MORISSEY · JULY 10, 2007

LOU REED · APRIL 30, 2008

MEGADEATH · MAY 8, 2012

JAY LENO · MAY 2, 2009

STAGEHANDS RELAXING DURING A BREAK · 2006

Still associated with Bonnaroo, Capps started a festival closer to his own heart in his hometown in 2009, when he launched an extraordinarily unusual music festival called Big Ears. Emphasizing minimalist and avant-garde music of a wide variety, Big Ears was a three-day festival that earned national attention. On its return in 2010, a major focus of the multi-venue festival was the Tennessee Theatre, where modernist composer Terry Riley appeared, as well as extremely popular alt-rock band Vampire Weekend. When music critics for the *The New York Times* and *Rolling Stone* described the festival, they inevitably described the Tennessee Theatre, one borrowing and popularizing the "Fabergé egg" quip.

Big Ears returned in 2014, and the Tennessee witnessed some of the festival's most memorable moments. Composer Steve Reich presented Wordless Music Orchestra performing his complex composition, "Music for 18 Musicians." But the most astonishing moment may have come on the afternoon of March 29, when Radiohead guitarist Johnny Greenwood, performing some of his own short compositions, much of it accompanied by traditional instrumentation, violins and cellos —until a message appeared on the screen above, suggesting that audience members type a certain address on their individual smart phone browsers "to participate in this performance." And throughout the old Tennessee Theatre, 21st-century cell phones chimed harmonically along with Greenwood's playing. It was a new interactive performance phenomenon, one of the first times in human history that it had been attempted. The effect was subtle, but surreal.

A few months later, Elvis Costello remarked that in planning his unusual 2014 solo tour, he had to include a third performance at Knoxville's Tennessee Theatre. "There's no telling what will come to mind when I take the stage at the Tennessee Theatre," he told reporter Wayne Bledsoe of the *News Sentinel*. "There are so many resonances in that place that you could be put in any mind."

The Tennessee Theatre is a theater icon with a thousand resonances: of Roy Acuff's first performance, and Chet Atkins' last; of Desi Arnaz, dancing the rhumba with a local pharmacist; of screenings of most of the greatest movies ever made; of sham clairvoyants and regurgitation specialists; of massive war-bond drives; of hundreds of first dates that led to marriages; of major opera stars and instrumental virtuosos; of authors John Updike and Maya Angelou; of suave Glenn Miller and his polished big band on live radio; of rock 'n' roll legends Bob Dylan, Ray Charles, and Lou Reed; of Tom Mix himself, and his talented horse, Tony.

A FULL HOUSE FOR MIGHTY MUSICAL MONDAY

MIGHTY MUSICAL MONDAY

The theater is one of the city's most astonishing marvels, but it's a challenge to show off, because it's not open every day. Mighty Musical Monday has become the public's most regular opportunity to behold the Tennessee Theatre, along with its wonderful Wurlitzer, without the expense of a ticket.

Perhaps unique in the region and the state, the Tennessee's Mighty Wurlitzer is a bona fide rarity, one of very few original theater organs still installed in their original movie palaces. That fact is not just the result of good luck. Just before the theater's major renovation, the Wurlitzer itself got a thorough $300,000 restoration, personally sponsored by retired merchant Wallace Baumann, who had been the Tennessee's most enthusiastic promoter since the 1960s.

In 2001, soon after the installation of the refurbished Wurlitzer, the theater's management discussed a new tradition for the theater. The organ's mechanics had advised that the rare instrument get some regular exercise to keep it in shape. Bill Snyder, the former UT chancellor who had been the house organist at the Tennessee for more than 20 years, and Becky Hancock, then the theater's general manager, discussed the matter and settled on launching a monthly lunchtime organ recital disguised as a variety show. Offering an optional sack lunch, "Mighty Musical Monday"—the adjective came straight from the big Wurlitzer—was an unexpected hit, especially among retirees.

continues on next page...

Although the lunchtime event started purely as an organ concert, with Snyder the only performer, in 2007 it expanded to include singers with opera or Broadway credits, like Daniel Neer and Mark Fox; jazz combos from the eccentric Johnson Swingtet to the nationally hailed Knoxville Jazz Orchestra; and other special guests, including the chorus from Snyder's alma mater, Central High, who perform an annual holiday show. In 2012 two-time Golden Globe nominee David Keith served as emcee—25 years after he premiered his movie, "The Curse," at the Tennessee. On Labor Day, 2014, renowned organ virtuoso Jelani Eddington performed as guest organist. And most have been escorted by Snyder's most regular sidekick, local Barney Fife impressionist Sammy Sawyer, who greets guests and sometimes does a turn onstage.

Eventually named in memory of the theater's longtime owner and benefactor, Jim Dick, Mighty Musical Monday has become another of the Tennessee's signature traditions.

The Tennessee Theatre began as a multi-layered paradox in 1928, a movie theater that presented some of the live-theater vaudeville legends of its day, with a big organ to accompany silent movies that were no longer really silent and a palatially exclusive-looking place familiar to anyone with a few buffalo nickels for a ticket. Much of that interesting paradox resonates in a newer century. Although it's an intimate venue, and not an especially large room as auditoriums go, it's reasonable to assert that millions of Americans have experienced the place. Tens of thousands of performers have given their best on its stage.

The room, not exactly like any other in the world, has a history connecting it to the live-radio era and the last days of vaudeville, most of the classic movies or the Golden Age of Hollywood when they were new, and performances by some of the world's truly great performers of two centuries. Recent years suggest its best days may be yet to come. If the theater's no longer open every day, as it was in the early days of talkies, with crowds watching a never-ending stream of movies and shorts from noon to midnight six or seven days a week, recent Broadway shows attract crowds that would have impressed any promoter of the Ziegfeld Follies. A 2014 run of *Jersey Boys* sold over 12,000 tickets to eight performances, the biggest turnout for any touring show in the Tennessee's history.

While scores of its 1920s movie palace peers have been demolished or remodeled beyond recognition, the Tennessee remains, and thrives, as one of the 21st-century's most popular theater venues and an inspiration to those who visit it for the first time, and even to those who grew up with it and know it well.

35mm film was the primary format for screening movies at the Tennessee Theatre until June 2014, when Regal Entertainment Group donated a digital projector. Film prints are no longer being produced by the movie companies, and digital projection will allow the Tennessee to continue screening films well into the 21st century. Executive Director Becky Hancock holds an old reel, for only 20 minutes of 35mm film, and a box containing the digital file that holds an entire 2+ hour movie.

The 2013 – 2014 season of Broadway at the Tennessee closed with a record-breaking run of eight performances of the wildly popular "JERSEY BOYS." It sold 12,076 tickets and grossed over $800,000, making it the most successful show to date.

Left to right: Quinn VanAntwerp, Nicolas Dromard, Hayden Milanes, and Adam Zelasko.

JERSEY BOYS · APRIL 29 – MAY 4, 2014

APPENDIX

Since the Historic Tennessee Theatre Foundation's formation in 1996, 92 community leaders have volunteered and contributed their expertise to oversee the transformation of the treasured movie palace into a magnificent performing arts and entertainment venue, ensuring its long-term preservation. Their vision and courage are an invaluable gift to future generations. This alphabetical list shows all HTTF Board Members and their years of service (through 2014).

JOE ARMSTRONG ✦	2002 - 2008
BEN ATCHLEY ✦	2002 - 2008
BOB BASKERVILLE	2002 - 2011
TIERNEY BATES	2011
WALLACE BAUMANN ◊ ‡	1996 - 2009
TERRY BAZZOON	2013
PATRICK BIRMINGHAM	2013 - PRESENT
BARBARA BLEVINS	2007 - 2008
DON BOSCH	2007 - 2013
BRUCE BOSSE	2001 - 2006
CHARLES BROADWATER	1999
JIMMY BUCKNER	2009 - 2013
FRED BUFFUM	2001 - 2007
TIM BURCHETT ✦	2002 - 2008
BOB CALLOWAY	2000 - 2006
BRECK CAMP	2008 - PRESENT
BILL CAMPBELL ◊	1997 - 2005
TOM CATANI	2007 - 2009
CHRIS CHANDLER	2012 - PRESENT
DOC CLAUSSEN	2012 - PRESENT
MICHAEL COMBS	2000 - 2010
LEWIS COSBY	2009
JOHN CRAIG	2011 - PRESENT
BETSEY CREEKMORE	2003 - 2014
JED DANCE	2006 - PRESENT
BILL DAVIS, SR. ◊	1996 - 2007
BILL DAVIS, JR.	2007 - 2010
MARLEEN DAVIS	2002 - 2011
DAVID DEWHIRST	2007 - 2010
ARTHUR DICK	2007 - 2013
JAMES A. DICK ◊ ‡	1996 - 2010
TIKI DIXON	2001
JAY DUNLAP ◊	1997 - 1999
GREG DUNN ◊	1997 - 2014

RACHEL FORD — 2007 - 2010
VINCE FUSCO — 2008 - PRESENT
JOHN FISHER ◊ — 1997 - 2007
KIMBERLY DIXON HAMILTON — 2007 - 2009
MIKE HAMMOND — 2006 - 2007
MARK HANSON — 2001 - 2003
BRUCE HARTMANN ◊ — 1996 - 2010
JIM HASLAM ◊ — 1996 - 2007
DAVID HENDERLIGHT ◊ — 1996 - 1999
CAROL HICKS — 2000 - 2001
HALLERIN HILL ◊ — 1997 - 1998
JENNY HINES ◊ — 1997 - 2013
FRANKLIN HUNDLEY — 2007 - 2010
BRENDA HUNTER — 2007 - 2009
LEE INGRAM — 2012 - PRESENT
ANDY JOHNSON — 2007 - 2014
TONJA JOHNSON — 2014 - PRESENT
RAJA JUBRAN — 2009 - 2010
DALE KEASLING ◊ — 1997 - 2009
CHRIS KITTRELL — 2014 - PRESENT
JOSEPH KOKER — 1999
PHIL LAWSON — 2009
BARBARA LEWIS ◊ — 1996 - 1999
MARK MAMANTOV — 2008 - 2014
JIM MARTIN ◊ — 1996 - 2009
LARRY MARTIN ◊ — 1997 - 2009
DIANA MORGAN — 2007 - 2010
MONTY MONTGOMERY ◊ — 1997
DAVID MOON ◊ — 1996 - 1999, 2002 - 2005

CYNTHIA MOXLEY ◊ — 1996 - 2001
JORDANA NELSON — 2014 - PRESENT
JIM PIPPIN — 2009
SAMMIE LYNN PUETT ◊ † — 1997 - 2001
RHONDA RICE — 2007 - 2013
ANGELA S. JOHN — 1999 - 2001
ERIC SCHWARZENTRAUB — 2007 - 2013
FRAN SHEA — 2006 - 2008
JAMES SHELBY ◊ † — 1997 - 2008
TOM SKAGGS — 2011 - PRESENT
BILL SNYDER ◊ — 1996 - 2007, 2010 - 2012
RICK STONE — 2008 - 2014
STEVE SOUTH ◊ — 1997 - 2007
LEANN STRIBLEY — 2007 - 2009
THOMAS "TANK" STRICKLAND, JR. — 2003 - 2010
GLENN SWIFT — 2007 - 2009
KIM TRENT — 2009 - 2013
ROBYN ULRICH — 2008 - PRESENT
JAN WADE ◊ — 1997 - 2006
JAMES WANSLEY — 2014 - PRESENT
MARTHA WEAVER ◊ — 1997 - 2008
MIKE WEST — 2009 - 2012
MARIANE WHITTEMORE — 2013 - PRESENT
MARK WILLIAMS* — 1996 - 2006
SUSAN WILLIAMS — 2014 - PRESENT
TRACY WILLIAMS — 2003 - 2007
TAMMY WILSON — 2014 - PRESENT
JONATHAN WINKLE — 2004 - 2006
NORMAN ZIGROSSI ◊ — 1997 - 2004

◊ *Founding Member*
† *Deceased*
✦ *Ex-Officio*

PHOTO CREDITS

WALLACE W. BAUMANN
MCCLUNG HISTORICAL COLLECTION
3 left, 28, 34 right, 60, 63 top right, 65 left, 70 left, 76, 86, 90, 92, 93 right, 96, 104, 106 left, 107 left & right, 108, 109 left & bottom right, 110 right, 111 top & bottom left, 113, 114 right, 115, 116, 120, 122, 124, 125, 126 middle, 128 middle & right, 129 middle, 138, 141 left, 144, 145 middle, 152 left, 166 middle, 175 left

FAMILY OF WALLACE W. BAUMANN
114 top left

LIBRARY OF CONGRESS
3 top & bottom right, 45 right, 48, 69 left, 72 right

FAMILY OF JAMES A. DICK
139

MOTION PICTURE DAILY
87

NELS AKERLUND
II, IX, X, XIII left, 175 right, 176, 177, 179, 180, 181 left, 200 left, 206, 211 right

TIM BURNS
42, 75, 100, 129 right, 130 right, 131, 132, 135 left, 136, 140 left, 142 left, right & middle, 145 left, 146, 147, 171 top left, 172 top left, 173 top left & bottom right, 174 top left

MCCLUNG HISTORICAL COLLECTION
6, 15 top & bottom right, 18, 89 left & top right, 114 bottom left

ALABAMA THEATRE
22

MARK HEINZ
106 right

DOCTORMACRO.COM
23 right, 41 left & top right, 57, 58, 63 bottom right, 65 bottom right, 67, 69 right, 72 left, 79, 80, 81 right, 84 left, 94 top & bottom left, 95 right, 97, 98, 99, 109 top right, 117, 118, 127 left, 128 left, 133, 134, 135 right, 145 right

DENARK CONSTRUCTION
168, 169, 170, 171 top right & bottom left, 173 top right & bottom left, 174 top & bottom right

CHRISTOPHER L.C.E. WHITCOMBE
FROM A DECEMBER 1897 CATALOGUE OF THE T.H. MCALLISTER CO.
5 left

KNOXVILLE OPERA / JC STUDIOS PHOTOGRAPHY
188 bottom left

SHAWN POYNTER
184

HISTORIC TENNESSEE THEATRE FOUNDATION
XIII right, 21, 24 left, 25, 30, 59, 89 bottom right, 130 left, 139 left, 140 right, 141 right, 148 left, 149, 159, 160, 161, 162, 166 right, 167, 171 bottom right, 172 top & bottom right, 178, 200 right, 201, 211 left

KNOXVILLE NEWS SENTINEL
83, 105, 107 middle, 110 left, 121, 129 left, 150, 151, 156, 166 left, 172 bottom left, 174 bottom left, 194, 195

SANBORN MAP & PUBLISHING CO., LTD
NEW YORK
11, 12

KNOXVILLE SYMPHONY ORCHESTRA
157 bottom right

EBET ROBERTS
158 bottom right

KNOXVILLE JOURNAL
KNOX COUNTY PUBLIC LIBRARY
50, 51, 54, 64 left, 66, 68, 69 middle, 71, 73, 74, 78, 81 left, 84 right, 88, 94 right, 119 right

THOMPSON PHOTOGRAPH COLLECTION
MCCLUNG HISTORICAL COLLECTION
foreword, 2, 3 middle, 4, 8 left, 9, 10, 14, 15 left, 16, 17, 19, 20, 23 left, 24 right, 32, 33, 34 left, 35, 36, 37, 38, 39, 40, 41 bottom right, 43 left & middle, 44, 49, 52, 53, 56, 64 middle, 70 right, 77, 95 left, 205

BECK CULTURAL EXCHANGE CENTER
5 right

ERICK KABIK
157 bottom left

ERIC L. SMITH
143, 148 right, 152 right, 153, 154, 155, 157 top left & right, 158 top left, right & bottom left, 164, 165, 181 right, 182, 183, 185, 186, 187, 188 top left, right & bottom right, 189, 190, 191, 192, 193

TENNESSEE ARCHIVE OF MOVING IMAGE & SOUND
KNOX COUNTY PUBLIC LIBRARY
8 right, 43 right, 45 left, 47, 62, 63 left, 64 right, 65 top right, 93 left, 102, 111 right, 119 left, 126 left

JEREMY DANIEL
195

HDWALLPAPER.HBWILD.COM
101

IMPAWARDS.COM
126 right

AISLE 1

LOUNGE

THANK YOU TO THE TENNESSEE THEATRE BOOK SPONSORS

The Board of Directors and staff of the Historic Tennessee Theatre Foundation gratefully acknowledge the generous support received from the following sponsors. Without them, this book would not have been possible.

Established in 1989, Regal Entertainment Group is headquartered in Knoxville, Tennessee. REG operates the largest, most geographically diverse theatre circuit in the United States — nearly 600 theatres housing more than 7,000 screens in 42 states and the District of Columbia, as well as American Samoa, Guam and Saipan. Each year approximately 229 million moviegoers enjoy viewing Hollywood blockbusters, family entertainment and award-winning films at Regal, United Artists and Edwards theatres.

With a history of continuing philanthropy, the company generously gives back to the communities it serves. Regal Entertainment Group and The Regal Foundation are extremely proud of the successful relationships fostered with charitable partners and their multi-faceted involvements in community service. Moreover, Regal employees are very active in local communities in which they live; the company as a whole is committed to public service and to maintaining a reputation of good citizenship.

Since the Historic Tennessee Theatre Foundation was formed in 1996, Regal has been a generous partner with the Tennessee Theatre in providing funding for the major renovation of 2003-2005, as a presenting season sponsor, and by providing projection equipment. Regal executives and employees serve on the HTTF board, committees and task forces and, when needed, supply invaluable knowledge and technical assistance. Since 2007 Regal has been a neighbor of the Tennessee, returning first-run movies to downtown Knoxville for the first time since 1972 with the opening of the Regal Riviera, which is located in the same spot as the historic Riviera Theatre.

Clayton FOUNDATION

The Clayton Family Foundation's mission is to provide support, leadership and funding to facilitate community growth and development. The goals involve supporting groups and organizations that seek to enrich current and future generations in communities where the Clayton family and Clayton team members live and work.

Education is a Foundation priority and the arts are a material component of a healthy and vibrant educational initiative. For decades, the Clayton family and related enterprises have supported programs and institutions that nurture creative expression, artistic collaboration, and civic engagement while complementing and enhancing the individual educational experience.

The Clayton Family Foundation was proud to be a lead donor in the renovation campaign to save the Historic Tennessee Theatre and continues to partner with this downtown Knoxville jewel. Supporting Education through the Arts is only part of the Clayton giving story, as the Foundation annually invests millions of dollars with an emphasis on:

Economic Development – programs that build an educated, dynamic workforce to attract and retain successful enterprise
Youth – programs that support and address the challenges faced by today's youth,
Education Initiatives – programs that advance innovative learning and economic achievement
Human Services – programs that improve the quality of life where we learn, earn, and return

"Being able to Return back to communities that have supported my extended family over the decades, as we Learned and Earned, is my dream fulfilled." – Jim Clayton

visit knoxville
TENNESSEE

As the official Convention and Visitors Bureau for the City of Knoxville and Knox County, Visit Knoxville promotes the rich history and culture of Knoxville every day. Nowhere does that history and culture come together more beautifully than at the historic Tennessee Theatre. The Tennessee Theatre draws visitors from around the world and serves as a unique gathering place for groups and organizations. Knoxville is blessed to have this treasure, and Visit Knoxville is fortunate to have the opportunity to work alongside the theatre's staff to promote it.

As the official and primary provider of visitor information for Knox County and the City of Knoxville, Visit Knoxville serves as the "go-to" for visitors, and assists locals on a daily basis. Few things bring more excitement than watching the face of an international journalist as he or she first walks into the lobby of the Tennessee Theatre. That same joy comes on educational tours Visit Knoxville provides members of our local hospitality industry, many of whom experience the sights and sounds of the theatre for the first time on these tours.

Visit Knoxville is passionate about collaborating with local tourism partners to promote this city and all the wonderful things it has to offer. We appreciate the contributions of the Tennessee Theatre and celebrate its history and future.

chevalier
THE PLAYBOY OF PARIS
FREE!
chevalier
THE PLAYBOY OF PARIS
FRANCES DEE

Lithographics inc.

In 1975 Lithographics began as the vision of two pressmen to pursue their passion to be the best printers in Tennessee. Today, Lithgraphics is recognized as Middle Tennessee's leading printer and continues its simple undertaking of helping clients grow their businesses. The 103 members of "Team Litho" are immensely proud to be the chosen printer of this documentation of a state treasure; we congratulate the Historic Tennessee Theatre Foundation and all of Knoxville on its restoration and preservation. Just as some thought the Tennessee Theatre would fade away and no one would miss it, some thought print would fade away. Here is to looking toward a bright future for all of us. Congratulations Tennessee Theatre — you are a unique thing of beauty.

INDEX

A

ABC / ABC Southeastern — 111, 113, 119, 122
Abel, Walter — 96, 99
AC Entertainment — 147, 149, 150, 151, 152, 166, 185
Acker, Janet — 137
Acuff, Roy — 61, 64, 72, 193
Adios Amigo — 119
Adkin, Sam — 71, 78
Adler, Arnold — 94
Adler, Dankmar — 27
Adler Theatre (Davenport, IA) — 30
Agee, James — 5, 7, 8, 107, 112
Agree, Charles — 22
Ah, Wilderness! — 73
Ain't Misbehavin' — 146
Akers, Bill, Jr. — 135
Akins, Claude — 141
Alabama Theatre (Birmingham) — 22, 26, 27, 30, 34, 111
Alexander, Lamar — 106
Ali, Hadji — 48
All the Way Home — 107, 112
Alpert, Jon — 154
Alumni Memorial Auditorium / Hall — 75, 81, 88, 96
Alvin Theatre (New York City) — 70
American Idiot — 185
Amos, Charles H. — 33, 34, 54
Anderson, Harry — 145
Anderson, Laurie — 183
Anderson, Lynn — 140
Anderson, Maxwell — 69
Andrew Johnson Hotel — 47, 88, 120
Andrews, Lois — 94
Angelou, Maya — 183, 193
Animal Crackers — 50, 57, 123
Appalachian Ballet Company — 143
Appalachian Exposition of 1910 — 64
Apple, Fiona — 183
Arcade — 5
Arden, Eve — 68
Arnaz, Desi — 84, 193
Ashe, Victor — 149, 167
Atkin Family — 13, 135, 137
Atkin Hotel — 13
Atkin House — 13
Atkin, Clay Brown (C.B.) — 13, 15, 17, 23, 31, 61, 70, 135, 136
Atkin, Frank — 13
Atkins, Chet / Chester Burton — 61, 63, 101, 155, 158, 185, 193
"Aunt Sally Visits Knoxville" — 5
Auriemma, Geno — 154
Austin, Gene — 48
Austin-East High School Jazz Band — 182
Ax, Emmanuel — 185

B

Bacharach, Burt — 185
Baez, Joan — 185
Ball, Lucille — 82, 84
Baltimore Hotel Orchestra — 67
Baltimore Lunch Room — 17
Barnes, Billy — 75, 76, 84, 92, 126, 128, 132, 144, 145
Barry, Marion — 106
Baumann, Wallace W. — 60, 113, 114, 119, 125, 127, 129, 131, 163, 168, 169, 170, 182, 194
Beard, Billy — 55
Beck Cultural Exchange Center — 106
Beechman, Laurie — 148
Beers, Jimmy — 67
Beery, Wallace — 49, 73
Bell, Joshua — 144, 157, 183
Bennett, Tony — 183, 191
Bergen, Polly — 109
Bergman, Ingrid — 112
Bernhardt, Sarah — 3
Bethel AME Church Choir — 182
Big Ears Festival — 165, 190, 193
Bigler, T.C. — 115
Bijou (By David Madden) — 92
Bijou Art Theatre — 11, 111
Bijou Theatre — 11, 13, 15, 16, 17, 29, 31, 48, 50, 55, 63, 75, 92, 93, 102, 111, 115, 116, 119, 129, 136, 139, 143, 149, 152
Bill Wallace of China — 112
Black Lillies, The — 182
Bledsoe, Wayne — 193
Blount College — 1
Blount, William — 1
Blue, Ben — 71
Bonnaroo — 184, 185, 193
Booker, Bob — 106
Booth Theatre — 34
Bourdain, Anthony — 186
Bow, Clara — 41, 42
Bowery — 5
Bowes, Major Edwards — 71
Branson, Lloyd — 18, 19
Brass Rail — 132
Bravo (TV Network) — 185
Bredesen, Phil — 182
Brice, Fanny — 67, 68, 69, 103
Brice, William — 139
Brigadoon — 146
Broadway (New York City) — 45, 48, 51, 54, 67, 69, 70, 71, 72, 78, 82, 139, 140, 141, 148, 161, 185, 195, 196
"Broadway Rhapsody" — 48
Brock, William M. — 55
Brown, Clarence – 43, 55, 69, 70, 73, 113
Browne, Jackson — 185
Brubeck, Dave — 183
Brunswick — 51
Bryan, Ross — 161
Bugg, Tom — 151, 152, 160
Bullock, Glenn — 115
Burke, Billie — 67, 68
Burns, Tim — 27, 119, 137, 143, 146, 161, 184
Burton, Gary — 143
Burwell Building — 6, 10, 15, 17, 18, 19, 23, 136, 139, 183
Burwell, Mary — 15
Byrne, David — 185, 187

C

C.B. Atkin Reality Company — 122
Calloway, Cab — 82, 142
Camp, Breck — 101
Campbell, Archie — 128
Capps, Ashley — 143, 147, 148, 149, 150, 151, 152, 161, 163, 183, 185, 193
Capra, Frank — 135
Capri Cinema / Capri-70 — 112, 123
Captain China — 94, 97
Carlson, Violet — 73
Carolina Theatre (Charlotte, NC) — 20, 21
Carrick, Samuel — 1, 30
Carroll, Earl — 65, 72, 73, 112
Carson, Sunset — 145
Carter Family Fold — 154
Casablanca — 88, 90, 98, 112, 131, 132
Casanova, Eve — 45
Cash, Johnny — 152, 154, 155, 157
Castle, Peggie — 94
Cats — 148
CBS — 145
Cella, Connie — 73
Central Street — 4, 5, 49, 111
Champe, Charlie — 5
Chancellor, Van — 154
Charles, Ray — 144, 152, 193
Chase, Chaz — 66
Cheverton, Bill — 137
Chicago — 22, 23, 27, 29, 67, 169
Chicago (band) — 185
Chicago Opera House — 12
Chicago Theatre — 23
ChildHelp USA — 152
Chilhowee Park — 4, 29, 46
Cho, Henry — 185
Cinderella Season: The Lady Vols Fight Back, A — 154
CinemaScope — 100
Civic Auditorium / Coliseum — 103, 129, 136, 139, 143, 144, 161,186,187
Clarence Brown Theatre — 136
Clark & McCullough — 72
Clark, Bertha Walburn — 75
Clay, Clement — 1
Clement, Frank — 99
Clute, Chester — 72
Cocoanuts, The — 50, 52
Coffeen, Robert C. — 143
Collins, Judy — 144
Colvin, Shawn — 150
Comer's (pool hall) — 93
Conklin, Abby — 154
Conroy, Pat — 149
Console, The — 114
Contreras, Cruz — 182
Conversion of Buster Drumwright, The - 140
Conway, Tim — 146
Cooper, Prentice — 91
Corea, Chick — 143
Cosby, Bill — 155, 160

Costa, Mary — 152
Costello, Elvis — 183, 185, 193
"Cotton Club Revisited" — 142
Couch, Aubrey — 9
Cowboy Copas — 131
Cowboy Junkies — 150
"Cradle of Country Music" Tour — 154
Crome, Ken — 163
Crosby, Bing — 66, 83
Crosby, Kim — 146
Crosby, Stills & Nash — 185
Crouch School of Music — 20
Crystal Theatre (Market Square) — 102
Cullum, J.D. — 140
Cullum, John — 129, 140
Curse, The — 141
Curtain Call at Cactus Creek — 94

D

D'Orsay, Fifi — 72
Dalton, Emmett — 7
Daly, Fanny — 74
Davidson, John — 146
Davis Manufacturing Company, The - 20
Davis, Bill, Sr. — 99, 150
Dearstone, Mickey — 149
Death in the Family, A — 7, 8, 108
DeLeo, Maryann — 154
Delmore Brothers — 71
Dempster, George — 99
Denark Construction — 167, 170
Denton, Bobby — 137
Devine, George — 96
Dick Broadcasting, Inc. — 137, 149
Dick, James A. / Jim — 137, 139, 140, 142, 143, 149, 150, 160, 163, 195
Difranco, Ani — 152
Dirty Guv'nahs, The — 185
Dixie Amusement Parlor, The — 5
Dixie Gem Coal Company, The — 54
Dorsey, Tommy — 66
Drumbar, William C. — 17, 55
Drumwright — 140, 141, 142
Duncan, John, Jr. / Jimmy — 25, 154
Dunn, Lin — 154
Dylan, Bob — 183, 193

E

Earl Carroll's Vanities - 65, 66, 67, 72, 73
Earle, Steve — 152, 183
East Tennessee Historical Society — 154
East Tennessee History Center — 183
Easterday, Ben Howard — 74
Easterday, Claude Raymond — 74
Eat, Pray, Love — 186
Eberle, Ray — 81
Ebsen, Buddy — 68
Eddington, Jelani — 183, 195
Eden, Barbara — 146
Edison Theatorium — 7, 11
Elk's Lodge / Club — 17, 64
Ella Guru's — 152
Emmanuel, Tommy — 185
Ennesse Theatre — 153
Erwin, Lee — 112, 113, 115
Evergreene Architectural Arts — 168
Everly Brothers — 101, 137, 148, 154
Everly, Don — 101, 148
Everly, Phil — 101
Evita — 146
Exchange, The (bar / restarant) — 139

F

Farr, Jamie — 146
Farragut Hotel — 13, 96
FCC — 99
Fillmore East — 143
Film Daily — 20, 21, 22
First Baptist Church — 26
First Presbyterian Church - 3, 20, 75, 161
First Presbyterian Churchyard / Cemetery — 1, 161, 170
Fisher Theatre (Detroit, MI) — 30
Fleck, Béla — 185
Fleet's In, The — 41, 42
Florida Theatre (Jacksonville) — 20, 21
Floyd, Carlisle — 143
Fool Killer, The — 109, 112
Forbes, China — 185
Ford, Jessie Hill — 140
Ford, Reverend W. Herschel — 74, 75
Fowler, Virginia — 105
Fox Theatre (Atlanta, GA) — 26, 67, 129
Francis — 94
Francis, Pearl — 96
Frederick, Pauline — 70
Friends of the Library — 149
Frost, Ralph — 128, 129
Frost, Robert / Bob — 128, 129, 131, 132, 137, 142, 149
Fulton, Barbara — 78
Fulton, Weston — 26, 76, 78

G

Garbo, Greta — 43, 48, 55
Garland, Judy — 68, 78
Gaskill, Gordon — 72
Gass, William — 7, 15, 49
Gem Theatre — 11, 105, 111
George A. Fuller Company — 7, 13, 23
Georgia Crackers — 57
Getty, Estelle — 145
Gibbons, Floyd — 78
Gilbert, Elizabeth — 186
Gilmore, Rachele — 186
Giovanni, Jones — 105
Giovanni, Nikki — 103, 105, 106
Girl of the Golden West — 186, 188
Glencoe — 170
"Golden Girls" — 145
Gone With the Wind — 85, 87, 92, 95, 145
Gonzales, Servando — 109
Gordon, Marianne — 141
Grace Moore Scholarship — 95
Grand Ole Opry — 51, 61, 71, 182
Graven & Mayger — 22, 23, 24, 25, 27, 29, 30, 167, 169
Graven, Anker Sveere — 22, 30
Gray, Loretta — 65
Grayson, Kathryn — 95, 96, 99
Green, Al — 183
Green, John Webb — 6
Greene, Jeff — 168
Greenwood, Johnny — 193
Grey, Erin — 141
Griffin, Kathy — 185
Griffin, Merv — 95, 96, 99, 132
Griffith, Nanci — 166
Griffith, Robert F. — 72
Gully Jumpers — 71
Gunter, Sue — 154
Gunther, John — 92
Guy, Buddy — 183
Gyllenhaal, Jake — 153

H

Haggard, Merle — 183, 187
Hall, Anthony Michael — 141
Hall, Mary Alice — 74
Hall, R.E. — 20, 21, 27, 29
Hampton, Lionel — 144
Hancock, Becky - 163, 166, 175, 194, 195
Hardy Holzman Pfeiffer — 155
Hardy, Harry — 67
Harkreeder, Sid — 71
Harrington, Pat — 146
Harris, Emmylou — 166, 183, 187
Hartmann, Bruce — 150, 163, 167
Haslam, Bill — 182, 184
Haslam, Jim — 150
Hayes, Helen — 69, 70, 71, 140
HBO — 154
Hearst Metrotone — 109
Helburn, Theresa — 69
Helton, Jo — 112
Hensley, Donna — 116
Hensley, Jim — 131, 136
Hiatt, John — 183
Hickam, Homer — 153
Hines, Jerome — 143
Historic Tennessee Theatre Foundation / HTTF — 150, 155, 163
Holbrook, Hal — 183
Hollywood Theatre (Detroit, MI) — 22
Holston Bank Building — 13
Holzman, Malcolm — 155
Howard, Eugene — 68
Howard, Willie — 68
Huff, John L. — 122
Hutton, Marion — 81

IJ

James, Forrest — 22
Jenkins, Carol Mayo — 182
Jersey Boys — 195, 196
Johnson, Andrew — 87, 88
Johnson, Cal — 5
Johnston, Joe — 153
Jones, Red — 61
Journal Arcade Building — 20
Junior League — 115
Just Add Ice — 152

K

Kaye, Danny — 65
Kearney, Michael — 108
Keillor, Garrison — 186
Keith, David — 195

Kennedy, William — 149
King, B.B. — 183, 185, 190
King, Pee Wee — 131
Kirkegaard Associates — 169
Kiwanis Club — 64
Knotts, Don — 146
Knox Theatre — 91
Knoxville Banking & Trust Building — 6, 13, 15
Knoxville College — 105, 106
Knoxville Drive-In — 119
Knoxville Heritage — 115
Knoxville High School — 44, 73, 128
Knoxville Journal — 16, 34, 51, 54, 61, 64, 66, 68, 69, 71, 73, 74, 78, 81, 84, 87, 88, 119
Knoxville Opera Company — 143, 148, 160, 182, 188
Knoxville Symphony Orchestra / KSO 75, 115, 137, 139, 143, 144, 148, 157, 163, 164, 182
"Koran, the Marvelous Mentalist" — 48
Krauss, Alison — 183, 187
Kristofferson, Kris — 183, 187

• L •

La Traviata — 99
La Vie Paree — 65
Larsen, Lyn — 163, 166
Larue, Lash — 145
Last of the Red Hot Lovers — 146
Lathan, Bobbi Jo — 140
Lee, Albert — 148
Legend, John — 185, 188
Les Miserables — 148, 188
Lincoln Theatre — 5, 11
Logan-Ernest Building — 16
Louvin Brothers — 154
Louvin, Charlie — 154
Lovett, Lyle — 147, 183
Lown, Bert — 67
Lucas, Nick — 65
Lucia di Lammermoor — 143, 186
Lutz, Adelia — 6
Lutz, J.E. — 6
Lyall, Robert — 143
Lynn, Loretta — 185, 188
Lyric Theatre — 11, 16, 17, 33, 68, 82, 91, 92, 102, 120

• M •

MacMurray, Fred — 81, 108, 109, 112
Macon, Uncle Dave — 71
Madden, David — 92
Main Street Knoxville — 147
Majestic Theatre — 7, 8, 11, 17, 33, 44
Manley & Young — 16
Marcus Show, The — 65
Market Square — 11, 92, 102, 149, 160, 183
Marsalis, Wynton — 183
Mary of Scotland — 69
Mary Poppins — 185
Matheny, Pat — 183
Maud the Mule — 6
May, Ralphie — 185
Mayger, Arthur Guy — 22, 30
McAdoo, William Gibbs — 4
McCarthy, Cormac — 92, 93
McCarty Holsaple McCarty — 160, 167
McCarty, Doug — 160, 161, 168
McCrary & Branson — 18, 19
McCullough, Paul — 73
McDougle, Edwin — 161
McEntire, Reba — 140
McGuire, Michael — 148
McQueen, Butterfly — 145
Mechanics Bank & Trust Building - 10, 20
Medical Arts Building — 47
Merivale, Philip — 69
MGM — 47, 113, 173
Midori — 144
Mighty Wurlitzer — 31, 34, 41, 42, 55, 59, 60, 66, 73, 76, 84, 92, 101, 104, 113, 114, 115, 125, 126, 127, 131, 132, 137, 139, 144, 163, 175, 182, 194
Miller, Glenn — 81, 82, 103, 193
Miller, Malcolm — 68, 70, 72, 73, 87
Miller's Building — 10, 160, 175
Minnesota Theatre (Minneapolis, MN) — 30
Miracle on 34th Street — 94
Miranda, Carmen — 90
Mix, Mabel — 63, 64
Mix, Tom — 63, 64, 144, 186, 193
Monroe, Vaughn — 101
Moore, Grace — 95, 96, 99
Morgan, Dennis — 126, 127
Morris, R.B. — 182
Morrissey — 185
Motion Picture Daily — 87, 90
Motion Picture News — 55
Mull, Reverend J. Bazzell — 150
Mull's Singing Convention — 150
Mundy, Helen — 22, 23
Murray, Ken — 81
My Morning Jacket — 183

• N •

National Film Registry — 152
National Register of Historic Places -140
NBC — 145
"NBC Presents Major Bowes Amateur Show on the Stage" — 71
Neal, Patricia — 128
New York City Opera — 160
New York Theatre Guild — 69
New York Times, The — 95, 193
News-Sentinel / Knoxville News-Sentinel 23, 29, 33, 84, 127, 150, 152, 193
Neyland, Robert — 46
Niceley, John — 186
Nickel Creek — 183
"Night Court" — 145
Nine Counties. One Vision. — 160
Norman, Lula Myrtle — 74

• O •

O'Connor, Donald — 94
O'Hare, Husk — 67
October Sky — 152, 153
Odd Couple, The — 146
Old Crow Medicine Show — 183, 185

• P •

Page, Lucille — 73
Page, Patti — 99
Palmer, Robert — 148
Paramount — 16, 17, 42, 43, 49, 51, 52, 54, 85
Paramount Theatre (New York City) – 22, 75
Park Theater — 109
Parmelee, Martin — 20
Parton, Dolly — 137
Patricia Neal Homecoming Film Festival — 128
Patterson, Margaret — 88
Patterson, Martha Johnson — 88
Patton, E.E. — 88
Pavarotti, Luciano — 148
Pavlova, Anna — 3, 87
Payne, Ashley — 151
Payne, John — 94
Pedro, Don — 41, 42
Peris, Luis — 168
Perkins, Anthony / Tony — 109
Perlman, Itzhak — 185
Peters, Roberta — 143
Petrie, Daniel — 141
Piece of the Action, A — 122
Pike Theatre — 90
Pilot Corporation — 150
Pink Martini — 185
Plaza Tower — 120
Polivnick, Paul — 144
Pollstar — 183
Popeye Club — 61, 63, 65, 66, 75, 76, 115
Poulton, Curt — 71
Poundstone, Paula — 183
Preisser, June — 68
Preservation Hall Jazz Band — 132
Preston, Catherine — 108
Preston, Robert — 107, 108
Pryor Brown Parking Garage — 93
Pryor, Richard — 119
Public Building Authority — 168
Publix (Theatre Chain Corporation) - 16, 22, 31, 34, 44, 55, 59, 60
Puett, Sammie Lynn — 163

• Q •

Qirko, Hector — 182
Quinn, Anthony — 112
Quinn, Martin — 7

• R •

Radio Keith Orpheum / RKO (Rochester, NY) — 30
Radiohead — 193
Ragsdale, Mike — 167
Raines, Ron — 148
Raitt, Bonnie — 185
Rapp & Rapp — 22
Red Cross — 88
Reed, Lou — 185, 192, 193
Regal Entertainment Group — 167, 184, 195
Regal Riviera — 11, 184
Reich, Steve — 193

Renaissance Knoxville — 160
Rex Theatre — 8, 10, 11
Rhodes, Grandon — 72
Rialto Theatre — 11, 20
Riley, Terry — 190, 19
Riviera Theatre — 10, 11, 16, 17, 19, 20, 22, 23, 31, 33, 44, 76, 77, 85, 90, 91, 93, 102, 106, 116, 122, 123, 125, 136, 147
Robe, The — 103
Robinella & the CC String Band — 182
Rogers, Kenny — 141
Rolling Stone — 193
Rollins, Avon — 106
Rollins, Sonny — 183, 189
Roosevelt, Teddy — 64
Rossini Festival — 163
Roxy Theatre — 11, 47, 75, 92, 93, 102
Rozsnyai, Zoltan — 139, 144
Rule, William — 20, 46
Russell, Easter — 132
Russell, John — 94
Russell, Leon — 147
Ryman Auditorium (Nashville, TN) — 51, 160

S

S&W Cafeteria — 76, 77, 136, 184
Safford, Jack — 74
Salesky, Brian — 160, 182
Salvation Army — 91
Santiago, Saundra — 146
Santrey, Henry — 65
"Saturday Morning at the Movies" — 145
Schiff, Andras — 144
Schneider, John — 141
Schwarzenbach, Annemarie — 76
Scott, Lizabeth — 93
Scruggs, Earl — 183, 185
Second Presbyterian Church — 131
Sedaris, David — 183
Sherrill and Weber — 77
Shugart, Bess — 131
Signal Amusement Company — 16, 17
Six Pack — 141
Sleeping Beauty — 152
Smalls, "Marshal Andy" — 145
Smiley, L.H. — 82
Smith, Trixie — 48
Smoky Mountain Wildflower Festival Coronation Ball — 81
Smolik, Darlene — 168
Snow White and the 7 Dwarfs — 78, 103
Snyder, Bill — 130, 131, 139, 149, 150, 163, 182, 184, 194, 195
So This Is Love — 95, 107
Sousa, Leone — 68
Southern Living — 155
Spamalot — 185
Spaulding, Preston — 125
Spiva, Tony — 123, 125, 127, 129
St. James Hotel — 51
St. John's Orphanage — 75
St. Oliver Hotel — 186
Stanley, George — 54
Stark Love — 23
"Stars of Tomorrow" — 63
State Theatre of Tennessee — 160
Staub, Peter — 3
Staub's Opera House / Theatre — 3, 4, 11, 13, 16, 23, 102
Stewart, Redd — 131
Stokely Athletics Center — 103
Strand Theatre — 8, 9, 11, 17, 31, 33, 64, 93
Street, Eugene — 82
Suffridge, Bob — 84
Sullivan, Louis — 27
Summitt, Pat Head — 154
Sundquist, Don — 154
Susannah — 143
Susskind, David — 108
Suttree — 92

T

Tap Roots — 92, 97
Tate & McCallie — 122
Taylor, Dub — 145
Taylor, Earl — 73
Teal, Ray — 65, 71
Tellegen, Lou — 45, 48
Tennessee Children's Dance Ensemble 181, 182
Tennessee Crackerjacks — 61
Tennessee Enterprises, Inc. — 16, 17, 20, 21, 22, 23, 29, 31, 33, 41, 49, 55, 59
Tennessee Johnson — 87, 88
Tennessee Theatre Classics, Inc. (TTC) 125
Tennessee Valley Authority / TVA — 46, 64
Tennessee Valley Players — 143
"Tennessee Waltz, The" — 99, 131, 132
Terry Apartments (Maplehurst) — 55
Terway, Tys — 84
Thompson, Jim — 5
Time Magazine — 8
Tivoli Theatre — 92
To Kill a Mockingbird — 106, 118
Too Many Girls — 82, 84
Tower Theatre — 90
Trevor, Kirk — 144, 157
Tritt, Travis — 166
Turner Park — 4
Turner, Jim — 140
Tyler, Hugh — 5
Tyree, Randy — 125
Tyson, Charles McGhee — 15

U

Uncle Dave Macon — 71
University Concerts (UT program) — 95, 128
University of Tennessee / UT — 1, 4, 30, 43, 53, 46, 55, 73, 75, 82, 87, 95, 96, 99, 106, 112, 113, 123, 131, 136, 143, 149, 154, 163, 183, 194
Updike, John — 149, 158, 193
"UT Wall of Fame" — 111

V

Valatenga Theatre Corporation — 75
Vampire Weekend — 193
Van Dijk Westlake Reed Leskosky - 168
Velez, Milagros — 84
Viceroys / V-Roys — 152
Vincent, Bert — 33

W

Walcott, Gregory — 112
Walker, Cas — 101, 148
Ward, Irma — 64
Warlick, Holly — 154
Warner Brothers — 95
Warwick, Dionne — 183
Waters, Harry — 48
WATE-TV — 101, 167
Watling, H.L. — 82
Watson, Doc — 183
WBIR — 145
Webb, Clary — 6
Webb, Robert — 6
Weldon, Joan — 73, 96, 99
West Bend Theatre (Wisconsin) — 30
West Town Mall — 113, 116
West, Buster — 73
Westlake, Paul — 168, 182
Wheaton, Wil — 141
White, Betty — 145
White, Lasses — 51
Widespread Panic — 185, 186
Wilby, R.B. — 75
Wilby-Kincey Theater Service Corporation — 75, 85, 91, 95, 111
Wilco — 183
Wilson, Jean — 31, 41, 47, 48
Winter Marquee — 166
Winter, Johnny — 147
WIVK — 137, 149
Wizard of Oz, The — 78
WNOX — 64, 66, 81
Woman in Hiding — 94
Woman of Affairs, A — 43, 58
Women's Basketball Hall of Fame — 154
Wonderland Theatre — 5
Woodruff's Furniture — 114, 131
Wordless Music Orchestra — 193
"World of Wonders" — 140
World's Fair, Knoxville (1982) — 137, 138, 140, 141, 142
Worsham Brothers — 16
Worsham, Earl — 18
Wright, Stephen — 160
WROL — 51, 101
WUOT — 1
Wurlitzer — see Mighty Wurlitzer

XYZ

Ziegfeld Follies — 67, 68, 69, 195
Ziegfeld, Florenz — 67